CHOLERA

About the Book and Authors

CHOLERA: The American Scientific Experience, 1947–1980

W. E. van Heyningen and John R. Seal

Cholera—the dehydration disease that can be fatal in just one or two days—has been one of mankind's most tenacious and enigmatic adversaries. Its well-documented history is the story of the vagaries of a disease that originated in the Ganges delta, where it causes annual epidemics, whose European incarnation is as old as the Battle of Waterloo, and which was responsible for six pandemics in the nineteenth century alone, three reaching the United States, claiming 300,000 lives altogether.

This book records the role of U.S. medical science in the most recent—and finally successful—campaign against cholera. Drs. van Heyningen and Seal describe the first large-scale American research encounters with cholera, in Cairo in 1947 and in Bangkok in 1959. The authors then trace the growth in U.S. scientific and political interest in the eradication of cholera and describe the medical research and training facilities founded by the United States in Asia. There were failures as well as successes—exhaustive field trials of cholera vaccine proved ineffective—but eventually a simple oral treatment was found, and, in the process, advances were made toward the treatment of other dehydration diseases.

The authors devote an entire chapter to the biochemistry underlying the physiology of cholera because its implications reach far beyond the disease itself and throw light on many aspects of normal and abnormal biochemistry. They also recall the debt of modern cholera research to earlier discoveries, which were too often neglected. This extraordinary history of one of the most important developments in medicine concludes with an account of how, with the emergence of the independent republic of Bangladesh, the U.S.-dominated cholera research laboratory was, with good will, transformed into a locally controlled international center for the study of diarrhoeal disease and related problems.

W. E. van Heyningen is an internationally recognized biochemist who has specialized in bacterial toxins. Until his retirement in 1979, he was master of St. Cross College and was also actively involved in research and teaching bacterial chemistry at the University of Oxford, England. He now holds emeritus and honorary positions there. **John R. Seal** received his medical degree from the University of Virginia School of Medicine. He has served as director of intramural research, scientific director, and deputy director of the National Institute of Allergy and Infectious Diseases. He currently is special assistant for prevention research at the National Institutes of Health.

CHOLERA
The
American Scientific Experience,
1947–1980

W. E. van Heyningen
and John R. Seal

Westview Press • Boulder, Colorado

Illustration credits: Figure 1.1 is reproduced through the courtesy of the F. Berry Rockwell Estate and the Library of Congress. The photographs (Figures 3.1, 4.1–7, 8.1–7 and 9.2) were kindly supplied by the National Institute of Allergy and Infectious Diseases, National Institutes of Health, Bethesda, Maryland, U.S.A.

3 - 1303 - 00061 9363

Published in 1983 in the United States of America by
Westview Press, Inc.
5500 Central Avenue
Boulder, Colorado 80301
Frederick A. Praeger, President and Publisher

Library of Congress Cataloging in Publication Data
van Heyningen, W. E. (William Edward)
Cholera: the American scientific experience, 1947–1980.
Includes bibliographical references and index.
1. Cholera, Asiatic—Prevention—International cooperation—History—20th century. 2. Medical assistance, American—Asia—History—20th century.
I. Seal, John R. II. Title.
RA644.C3V36   616.9'32   82-2729
ISBN 0-86531-400-4   AACR2

Printed and bound in the United States of America

Contents

Tables and Figures

Preface

This book derives from four sources.

First Source. Unpublished papers originating from the National Institutes of Health (NIH) of the Public Health Service of the United States Department of Health and Human Services (formerly Department of Health, Education, and Welfare—DHEW): (1) Minutes of meetings, memoranda and reports of the Ad Hoc Committee on Cholera, January to November 1959. (2) Minutes of meetings and memoranda of the Cholera Advisory Committee (CAC), May 1960 to March 1972. (3) Reports by the Director, NIH, on behalf of the CAC to the Secretary-General of the Southeast Asia Treaty Organization (SEATO) on the SEATO Cholera Research Program, 1960 to 1972. (4) Minutes of the Cholera Toxoid Advisory Subcommittee of the CAC, later of the U.S. Cholera Panel of the U.S.-Japan Cooperative Medical Science Program (U.S.-Japan CMSP), June 1973 to September 1977. (5) Various papers relating to cholera, and in particular those embodying proposals for institutions to succeed the Pakistan-SEATO Cholera Research Laboratory (PSCRL) at Dacca prepared at the instigation of the Agency for International Development (AID) of the U.S. Department of State. (6) Annual proceedings of the directing council and of the technical committee of the PSCRL. (7) Corresponding files of the Cholera Research Program Office, the National Institute of Allergies and Infectious Diseases (NIAID) and the NIH.

Second Source. Transcripts of tape-recorded interviews by W. E. van H. with the following 46 persons concerned with cholera research in the United States, the United Kingdom, the PSCRL in Dacca, the Johns Hopkins University Center for Medical Research and Training (JHCMRT) in Calcutta, the U.S. Naval Medical Research Unit Number 3 (NAMRU-3) in Cairo and the U.S. Naval Medical Research Unit Number 2 (NAMRU-2) in Taipei between 1947 and 1978, the NIH between 1959 and 1980, and other institutions, giving the institution of presumed first contact with the cholera problem: the late Jamuil Alam, PSCRL; Earl

S. Beck, NIH; Abram S. Benenson, PSCRL; R. Quentin Blackwell, NAMRU-2; General Joe M. Blumberg, U.S. Army 406th Medical General Laboratory; Philip S. Brachman, Communicable Disease Center (CDC, now Centers for Disease Control); Sir Graham Bull, NAMRU-2; Charles C. J. Carpenter, JHCMRT; John J. Conroy, U.S. Embassy, Thailand; John P. Craig, PSCRL; George Curlin, PSCRL; the late Geoffrey Edsall, Walter Reed Army Institute of Research (WRAIR); John Feeley, Bureau of Biologics, Food and Drug Administration (BOB); Richard A. Finkelstein, University of Texas at Austin (UTA); Samuel Formal, WRAIR; Eugene J. Gangarosa, WRAIR; Robert S. Gordon, PSCRL; William B. Greenough, III, PSCRL; Carolyn Hardegree, BOB; Thomas Hendrix, Johns Hopkins Medical School (JHMS), Baltimore; Norbert Hirschhorn, PSCRL; Richard Hornick, University of Maryland School of Medicine (UMSM); Colonel Robert J. T. Joy, Uniformed Services University of the Health Sciences (USUHS), Bethesda; Alexander Langmuir, CDC; Charles E. Lankford, UTA; Michael Levine, PSCRL; Maclyn McCarthy, Rockefeller Institute, New York; Carl Miller, BOB; David R. Nalin, PSCRL; Franklin Neva, NAMRU-3; Robert Oseasohn, PSCRL; Doris Parkinson, NIH; Clifford Pease, AID; Mrs. Hope Phillips, widow of Robert A. Phillips, NAMRU-3; Nathaniel F. Pierce, JHCMRT; Margaret Pittman, BOB; R. Bradley Sack, JHCMRT; James Shannon, former Director, NIH; Joseph Stockard, PSCRL; Martha Vaughan, NIH; the late Willard F. Verwey, University of Texas Medical Branch, Galveston; Capt. Craig Wallace, NAMRU-2; Capt. Raymond H. Watten, NAMRU-2; Theodore E. Woodward, UMSM; William E. Woodward, PSCRL; and John Yardley, JHMS. We are most grateful to all these distinguished persons for having given so much of their time and their patience.

No specific references are made in the text to material derived from the first and second sources above. Copies of papers, tape recordings and transcripts are deposited in the Wellcome Unit for the History of Medicine, University of Oxford.

Third Source. The medical and scientific literature concerning cholera, or relevant to it in one way or another, in American, British, French, German and Indian journals between 1817 and 1980. Specific references to this material are given in the text.

Fourth Source. The personal experience of the authors. In his Navy career, J.R.S. was associated with many of the military workers on cholera and served as a member of the CAC between 1961 and 1965. Joining the NIAID in 1965, he became the chairman of the CAC until it dissolved in 1972, in that role serving as the NIH manager of the SEATO Cholera Research Program. Since 1972, in other administrative positions in NIAID, he has been cognizant of the activities of the U.S.-Japan CMSP Panel on Cholera and developments in Bangladesh.

W. E. van H. was concerned with the cholera problem from 1968 to 1980, serving as a consultant to the PSCRL and being an invited participant in meetings and the CAC, workshops and conferences sponsored by the CAC, PSCRL and the U.S. Cholera Panel of the U.S.-Japan CMSP. From 1970 to 1978, he did research on the cholera toxin receptor in his laboratory in the Sir William Dunn School of Pathology, University of Oxford.

Chapters 8, 9 and 10 are technical. The authors hope that Chapters 8 and 9 are comprehensible to interested readers of all disciplines, but Chapter 10 may be of interest only to biochemists. The emphasis on cholera toxin stems from the fact that this newly discovered product of the organism and its role in the pathogenesis of the disease captured the interest of American scientists involved with the developments here recorded. The inclusion of Chapter 10 is necessary since it was a direct outgrowth of the SEATO Cholera Research Program making cholera toxin available as a research reagent to a wide variety of biochemists, pharmacologists, physiologists, and other researchers. One of the more remarkable products of the program was the demonstration of the utility of the toxin in the laboratory for research unrelated to cholera.

W. E. van H. is deeply in debt of gratitude. He thanks the American people for their altruistic devotion, through their public health, political and academic agencies, to a world-wide problem that is of very little direct concern to themselves; he thanks the National Institute of Allergy and Infectious Diseases for making possible the numerous inquiries that needed to be made and providing the administrative assistance that was necessary, and in particular he thanks Mr. Kenneth O. Cooke, Mrs. Denise Boettcher, and Mrs. Jo Morris for considerable and considerate assistance; and he thanks Dr. Martin Cummings and his staff at the National Library of Medicine for expert advice and assistance. He is deeply grateful to Dr. Dennis Shaw, keeper of scientific books of the Bodleian Library, Oxford, for generous provision of a comfortable room in the Radcliffe Science Library, whose staff were always unfailing in the provision of learned assistance.

He thanks his former collaborator, Dr. Carolyn King, in the Sir William Dunn School of Pathology, University of Oxford, for a careful survey of the development of the understanding of the chemistry of cholera between 1970 and 1978 upon which Chapter 10 is based. He also thanks Mrs. June Clark, administrator of the Sir William Dunn School, for much support, and Mrs. Carol Phillips of St. Cross College for skillful assistance as well as enthusiastic lay appreciation, and Mrs. Lynda Hayworth. He is grateful to Professor Margaret Gowing of the history faculty and Dr. Charles Webster and Miss Margaret Pelling of the Wellcome Unit for the History of Medicine, University of Oxford, for encouragement in this, his first attempt at scientific history. Most of all he is grateful, deeply grateful, to his present collaborator, J.R.S., who proposed the writing of this book in the first place, and without whose encyclopaedic and unfailing support not only would this book never have been written, but many of the main events recorded in it would not have happened.

The authors would like also to record their appreciation of the friendly and efficient assistance they have received from the staff of Westview Press, and their awed admiration for the hawk-eyed vigilance of the editors.

Photographs appearing in the book unless otherwise attributed are through the courtesy of the Pakistan-SEATO Cholera Research Laboratory.

W. E. van Heyningen
John R. Seal

CHOLERA

I

The Disease

1. Introduction

Few major infectious diseases have moved with the times as successfully as cholera.

Editorial, *Proceedings of the Royal Society of Medicine,*
May 1977

There have been three watersheds in the history of the involvement of the Western world in cholera. The first, early in the last century, marked the end of the isolation since times immemorial of the West from cholera, when the disease erupted from India in six pandemics at intervals of one or two decades and invaded Europe five times and the Americas three times. It struck Britain with a terror such as had not been experienced since the Plague, which, to use Creighton's words, "had been the grand infective disease of Britain from the year of the Black Death, 1348–9, for more than three centuries, down to 1666" [86]. Diarrhoeal diseases (of which cholera is one) were not unknown in Europe and in fact often went under the name of "cholera" of some sort or another, such as "Cholera Nostra", but, to use Creighton's words again, the newly imported "Indian or Asiatic cholera, which first showed itself on British soil in one or more houses on the Quay of Sunderland in the month of October 1831, was a 'new disease' in a more real sense than anything in the country since the sweating sickness of 1485". But we must be wary of dramatics: "We are all the dupes of words or of their emotional colour", wrote Greenwood, comparing plague and the far more lethal disease with the "emotionally colourless [name of] influenza" [180]. Pelling has pointed out that "as a cause of death and debility in mid-nineteenth century England, cholera was surpassed among epidemic diseases by 'common continued fever' (chiefly typhoid, relapsing fever and some typhus), scarlet fever, smallpox, and measles, and accounted for only a very small proportion of the area of highest mortality, which occurred among infants and young children" [328]. She goes on to state that

> cholera has, however, attracted some of the kind of attention from historians that other diseases, excepting plague, have conspicuously lacked. There are many reasons for this: the shock value of cholera[1] abundantly recorded at the times of its appearance; its coincidence with other dramatic and disturbing forces, particularly the social and the political; its assumed relation to innovation in institutional and administrative structures; the comparative superiority of the records of its appearances; and the abundance of its literature. The *Surgeon-General's Catalogue* alone records 777 separate works on cholera published in London, including authors' contributions to journals (medical only), for the years 1845–1856.

At the very beginning of this era of nineteenth-century involvement of the West in the cholera problem, some acute observations were made by W. B. O'Shaughnessy as to the nature of the disease, and he drew the proper conclusions as to its treatment, but they were largely misunderstood and ignored, and their application was delayed for nearly a century. In the mid-nineteenth century, a very sound observation was made by John Snow on the water-borne cause of the disease, but it was not until it was confirmed by Robert Koch 30 years later that it was acted on by the introduction of serious sanitary measures. Towards the end of this year, the search for the poisonous agent of cholera— its toxin—was initiated by Koch, but at the same time put by him on the wrong scent, so that its discovery was delayed for 75 years. The modern history of cholera is to a surprising extent a history of rediscoveries of earlier major discoveries.

The second watershed, at the turn of the century, marked the dying away of cholera in the Western world, partly due to the improved sanitary measures that the disease called down upon itself through a dozen international sanitary conferences from 1851 to 1912 [210], and partly, perhaps largely, due to natural, as yet not understood, causes alluded to by Greenwood:

> As seems so often to be my fate, I must end on a note of interrogation. Why did the Indian variety of cholera acquire a dispersive power a little

---

1. It was shocking too when it first came to the United States in the nineteenth century. "In point of numbers, few Americans died of cholera, but for each of its victims, malaria and tuberculosis claimed scores. Unlike them, however, it was novel and horrifying, a crisis demanding response in every area of American life and thought" [377]. There may actually have been far more deaths from cholera in the United States than in Great Britain; see Table 1.1.

more than a century ago? Why did it ravage Europe for more than a generation and then lose interest in us? Without going the whole way with Sticker I am prepared to go some distance and to doubt whether the decisions of national and international committees on the blockading of land and sea frontiers have played a much more important role than the fly on the wheel [180].

As a consequence, interest in the disease died away in those parts of the world that were scientifically best equipped to deal with it and to do research into its nature.

The third watershed, at the turn of the 1950s, marked the end of the long period of stagnation in interest in the disease, at any rate in the West. It culminated, fittingly, in the publication in 1959 of Pollitzer's comprehensive and conscientious monograph on cholera [360].

Pollitzer's monograph appeared just too soon to record the beginning of the new era of progress in the understanding of cholera, which it is the object of the present history, however inadequately, to record. These beginnings were marked by the publication in the same year as the monograph, 75 years after Koch had postulated the existence of a cholera poison, of a report by S. N. De in Calcutta on the discovery of cholera toxin. And this discovery came in timely concatenation with new outbreaks of cholera beyond the borders of its homeland. In 1958, an epidemic of cholera in Bangkok attracted the interest of American investigators—an interest that had already been foreshadowed by the intervention of the U.S. Navy in an outbreak in Egypt in 1947. The Bangkok outbreak was the scientific, if not the bacteriological, curtain-raiser for the seventh cholera pandemic, which erupted in the Philippines in 1961. This was the beginning of the invasion of a greater part of the world than had previously been affected by the cholera vibrio— not the classical *Vibrio cholerae*, but the hitherto largely ignored and apparently harmless biotype *Vibrio eltor*, which, though meeker, is in fact more sinister because it is more able to survive. By now, the Americans, though not themselves affected by the disease, had the will, and enough experience, to deal with it. Out of these beginnings there grew over the last two decades an immense effort of investigation in Dacca and Calcutta, and in the United States. It has resulted in an explosion of knowledge not only about the nature and the treatment of cholera, and of other even more serious because more wide-spread diarrhoeal diseases affecting countries all over the world, but also about the scientific principles that are fundamental to the normal as well as to the abnormal functioning of the animal organism.

Thus, the editorial statement quoted at the head of this introduction is apposite, but only as long as it is applied to this third era of Western involvement in the cholera problem; as it applies to the previous two eras, it must be considered ironic.

2. The Six Cholera Pandemics of the Nineteenth Century

There is some disagreement about cholera's antiquity and about its homeland. De, one of India's noted cholera investigators (whom we will meet again), maintains that cholera is—or rather, was—not an exclusively Asiatic disease. He claims that cholera was present in the classical world and Arabia[2] and in Europe in the seventeenth and eighteenth centuries [96]. Howard-Jones disagrees; he points out that ever since the term "cholera" appeared in Hippocratic writings nearly 2,400 years ago it has, until the late nineteenth century, been a nosological mess, standing for all kinds of ill-defined sporadic gastrointestinal derangements of diverse origins, none of them having any relation to true Indian, or Asiatic, cholera [209]. The fact of the matter, as Greenwood has pointed out, is that while clinical *cases* of European "cholera" may have been very similar to *cases* of real Asiatic cholera, "epidemiologists agreeing in little else agree that the particular manifestations of cholera which showed themselves in Europe after Waterloo differed epidemiologically from anything which had been seen before. This difference may be summarized in a phrase as a difference in *dispersiveness*".

Although the presence of true cholera in Europe before the Battle of Waterloo must on balance be considered most unlikely, there is little doubt of its prolonged existence in India. Pollitzer records strong suggestive evidence that it has been there since historical times. Although it swept throughout India and neighbouring countries from time to time, its natural home has always been the delta of the Ganges[3] in Bengal—West Bengal in India, with its capital, Calcutta, on the Hooghly River; and East Bengal that was in India, then was East Pakistan, and now is Bangladesh with its capital, Dacca, on the Padma River.

This is a region of dense population, poor sanitation and a large surface area of water, where the temperature exceeds 17° C and the humidity exceeds 40 percent for a long period each year. These conditions

2. But Pollitzer points out that when Arabian medical writers were confronted by the outbreak of cholera in Oman in 1821 they had no name by which to designate the disease.

3. The holy River Ganges suffers two indignities near the end of its long journey from its source in an ice cave at the foot of a Himalayan snow-bed to its steaming delta on the Bay of Bengal: first, when it is joined by the mighty Brahmaputra (or Jamuna) River and becomes the Padma; then, when in this guise it is joined soon after by the Meghna and yields its name once more to that short if voluminous tributary. Nevertheless, the delta is still known as "the many mouths of the Ganges".

contribute to keeping the disease alive and endemic, ready to become epidemic in its season every year.

Towards the end of the eighteenth century, there were several severe outbreaks of cholera in India. In 1770, it was endemic in the Madras and Travancore regions. In March 1781, it attacked British troops on the march at Ganjam, between Madras and Calcutta, as if they had been struck by a planet (see p. 48), then moved on to Calcutta. From there, it moved to the holy place of Hardwar on the right bank of the Ganges, about 200 miles north of Delhi, and killed 20,000 pilgrims in less than 8 days. There were further devastating outbreaks in Arcot and Vellore in 1787 and 1794, and again in Ganjam in 1790. Thus, by the time the cholera came to Britain in 1831, the British had already had experience of it in India. The outbreak in Bengal in 1817, "from which", as Creighton states, "the modern history of cholera dates" [86], and the prevalence of cholera in the Madras Presidency shortly after, were the subject of several reports by British medical men serving with the East India Company or the British army or navy. Those who had seen cholera in India brought word back to Britain of the formidable new pestilence, and in the 1820s articles on cholera appeared for the first time in the British medical press.

In 1817, the first pandemic of cholera started with an unusually violent epidemic at Jessore, nearly halfway between Calcutta and Dacca, having probably originated in the hinterland of Bengal between the Ganges and the Brahmaputra. It spread rapidly through India and then eastward to China and Japan, and westward as far as the Syrian border of the Mediterranean Sea. It touched Armenia at Tiflis and European Russia at Astrakhan but went no further. By common consent, the date of 1817 is taken as the beginning of a new era in the history of cholera, but Pollitzer implies that the beginnings of the beginning were earlier, with the outbreaks in India mentioned in the previous paragraph. He states, "It was only during the last three decades of the eighteenth century when, as noted already, *for the first time in its known history the infection showed a marked tendency to spread far afield* [emphasis added], that further information on an invasion of contiguous or neighbouring countries became available". Creighton, referring to the outbreaks in India of 1781, 1783 and 1790, states that they

> were undoubtedly from the same epidemic infective cholera that was seen fifty years after in Europe. But there were occasional great explosions, which arose suddenly and ceased abruptly; whereas from about 1817 onwards the infections became, as it were, a seasonal product of the soil of Lower Bengal year after year, and at the same time began to range widely beyond its

"endemic area" to other provinces of India, beyond the North-Western frontier to Central Asia and to Europe, and across the ocean to America.

And Greenwood quotes the historian Sticker:

> What was new [the events of 1817] in the history of Indian cholera and rightly caused apprehension there as well as here was the further intelligence that this destructive epidemic no longer confined itself to a particular area and at the accustomed season of the year appeared simultaneously in several places, but set itself in motion, under the influence of some mysterious impulse began to travel, attaching itself to the lines of human intercourse, spread widely in various directions, exacting everywhere hecatombs of victims.

Creighton states that "the antecedents and circumstances that made the year 1817 so critical for cholera in India, and for its diffusiveness far beyond India, constitute one of the greatest problems in epidemiology." He did not think that the "personal habits [dispensation with systematic provision of faecal matters] of the peasantry, *not unknown in other countries* [emphasis added] and immemorial in Lower Bengal itself, should have led to a definite disease-effect in a certain year of the 19th Century and perennially thereafter", but that something must have been moving towards this effect before and eventually reached such a degree of aggravation as to make a specific result manifest. He believed that two things happened: One was a gradual change in the beds of the rivers, altering the relative amounts of water flowing above and under ground, thus affecting the decomposition processes in the soil; the other was the increase in the number of cultivators per square mile under British rule "owing to the cessation of intertribal wars, and of famines which were chiefly caused by the overflow of rivers no longer subject to floods, and of wilful and barbarous checks to population". One might smile now at such colonialist complacency, and at Pettenkorf's doctrine,[4] but considering only the facts of dense cultivation and a changed water-table, both of which might conceivably foster the well-being of the cholera vibrio, is there perhaps not a ring of good sense in the admirable Creighton's ideas? A recent article in *Scientific American* mentions a suggestion that the change in the epidemiological character of cholera was due to starvation during famines in Bengal caused by failures of harvests in the cold summer of 1816 that followed the eruption of Mount Tambora in the Dutch East Indies in 1815. The

---

4. Creighton in 1894 still adhered to the doctrine of Koch's opponent, Pettenkorf, which held that epidemics occur when the ground-water is at a low level, and that disease bacteria do not pass directly from the sick to the healthy, but pass into the soil, where they ripen when the soil is dry.

eruption ejected 25 cubic miles of debris into the air and reflected the heat of the sun away from the Earth [409]. But the change in cholera had begun 40 to 50 years earlier, and in any case a causative connexion between malnutrition and cholera, especially the epidemiology of cholera, is not established. Selwyn goes so far as to imply that there was not so much a change in an old disease but the birth of a new one, for he states firmly, and contrarily to the evidence adduced by, for example, Pollitzer, that cholera is a relatively young disease: "Before 1781 there were no authenticated epidemics of true 'Asiatic cholera'. . . . Around this time a subtle genetic change must have occurred in a member of the vibrio genus. This heralded the triumphal progress of true cholera beginning in Jessore, near Calcutta, in 1817 when the pandemic set out" [395].

The five subsequent pandemics reached Western Europe, three of them producing four epidemics in Great Britain; two pandemics reached the United States of America, producing three epidemics. There are no estimates for mortality in the first two American epidemics, but guesswork suggests the cholera killed perhaps twice as many people in all three epidemics in the United States as it did in the four epidemics in Great Britain (Table 1.1).

The second cholera pandemic set out in 1829[5] and reached Moscow in the autumn of 1830. After a lull in the winter, it advanced westward again vigorously in the spring of 1831 through the Baltic States and Poland. It reached the port of Hamburg in October, watched anxiously by the British with their close shipping connexions with the Baltic and German ports.[6] The most anxious British port was Sunderland, on Tyneside in the northeast of England, and, indeed, on 9 October it had its first case, and on 12 October its first death, but it was not until noon on Wednesday, 26 October 1831 that Britain's first officially acknowledged victim of cholera, William Sproat, died in a house on Fish Quay in Sunderland.[7] It spread over most of Britain, killing more than 23,000 people in England and Wales but strangely avoiding London and Birmingham.[8] Now it was the turn of the Americans to quake in their boots, and inevitably the cholera touched their shores in the

---

5. The dates of onset of the pandemics differ with different authors—these are taken from Pollitzer.

6. They had already had a foretaste in June, with the disease on board warships coming from Riga anchored in quarantine off the Medway below London.

7. For a popular account of the British waiting and preparing for the cholera, and of the four assaults they endured, see Longmate's *King Cholera* [256].

8. For an account of the cholera in nineteenth-century England, its relation to the industrialization and growth of towns, the public health concerns and the major developments in English epidemiology, see Pelling [328].

Table 1.1
The six cholera pandemics of the 19th century and the epidemics they
produced in Great Britain and the United States of America

Pandemics	Epidemics	
(Pollitzer [360])	Great Britain (Pelling [328]*)	United States (Chambers [66]**)
1. 1817	none	none
2. 1829	1. 1831, 23,000 dead	1. 1832, 50-150,000 dead
	2. 1849, 53,000 dead	2. 1849, 100,000 dead
3. 1852, the worst on record	3. 1853-4, 23,000 dead	none
4. 1863	4. 1866, 14,000 dead	3. 1866, 50,000 dead
5. 1881, much less havoc than earlier ones	none	none
6. 1889, Western Europe only slightly affected	none	none

*   Data for England and Wales only; Scottish data unknown.

** "..even so the mortality in '66 did not compare to that of previous
epidemics. While estimates for the whole country were not even attempted
for either of the previous epidemics in '33 a mortality of 5 percent, 10
percent or even 15 percent of the population of a locality was not unusual;
the mortality in '49 seldom reached 10 percent; while in '66 we know of no
considerable community where the mortality reached 5 percent".

summer of 1832. Officially, it arrived in Montreal on 6 June and moved
down to New York on 23 June, but it seems more likely that it was
imported into New York via an infected ship earlier than and independently of the Canadian outbreak, and that the fact appears to have
been suppressed by the New York Board of Health.[9] It reached most
of the major cities of the United States and by 1834 had crossed the

9. See Rosenberg's account, based on contemporary newspapers and medical journals,
of the cholera in nineteenth-century United States, largely concerned with New York
[377]. For a popular account based on a U.S. government report, see Chambers [66]. Like
the Europeans, the Americans were inclined to believe that cholera was intended for the
poor and the indiscreet ("The penalty of indiscretion must be paid!"), but in October
1832 a weekly journal did report that "a number of very respectable persons have died
of the cholera at Chambersburg" [309].

Rocky Mountains and pressed onward to the Pacific coast. It is said also to have reached South America and Central America. In 1834, it flared up again in France[10] and spread to Africa along the Mediterranean coast and down the east coast to Zanzibar. In 1848, it swept again over most of Europe, and it produced the most lethal attack that Britain endured, killing 53,000 people in England and Wales (Table 1.1). It returned again to the United States, from New York to the Rocky Mountains, although not justifying the title "America's greatest scourge" [66], and in 1850 attacked San Francisco overland and by sea from Panama.

The third pandemic started in 1852. It arose partly from recrudescences of the the second pandemic and partly from repeated importations of the disease. In England and Wales, it killed 23,000 people in 1854 (Table 1.1) but was more severe in Southern Europe, and that year was considered by Pollitzer to be one of the worst cholera years on record. It appeared in China and Japan, in North Africa and later in East Africa, and in South and Central America, but not in North America.

The fourth pandemic started in 1863. It found its way to Europe, not by its accustomed route through Persia and the Caspian ports, but by means of pilgrims through Mecca to Egypt and Constantinople and thence to Italy and southern France. It killed half a million people on the continent of Europe, but in Britain, where it was to produce the last serious outbreak, the toll was only 14,000. It travelled extensively through Africa, from North Africa as far south as Kenya and Tanganyika on the east and Gambia and Portuguese Guinea on the west. It produced its last assault on the United States in 1866, travelling on newly laid railroads to the South and the Middle West, killing perhaps 50,000 people, considerably fewer than in the previous attacks of 1832 and 1849.

The fifth pandemic (1881) caused much less havoc than its predecessors. It is notable for us, for it was the one studied in the summer of 1883 by the French and German cholera commissions under Isadore Straus and Robert Koch in Egypt, and later by Koch in Calcutta. It reached Egypt again through Mecca, and produced an epidemic in Toulon and in Italy in 1884. Although cases were imported into Britain, the disease was thwarted from going any farther by adequate sanitary measures. The cholera also failed to get into New York from any infected ships arriving there in 1887 and 1892. Pollitzer maintains that this was due to the "rapid establishment of a correct diagnosis through laboratory

---

10. Three villages in France (in the Departments of Aisne, Seine-et-Oise and Saône-et-Loire) were named "Choléra". For a fictional account of the later attack in Provence, see Giono's novel with the terrifying title of *Le Hussard sur le toit* [159].

methods, this being the first time that bacteriology was used for such a purpose", but one wonders whether bacteriological confirmation of such an expected and readily recognizable disease really was essential under the circumstances—it could hardly have initiated quarantine, but only confirm its necessity, and might even have delayed matters rather than expedite them. Although cholera did not enter North America, it did produce the most serious outbreak of the period in Argentina and Chile.

The sixth pandemic, which lasted from 1899 to 1923, was essentially the last outbreak of cholera in the West. It caused many deaths in Mecca and Egypt, and in Russia, but its visitations to Western Europe were restricted to sporadic cases or abortive outbreaks. It failed to reach the Americas.

3. The Nature of the Disease

And thou shalt have great sickness by disease of thy bowels, until thy bowels fall out by reason of the sickness day by day.

2 Chronicles 21:15

Cholera is a disease of the bowels' turning to water, and the water being discharged from both ends of the alimentary tract by vomiting and diarrhoea, mainly by diarrhoea. Premonitory symptoms are rare, and the onset of the disease is generally abrupt, with diarrhoea and vomiting sometimes even occurring in sleep, usually some hours after the last meal, when the stomach and small intestines are empty. At the first SEATO Conference on Cholera in Dacca in December 1960, A.K.M. Abdul Wahed, who had had 40 years of experience of cholera in Bengal, described the disease in this way:

After the normal contents of the bowel have been evacuated, the typical rice-water stool of cholera starts. . . . Large quantities (one to four pints) are passed at intervals of 1/2 to 1 hour in the earlier stages and lesser amounts (6 to 8ozs) in between at frequent but irregular intervals. The total number of stools may be 12 to 15 in 24 hours in mild cases and 20 to 30 in severe cases [i.e., up to 30 litres a day]. Vomiting occurs simultaneously with the rice-water stool. It is not associated with nausea or retching. Diarrhoea and vomiting produce the typical picture of cholera, typified by cold clammy skin, poor pulse which is frequently imperceptible, tachypnoea [rapid breathing], pinched faces, sunken eyes, shrivelling of the skin of the hands and feet and cyanosis [blueing] of the nail beds. The tongue is clean but dry, and the voice is hoarse. The patient is restless but quite alert. Frantic demand for water to alleviate thirst is a very important feature. . . . Cholera patients

FIGURE 1.1. American medical science did not slumber in 1883, it hardly existed. The concern in America about importation of the fifth cholera pandemic of 1881 sent young Dr. Joseph Kinyoun to study with Pasteur and Koch in Europe. Returning, he set up a bacteriological laboratory in the Marine Hospital, Staten Island, N.Y., in 1887. The present National Institutes of Health is directly traceable to that laboratory. *Vibrio cholera* were isolated by Dr. Kinyoun from immigrants in 1887 and 1888, but strict quarantine was credited with preventing its entry. This cartoon by Kendrick was published in *Life*, 2 August 1883.

are mentally quite clear though totally exhausted and prostrated. Many have intense fear of impending death [444].

One of the earliest visitors to Tyneside after the cholera arrived there was a Frenchman, François Magendie, teacher and collaborator of Claude Bernard, Professor of Medicine at the Collége de France and physician at the Hôtel-Dieu, the oldest and most famous of the Paris hospitals. The French had been anxious to learn more about cholera and had sought permission to go to Russia to study the disease, which had arrived in Moscow in 1830, but Tsar Nicholas I would not recognize the newly created King Louis-Philippe (*le Roi-Citoyen*) and had ordered his ambassador in Paris to refuse passports to French subjects wishing to enter Russia. By the time the French eventually got permission to visit St. Petersburg in February 1831, the cholera epidemic was over, so on 21 October, very shortly after the cholera had reached Sunderland (and before the first "official" victim had succumbed), Magendie asked the Academy of Sciences of Paris to send him there. He arrived on 2 December, and in a letter he sent to the President of the Academy the next day he wrote

> a person in the best of health, when he is smitten by the cholera, is in an instant transformed into a corpse! There is the same state of the eyes, the same aspect of the face; the same coldness of the limbs; the same colour of the skin, etc. Were there not the intelligence left, so to speak, intact, were there not a remnant of the voice even though almost imperceptible, one would proceed to burial at the actual moment of attack. . . . to put it all in one word, the disease which is under my eyes in an instant *cadaverizes* the person whom it attacks.

Later in London, asked what he thought of cholera, he replied (so it is said), "I think it is a disease which begins where others end, with death" [313].

Magendie was followed nine days later by a remarkable young British physician from London, William Brooke O'Shaughnessy. Victoria was not to ascend to the throne for yet another six years, but already a Victorian taste for melodrama had found scope for expression in harrowing descriptions of the disease, which nonetheless were accurate, even without Abdul Wahed's long experience, and not unduly embellished. Witness O'Shaughnessy's description of a patient:

> On the floor . . . lay a girl of slender make and juvenile height, but with the face of a superannuated hag. She uttered no moan, gave expression of no pain, but she languidly flung herself from side to side, and from the supine to the prone position. The colour of her countenance was that of lead—a

silver blue, ghastly tint; her eyes were sunk deep into their sockets, as though they had been driven an inch behind their natural position; her mouth was squared; her features flattened; her eyelids black; her fingers shrunk, bent, and inky in their hue. All pulse was gone at the wrist, and a tenaceous sweat moistened her bosom. In short, Sir, that face and form I can never forget, were I to live beyond the period of man's natural age [318].[11]

American descriptions of the disease at that time were also harrowing. A surgeon in the U.S. Army reported in 1832:

The face was sunken, as if wasted by lingering consumption; perfectly angular, and rendered particularly ghastly by the complete removal of all the soft solids, and their places supplied by dark lead colored lines; the hands and feet were bluish white, wrinkled as when long macerated in cold water; the eyes had fallen to the bottom of their orbs, and evinced a glaring vitality, but without mobility; and the surface of the body was cold and bedewed with an early exudation. I stood gasping in mute horror upon the revolting object, when a sudden spasm convulsing his limbs caused him to screech in a voice so unearthly, that I involuntarily covered my ears with my hands [309].

The conditions thus described in the cholera patient are due to dehydration. All the water lost in the vomitus and stools must come from somewhere, and it comes from the blood, which consequently thickens and is often likened to tar; and the blood in its turn draws water from the tissues of the body, that is, from the intercellular spaces, and finally from the cells themselves. But in addition to being dehydrated, the cholera patient is demineralized and dealkalinized because with the water he loses are the mineral and alkaline salts dissolved in it. This demineralization and dealkalinization is no less harmful than liquid dehydration. Cholera diarrhoea is thus the exteriorization and consequent loss of the body fluid, the *milieu intérieur*.

At this stage, we must touch on some of the concepts and terms that come into considerations of that liquid *milieu intérieur*, since it constitutes the immediate environment of the organism, resembling and replacing the external environment of early forms of life, that is, sea-water. Claude Bernard thus expresses its role:

11. The pages of the British medical journals of the nineteenth century, particularly those on cholera in *The Lancet*, could provide a rich and virgin lode of source material for many a Ph.D. thesis on English literary style of the period. Indeed, a suggestion to the effect was recently accepted with avidity by a Professor of English.

Table 1.2
Concentration (mEq/l) of principal ions in various normal and cholera
pathological body fluids and in intravenous replacement (i.v.r.f.) and
maintenance fluids (i.v.m.f.) and oral replacement fluids (o.r.f.)

Line	Reference	Fluid	Author/ Date	$^+$NA	$^+$K	$^-$Cl	$^-$HCO$_3$
1	29	Seawater		478	10	535	0.47[a]
2		Seawater 1/3 dilution		159	3.3	178	0.16[a]
3	321	Blood, normal	O'Shaugh- nessy, 1832	135	-	103	16
4	456	Blood, normal	NAMRU-2, 1959	151	4.6	111	28
5	239	Sweat		87	5	90	-
6	34	Tears		145	24	128	26
7	320	Blood, Cholera	O'Shaugh- nessy, 1831-32	45	-	37	-
8	456	Blood, Cholera	NAMRU-2, 1959	158	4.8	119	18
9	456	Stools, Cholera	NAMRU-2, 1959	137	16	107	45
10	48	i.v.r.f.	O'Shaugh- nessy, 1831[b]	117- 198	0	62	7-17
11	243	i.v.r.f.	Latta, 1831-32	58	0	49	9
12	372	i.v.r.f.	Rogers, 1921[c]	278	0	230	56

there are in fact two environments for the animal: a *milieu extérieur* in which
the organism is placed—the atmosphere if it breathes, fresh or salt water if
it is aquatic—and a *milieu intérieur* in which the elements of the tissues
live. A creature exists, not in the *milieu extérieur*, but in the liquid *milieu
intérieur* formed by the circulating vital liquid which surrounds and bathes
all the anatomical elements of the tissues; this is the lymph or plasma, the
liquid part of the blood, which penetrates the tissues in higher animals and
constitutes the ensemble of all the interstitial fluids, the basis of all local
nutrition, and the source and coming together of all elementary exchanges.
A complex organism should be considered as the sum of all the simple
anatomical elements living in the liquid *milieu intérieur*.

The stability of the *milieu intérieur* is the condition for free and independent
existence; the mechanism which permits this is that which ensures in the

Table 1.2 (cont.)

Line	Reference	Fluid	Author/ Date	$^+$NA	$^+$K	$^-$Cl	$^-$HCO$_3$
13	218	i.v.r.f.	NAMRU-3, 1948	179	3.4	123	60
14	456	i.v.r.f.	NAMRU-2, Bangkok, 1959[d]	163	11	148	26
15	447	i.v.r.f.	NAMRU-2 Philippines, 1962[e]	174	0	115	60
16	337	i.v.r.f.	Phillips, Dacca, 1960	135	15	105	45
17	58	i.v.r.f.	Traditional Indian, 1966	175	0	153	22
18	178	i.v.r.f.	PSCRL 5/4/1, 1964	133	13	99	48
19	58	i.v.r.f.	JHCMRT, 1966	156	0	104	52[f]
20	347	o.r.f.[g]	JHCMRT, 1968	110	9	79	40
21	297	o.r.f.[h]	PSCRL, 1968	119	8	80	48
22	268	o.r.f.[i]	JHCMRT, 1973	90	0	60	30

a) Includes carbonate; b) attributed by Carpenter [48]; c) calculated by Carpenter [58] ; d) 8/1 saline/bicarbonate with KCL added; e) 3/1 saline/bicarbonate; f) lactate, equivalent to HCO$_3$; g) contains 160 mMoles glucose/1; h) contains 111 mMoles glucose/1; i) contains 121 mMoles glucose/1.

milieu intérieur the maintenance of all the conditions necessary for the existence of the elements [our translation] [27].

It was Macallum who gave historical and phylogenetic meaning to the constancy of Claude Bernard's *milieu intérieur* when, in 1926, he demonstrated the remarkable resemblance between the salt composition of the blood sera of various animal species and that of sea-water, the *milieu extérieur* in which the beginnings of life arose about 2.5 billion years ago [263]. He pointed out that just as in the embryonic development of the animal organism there were successive changes in structure in which could be found indications of its remote ancestral history, so too the cells of the animal tissue had endowments transmitted from the past, and so even had the chemical composition of the fluids that bathed them. The constancy of the proportions of the ionic elements of this fluid and the similarity of these proportions to those of sea-water indicated that they were of more than casual origin and that they might have a paleogenetic character.

Table 1.2, lines 4 and 2, show that the relative proportions of the principal ionic elements of human blood plasma water, sodium (Na^+), potassium (K^+), chloride (Cl^-) and bicarbonate (HCO_3^-) are similar to those of sea-water, although sea-water is three times as concentrated as plasma water. The proportion of chloride of plasma water is markedly lower than that of sea-water, but the proportions of the sums of the negative ions (anions), $Cl^- + HCO_3^-$, are very similar. Chloride takes the place of bicarbonate in sea-water because, in the relatively alkaline sea, soluble bicarbonates in calcium and magnesium are converted to insoluble carbonates and precipitated, eventually to become rock strata of chalk, dolomite and limestone.

It would be respectful to consider for a few moments the origins of the salts of the sea upon which this essential *milieu intérieur* is based. They are derived from the rocks of the Earth's crust and thus we are tied by our blood to the earth we stand on—we are its kin.

The Earth's crust consists predominantly of silicates and alumino-silicates of iron, calcium, sodium, potassium and magnesium. Other elements are less common by one or more orders of magnitude. Under the action of water containing atmospheric carbon dioxide (carbonic acid), the silicates are weathered, and those elements (Ca^{++}, Na^+ and Mg^{++}) that have soluble bicarbonates go into solution and flow to the sea. Silicon, aluminium and iron are transported predominantly as sediment, and even those amounts of them which dissolve are quickly precipitated when they reach the sea. Thus, the only important positively charged ions (cations) in the sea are Ca^{++}, Na^+, K^+ and Mg^{++}. The relative proportions of these cations in the sea are greatly modified by its slight alkalinity (pH 8–8.4), which converts bicarbonate to carbonate; calcium and magnesium are accordingly removed, as we have seen, as chalk, limestone and dolomite. Potassium is much more strongly absorbed onto clay sediments than is sodium and is therefore also preferentially incorporated in the formation of new sedimentary rocks; thus, the 2 to 1 ratio of sodium to potassium in the Earth's crust is increased to about 50 to 1 in the sea. Since chlorine is very much less abundant in the Earth's crust than sodium (by a factor of 200), and since carbonic acid is the essential agent of weathering, it might be expected that the main constituent of the salts in the sea would be sodium carbonate rather than sodium chloride. As we have seen, the reverse is true, due to the low solubility of calcium carbonate, so that the calcium inflow to the sea keeps the carbonate concentration low, and also due to the fact that virtually all chlorides are soluble, so that there is no mechanism for the removal of chloride from the ocean.

Blood plasma, the fluid in which the red blood corpuscles are suspended, is a solution containing about 9 grams of salts and 80 grams of protein per litre of water.[12] We will not be concerned much with the protein, but only with salts that occur more abundantly in plasma, i.e., the neutral chlorides of sodium and potassium and the alkaline bicarbonate of sodium. These salts are electrolytes, that is to say, when they are in solution in water they dissociate into their constituent electrically charged particles, or ions—positively charged cations and negatively charged anions, i.e., sodium (Na^+), potassium (K^+), chloride (Cl^-) and bicarbonate (HCO_3^-). Ions attract water, and the greater their concentration, the greater their attraction. This is the driving force of osmosis—water will always move through a semi-permeable membrane (such as the wall of a blood vessel or a tissue cell) from a solution of lower concentration of ions to one of higher concentration. Solutions with the same concentration of ions, and therefore the same attraction for water, are isotonic and iso-osmotic with each other. In considering concentrations of ions, we must be concerned not with their gram weight per unit volume of solution, but rather with their equivalent weight, which is proportional to the atomic weight of the atoms, or the molecular weight of the molecules or complex ions concerned. The atomic weights of sodium, potassium and chloride ions are approximately 23, 39 and 35.5, respectively; the bicarbonate ion, HCO_3^-, composed of the three elements hydrogen, carbon and oxygen, has a "molecular" weight of 61. Thus, for example, a solution of 58.5 grams of sodium chloride (23 g Na^+ + 35.5 g Cl^-, or one gram equivalent of each ion) per litre would be equivalent to, and isotonic or iso-osmotic with, a solution containing 100 g potassium bicarbonate (39 g K^+ + 61 g HCO_3^-) per litre. It is convenient and customary to express these concentrations as milliequivalents per litre (mEq/l), and thus these two isotonic solutions each contain 1000 mEq/l of the salts (or their constituent ions). The approximate concentrations of these ions in normal plasma water are: Na^+, 140 mEq/l; K^+, 5 mEq/l; Cl^-, 100 mEq/l;

12. The concentrations of salts in plasma should refer to their amounts per unit volume of plasma water, rather than of whole plasma, because the protein occupies an appreciable volume in a sample of plasma, and thus must be deducted; otherwise, the salts would appear to be dissolved in a falsely larger volume and thus their concentrations would seem to be lower than they really are.

HCO_3^-, 25 mEq/l.[13] (The far higher gram concentration of protein in blood amounts only to 16 mEq/l, because the molecular weights of proteins are very high compared with those of salts, about 40,000 in the case of plasma proteins.) The chlorides of sodium and potassium are neutral, i.e., neither acid nor alkaline, because they are, to put it in an old-fashioned way that will suffice for the present, salts of strong bases, sodium and potassium hydroxides (NaOH and KOH), and a strong acid, hydrochloric acid (HCl). The more abundant NaCl is important to plasma because it contributes largely to its tonicity, or osmolality; the less abundant KCl is important because potassium is an essential constituent of all tissue and blood cells and is necessary, for example, for the proper functioning of the heart. The bicarbonate of sodium ($NaHCO_3$) is alkaline because it is the partial salt of a strong base and a weak acid, carbonic acid (H_2CO_3), the hydrated form of carbon dioxide ($CO_2 + H_2O = H_2CO_3$), the concentration of which is regulated by continuous formation in the course of normal metabolism in the body and continuous elimination through the lungs. The loss—which we shall soon see—of $NaHCO_3$ from the blood in cholera reduces its alkalinity, although hardly ever actually to the point of acidity.[14] Nevertheless, this condition of dangerously reduced alkalinity of the blood is now generally referred to as "acidosis". The other anions (e.g., calcium, magnesium) and cations (e.g., phosphate, acetate) of plasma occur in low concentrations and are of no particular relevance to cholera.

In India, where there had been long experience of cholera, there was no understanding of the nature of the disease by the British physicians who were there during the first three decades of the nineteenth century. On the whole, since the black and tarry blood looked unhealthy, the thought was to get rid of it by bleeding, or by the application of leeches, even though the paucity and the thickness of the blood made this difficult. "Eliminative treatment" through one end or the other of the gut was also practiced, either by the administration of strong purgatives such as croton oil or calomel, or of emetics such as mustard oil or antimony salts. The unhappy patients were also cauterized with hot

---

13. See Table 1.2. Blood and tears have comparable concentrations of these ions (except that tears have about five times the concentration of K^+); sweat has an appreciably lower content of Cl^-.

14. The acidity of a fluid is proportional to the concentration of hydrogen ions, [H+], in it. This, for reasons that need not concern us now, is generally expressed in an upside-down way as pH, the logarithm of the reciprocal of [H+]. pH 7 is neutral, pH>7 alkaline, pH<7 acid. Normal blood has a pH of 7.4. "Acidotic" blood in cholera may go down to a pH of 7.2, rarely to pH 6.95, but this apparently small change in pH signifies a considerable loss of alkalinity, as we shall see.

irons or had blisters raised on them by the application of boiling water, nitric acid or sulphuric acid [208].

But as soon as cholera came to Europe, it was realized by some observant spirits what the true nature of the disease was. However, as Pollitzer has said, "Observations which have stood the test of time were made by a handful of advanced workers at comparatively early dates, but the facts observed by them were ignored or disputed by the vast majority of those taking an interest in the problem of cholera who were engaged in abstruse beliefs and practices of their own". When the malady reached Moscow for the first time by the autumn of 1830, the Governor-General, Prince Dimitri Galitzin, appointed a Temporary Medical Council to advise on its prevention and treatment.

One of the members of this Council was a German expatriate, Jaehnichen, physician to the Institute of Artificial Mineral Waters in Moscow, and Howard-Jones states (giving no reference) that at one of the first meetings of the Council, in the autumn of 1830, he proposed that water should be injected into the veins [208]. Jaehnichen himself makes no mention of such a proposal in a pamphlet published in 1830 [212a], nor is it mentioned in a paper dated 25 December 1830–January 1831 submitted in the *Gazette médicale de Paris* [213]. It perhaps is more likely that he made the suggestion later, following the investigations made by his colleague at the Institute of Artificial Mineral Waters, the chemist Hermann [see 208], a fellow German expatriate with whom he shared a house. Hermann was the first to make chemical analyses of the blood and stools of cholera patients and of normal people, and for this much credit is due to him, especially since some of the conclusions he drew were correct, even if most of his analyses were not. In a paper published in mid-1831, he claimed that normal blood serum was acid (wrong) due to the presence of acetic acid (wrong), and that cholera serum was alkaline, whereas the cholera stools were acid (wrong) with acetic acid (wrong). The proportion of the volume of the blood clot (i.e., the red cells plus clotted fibrin) rose from 43 percent in normal patients to 60 percent in cholera patients (right enough). Hermann concluded that the watery stools and vomit of cholera were formerly part of the blood (right), and that the immediate cause of death was the thickening of the blood and the consequent decrease in its circulation (partly right). He also concluded "das die Absorptionsfähigkeit des Darmakanals wahrend der Cholera absolut ertodtet seyn muss"—i.e., the absorptive capacity of the alimentary tract must be absolutely killed in cholera (half-right)—and supported this conclusion with a chance observation that was, more or less, prophetic of an observation to be made by R. A. Phillips in the Philippines 130 years later. He noted that the stools of a cholera patient who had happened to drink artificial mineral water (containing sodium carbonate, something Hermann should know about) shortly before the diarrhoeal attack contained sodium carbonate, i.e, the sodium carbonate was not absorbed by the gut, whereas it was absorbed in normal individuals [194].

Hermann deplored the fact that Jaehnichen's proposal (whenever and wherever it was made) of "Wassereinspritzungen in die Venen zu versuchen" was not considered. However, F.C.M. Markus, medical secretary to Prince Galitzin's Council, stated later that, since Hermann had found acetic acid in cholera stools, Jaehnichen had proposed the injection of water lightly acidulated with acetic acid. Jaehnichen encountered numerous difficulties in carrying out this proposal and was able only once to inject water (whether acidulated or not is not clear) in the veins of a woman who had been in agony for a day. It was not possible to introduce more than 6 oz of water, which had no result but for the reappearance of the radial pulse for 15 minutes, and the patient died after two hours. Thus ended the first recorded attempt at the rehydration of a cholera patient, but the outcome does not seem to have discouraged Markus, for he says, in a paper published in 1832, that he cites the proposal and the experiment in order to establish priority for Russian [sic] doctors against claims made "much later" by French and English doctors [272]. But intravenously injected water, alone or with a little acetic acid, would not help a cholera patient, who suffers not only from a lack of water in his blood but also of equally essential minerals.

As Markus implied, the idea of rehydration had by the time of his writing been taken up in Great Britain. The young London physician William Brooke O'Shaughnessy, a week before he followed Magendie to Sunderland on 11 December 1831, had, on the basis of descriptions of the disease which he had not yet seen, put forward a "Proposal of a New Method of Treating the Blue Epidemic Cholera by the Injection of Highly Oxygenised Salts into the Venous System" at a meeting of the Westminster Medical Society on 3 December [317]. His idea was to restore oxygen to the black blood of cholera patients in hopeless condition by the injection of potassium chlorate solution, which he had tried on a dog without ill-effect. He rejected the idea of injecting sodium chloride (which, as we will see, he was soon to recommend) on the grounds that it had no oxidizing capacity. In this paper, he referred in disparaging terms to Hermann's analyses of cholera blood, especially the mention of free acetic acid (which was also questioned editorially at about the same time in a translated extract of Hermann's paper [108a]). When he got to Sunderland and saw his first cholera patients, he approached the problem of the disease with good common sense: "The habits of practical chemistry which I have occasionally pursued, naturally led me, as well as others, to enquire whether in the remote causes, the pathology and physiology of the disease, any data could be discovered which might lead to the application of chemistry to its cure". His intention was to rectify the condition brought about by the disease, rather than deal with its agent, which, "in such utter darkness, I repeat, are we regarding its true constitution, that to attempt to supply an antidote on the recognized chemical principles which toxicologists have determined, could possibly be attended with no beneficial or even encouraging results [318]". He analysed the blood and stools of cholera patients and confirmed his scepticism of Hermann's curious ideas about acetic acid. By the end of December, he reported to the *Lancet* an outline of the results he had obtained:

> 1. The blood drawn in the worst cases of *the* cholera, is unchanged in its anatomical or globular structure. 2. It has *lost a large proportion of its water*, 1000 parts of cholera serum having but an average of 860 *parts of water*. 3. *It has lost also a great proportion of its* NEUTRAL *saline ingredients*. 4. *Of the free alkali contained in healthy serum, not a particle is present in some cases, and barely a trace in others*. 5. Urea exists in cases where suppression of urine has been marked symptom. 6. *All the salts deficient in the blood, especially the carbonate of soda, are present in large quantities in the peculiar white dejected matters*". (O'Shaughnessy's emphasis [319]).

This brief statement contains all the essential truths about the chemical consequences of cholera that are the foundations upon which the modern therapy of the disease is based, but the truth was not genuinely to be grasped for many years.

On 7 January 1832, O'Shaughnessy gave a report to the Central Board of Health in London detailing his analyses in Tyneside and in London. This was published by the Board as a 72-page monograph [321], which was extensively reviewed in the *Lancet* of 31 March [320]. As well as showing a clear understanding of the function of the "colouring matter of the blood" (i.e., the haemoglobin) in transporting carbon dioxide and oxygen, this report gave analyses of normal and choleraic blood and stools which stand the test of time very well. O'Shaughnessy showed that the ingredients defective in the blood appeared in the dejections, or, in other words, that "the addition of the dejection to the blood, in due proportion, would have restored the latter to its normal constitution". As to the treatment of severe cases of cholera, he stated, "I would not hesitate to inject some ounces of warm water into the veins. I would also, without apprehension, dissolve in that water the mild innocuous salts which nature herself is accustomed to combine with the human blood, and which in Cholera are deficient".

His data for normal and cholera blood and for intravenous replacement fluid (translated from grains per ounce to milliequivalents per litre) are shown respectively in lines 3, 7 and 10 of Table 1.2.

O'Shaughnessy himself never practiced intravenous therapy on a cholera patient, but his principle was soon to be applied with great success by Thomas Latta of Leith, as we shall see below, and, in fact, O'Shaughnessy made no further contributions to the cholera problem. He had been born in Limerick in 1809 and was thus only 22 years old when he went to Sunderland in 1831 and only newly qualified as a physician, having taken his M.D. at Edinburgh the previous year. In 1832, he was appointed cholera inspector for the Camberwell and Newington Districts of London but left for India the next year in the service of the East India Company. He was appointed assistant-surgeon in Bengal in August 1833. The only reference to any interest he showed in cholera in India is in a report of a meeting of the Medical and Physical Society of Calcutta (of which he was Foreign Secretary) in July 1836 giving an account of the treatment by one Dr. Stewart of a case of cholera by the intraveous injection of 4 pints of water containing 2 scruples of carbonate of soda and 3 drachms of muriate (chloride) of soda, but without success. A committee was appointed "to experiment upon and report on the extent to which injections into the veins may be practised with safety upon animals, and likewise the effects of aqueous solutions of saline substances at different temperatures. Dr. O'Shaughnessy to be secretary of the committee [420a]". Further search reveals no subsequent report of this committee, or any reference to O'Shaughnessy and cholera. O'Shaughnessy died in England (at Southsea) in 1889, and his obituary notices (under the name of Sir William O'Shaughnessy Brooke) in the *British Medical Journal* (4 January 1902), the *Times* (11 January 1889) and the *Telegraphic Journal and Electrical Review* (18 January 1889), as well as entries on him in the *Dictionary of National Biography*, Boase's *English Biography* and the *English Cyclopaedia*, make no mention of his work on cholera, doubtless because by the time they were written the treatment of cholera by intravenous rehydration according to his principles had not, after more than 50 years, been taken up, and was, indeed, in some disrepute. The fact which won him so much recognition was something else—the introduction of the electric telegraph in India. A few years after O'Shaughnessy's arrival in India, his mind began to turn to other things, including chemistry, electric batteries and motors, and particularly the telegraph. By May 1839, he had erected an experimental wire near Calcutta and, after overcoming initial official apathy, succeeded by 1855 in laying down a network of 4000 miles of telegraph lines between Calcutta, Agra, Bombay, Peshawar and Madras. He had to surmount immense difficulties, extending his lines with untrained workmen through dense untracked jungles and over mile-wide unbridged rivers. His project was completed just before the Mutiny, and it was said that "the telegraph saved India". He returned from India in 1856 and was knighted and later transposed his name to Sir William O'Shaughnessy Brooke [169].

In May 1832, Thomas Latta, a physician of Leith in Scotland, attempted rehydration of a cholera patient according to O'Shaughnessy's principles. His account of his experience is worth repeating at some length, for it tells us much about cholera and its treatment, and about Thomas Latta himself: "So soon as I heard the result of Dr. O'Shaughnessy's analysis, I attempted to restore the blood to its natural state, by injecting copiously into the larger intestine warm water, holding in solution the requisite salts—".[15] This treatment appeared only to aggravate the patient's condition, so he

at length resolved to throw the fluid immediately into the circulation. In this, having no precedent to direct me, I proceeded with much caution. The first subject of experiment was an aged female, on whom all the usual remedies had been fully tried, without producing one good symptom; the disease, uninterrupted, holding steadily on its course. She had apparently reached the last moments of her earthly existence, and now nothing could injure her—indeed, so entirely was she reduced, that I feared I should be unable to get my apparatus ready ere she expired. Having inserted a tube into the basilic vein, cautiously—anxiously, I watched the effects; ounce after ounce was injected, but no visible change was produced. Still persevering, I thought she began to breathe less laboriously, soon the sharpened features, and sunken eye, and fallen jaw, pale and cold, bearing the manifest impress of death's signet, began to glow with returning animation; the pulse, which had long ceased, returned to the wrist; at the first small and quick, by degrees it became more and more distinct, fuller, slower, and firmer, and in the short space of half an hour, when six pints had been injected, she expressed in a firm voice that she was free from all uneasiness, actually became jocular, and fancied all she needed was a little sleep; her extremities were warm, and every feature bore the aspect of comfort and health. This being my first case, I fancied my patient secure, and from my great need of a little repose, left her in charge of the hospital surgeon; *but I had not been long gone, ere the vomiting and purging recurring, soon reduced her to her former state of debility.* I was not apprised of the event, and she sunk in five and half hours after I left her. As she had previously been of a sound constitution, I have no doubt *the case could have issued in complete reaction,*

15. Carpenter has pointed out that "the fluids suggested by O'Shaughnessy were very close to those which are used for the treatment of cholera today—the differences between the fluids would be chemically inconsequential in the majority of adult patients if the patients were permitted to drink *ad libitum*" [48].

had the remedy, which already had produced such effect, been repeated [emphasis added] [243].

The very sick cholera patient no longer has diarrhoea because there is no more fluid to lose, but if the fluid is restored it will be lost again as long as the epithelium of the gut is lined with cells poisoned by the cholera toxin. This will last for some hours or days, until the infecting cholera vibrios are eliminated from the gut, as they always are in the natural course of events, and the poisoned epithelial cells are shed and replaced by new, unpoisoned cells. Until this takes place, fluid loss must be balanced by intravenous replacement. Latta realized that rehydration should be continued, although he could not have understood the reasons—perhaps he had a good physician's instinct. At any rate, with his next patients he demonstrated that persistence in rehydration brought success. He recommended that when diarrhoea recurred after rehydration the intravenous injection should be repeated, not too quickly, and "persisted in, and repeated as symptoms demand, or until reaction is completely established". He stressed, as R. A. Phillips was to do 128 years later, the need for initial rapid administration of fluids (up to 90 ml per minute), and, when the patient was adequately rehydrated, for the constant matching of fluid loss with replacement.

But few physicians paid attention to Latta's advice. This was perhaps partly due to Latta's death in 1833 and to the recession of the cholera epidemic in the same year (and possibly also to O'Shaughnessy's departure to India in that year). During the subsequent cholera epidemics in Britain, intravenous rehydration was still regarded as producing only a temporary alleviation of the symptoms of cholera (and allowing a less painful death). Even the highly sensible John Snow, in 1856, accepted that the rehydrated patient only "for a time seems well [403]", and so, as we shall see, did Sir Leonard Rogers after a further 50 years. In Victorian times, there was much controversy over the merits of eliminative treatment (blood-letting, induced purging and emesis) and of conservative treatment (rehydration).[16] Rehydration was retried from

16. For a vivid and well-informed fictional rendering of this debate, see Farrel's novel, *The Siege of Krishnapur* [115].

17. Some tried immediately after Latta: For example, a correspondent to the *London Medical Gazette* of September 1832 reported 28 cures out of 30 patients treated with saline compared with 78 deaths out of 78 patients treated in other ways [4]. In New York in 1832, intravenous injection of 0.6 to 0.9 l or more of a solution containing 47

time to time for 80 years after Latta first tried it, only to be given up.[17]
Even if it had been tried persistently, it would not have been without
its troubles. In the early days, before the germ theory of disease had
been established, the use of unsterilized saline could have led to
septicaemia, and the use of undistilled water containing pyrogens (fever-
producing substances) could have (and apparently did) lead to the
production of high fever. But we shall see that interest in rehydration
was revived early in this century and that in the end it triumphed
beyond any dreams that O'Shaughnessy or Latta may have had.

4. The Cause of the Disease

When cholera struck Britain for the second time, in 1853, the in-
comparable John Snow, in his spare time from doing research on
anaesthetics and applying the knowledge thus gained on Queen Victoria
and other patients, showed that the cholera "poison" was of a particulate
nature carried from one person to another by being swallowed and
increasing in the alimentary tract. He proved unanswerably that the
"poison" was carried by water contaminated with sewage, and he
suggested preventive measures based on personal cleanliness, avoidance
of faecal contamination of food and drink, and destruction of the
"poison" in food by cooking [403]. We now know that cholera results
from the infection and colonization of the small intestine by the Gram-
negative bacterium *Vibrio cholerae* (or, as we shall see, its biotype *Vibrio
eltor*). Robert Koch is generally credited with the discovery of the
organism, which he called the Kommabacillus (*Bacillus virgulus*), in 1883
[232], but in fact he had been anticipated by 30 years by Snow's Italian
contemporary Filippo Pacini, who observed myriads of curved organisms
swarming in the intestinal contents of cholera victims and ascribed the
cause of the disease to them, giving them the name *Vibrio cholerae*
[324]. Others also saw such organisms at the same time, but did not
ascribe the disease to them [210]. This discovery by Pacini was recognized
more than a century later by the Judicial Commission of the International
Commission on Bacteriological Nomenclature (1965), which ruled that

mEq NaCl/l and 16 mEq NaHCO$_3$/l was used to cure several people "even in the *last*
stage previous to death". No reference was made in this report to O'Shaughnessy or
Latta, but there was time enough for their reports to have travelled from Britain to
America [309]. There do not appear to be any further reports of attempts at intravenous
therapy of cholera in America, at least not in Rosenberg's or Chambers's accounts. Borodin,
the Russian physician-chemist-composer, is said to have been cured of cholera in 1885
by a laboratory colleague giving him an injection of saline [102]. Tchaikovsky did not
have this advantage and died of cholera.

the official name of the cholera bacillus should be *"Vibrio cholerae* Pacini 1854" [39a].[18]

Snow and Pacini made their observations during the second great cholera pandemic in Europe. After cholera had struck Europe for the fourth time, the First Conference for the Discussion of the Cholera Question was held at the Imperial German Health Office in Berlin on 26 July 1884 [233]. The menace was persistent and the pressure to deal with it had increased. In the meantime, the germ theory of disease was on the point of becoming established, and therefore the possibility of understanding the nature of cholera was improved. However, as Koch pointed out at the conference, studies on cholera had not been able to profit much from the progress made in studies on other infectious diseases during the previous 10 years because there had been no demand for inquiries into cholera in Europe; and while there had been much cholera in India, no one had been available to study it by the new methods of research. In the late summer of 1883, French and German commissions under Isadore Straus and Robert Koch, respectively, had been sent to Egypt to investigate the cholera outbreak there, and Koch had gone from Egypt to Calcutta for further study of the question. The object of the First Conference was to receive and discuss his report on his investigations in Egypt and India. The great pathologist Virchow, who had, as we shall see, his own views on the nature of the disease, presided over the meeting. There can be no doubt that Robert Koch was "by common consent the greatest pure bacteriologist [40]". Who else? Nor can there be any doubt that at this momentous conference Koch firmly established the "comma bacillus" as the causative organism of cholera; but he achieved this as much with the weight of his undeniable authority (and to judge from his writing, the force of his personality) as with his science. In effect, he persuaded the world to accept what had already been discovered—and clearly pointed out—by those who had preceded him by 30 years in his observations on cholera, but since he never referred to their observations he could perhaps be said to have been either insufficiently informed or lacking in generosity. It was not he who discovered the cholera vibrio as a practically pure culture

18. Howard-Jones has written a spirited defence of the fundamental importance of Snow's and Pacini's contributions to the understanding of cholera. They both competed for the Bréant Prize (for advancing science on the question of cholera) in 1858, but neither won; in fact, the judges awarded no prizes that year, thereby gaining for themselves some kind of niche in the negative history of cholera [209].

19. Pacini was not honoured in his own country, either, but he was in Britain. In 1865, he wrote: "When my scientific labours, having made the tour of Europe, will have returned, arrayed in foreign garb, to Florence, they will have permission to enter the

in the intestinal contents of cholera patients—it was Pacini.[19] It was not he who demonstrated conclusively that the cholera vibrio was water-borne—it was Snow. This is to emphasize the validity of the work of Koch's predecessors, not to deny the value of Koch's own work.

Koch had observed the comma bacilli in the intestinal contents (but not in the blood or tissues) of all of the many cholera victims he studied and had failed to observe it in healthy people or people suffering from other (mainly intestinal) diseases than cholera. He considered three arguments: (1) That the cholera process was not due to the bacilli, but was favourable for their development. In that case, everybody must have the bacilli in them before having cholera, since cholera was a wide-spread disease; but this was not so because, as we have seen above, the bacillus was never seen in healthy people or in those suffering from other diseases. (2) Another cart-before-the-horse argument, namely, that the disease was the cause rather than the result of the bacilli—that during the disease some normal bacterial colonizer of the gut underwent an alteration and assumed the form and character of the cholera bacillus. As to form, Koch stated that he knew of no case of a bacterium changing its form; as to character, he presented an argument of apparently unnoticed circularity—that the only change in character that he knew of was a loss of pathogenicity, as sometimes observed with anthrax bacilli. But this, he argued, was exactly the opposite of what would happen "if the harmless intestinal bacteria changed to the dangerous cholera bacilli". But who claimed the cholera bacilli were dangerous? Not those who would put the cart before the horse! Why should they? According to them, the dangerous condition changed the bacilli, and the bacilli did not bring about the dangerous condition. (3) The third argument he considered, and accepted, was that the comma bacilli caused cholera. He knew of no other explanation for the disease than that the comma bacilli preceded it and caused it. One of Koch's "postulates" (so called by others) for establishing that a given germ causes a given disease was that the germ should be grown in pure culture. The *raison d'être* of such a pure culture was to fulfill another

schools, and by then I shall be enjoying tranquil repose in Trespiano" [i.e., the grave]. An annotation in the *Lancet* of 1884 commented: "This bitter forecast has been verified almost to the letter, Pacini's doctrine, rehabilitated by the German Cholera Commission, being now adopted by his compatriots and taught in the Istituti Pathologici of Italy a year after his death" [2]. The word "rehabilitated" in this annotation appears recently to have been misunderstood by an Italian author and taken as "acknowledged", which, sadly, is the opposite of the truth [144].

of Koch's postulates—that the disease should be reproduced by inoculating the pure culture into experimental animals. But no sooner had
Koch stated this postulate in 1883 than he had to renounce it in February
1884 [233], a few months before the Berlin Conference.[20] He had failed
to produce cholera experimentally and argued that there was no possibility of doing so because cholera was no more a disease of animals
than rinderpest was disease of humans. But although Koch had tem-
porarily to abandon experiments on animals, he was able to claim—
with justice—that he had on hand some observations that were quite
as good as experiments on man. The most important of these was the
frequent infection of persons in India through contact with cholera linen,
in which he had always found the cholera bacilli in pure culture. Here
was man unwittingly swallowing pure cultures of cholera bacilli and
contracting cholera. He also cited instances of large numbers of people
living on the banks of village tanks (ponds, the only water supply)
getting cholera after these tanks had become contaminated with comma
bacilli through the deposition of cholera dejecta in one way or another.

5. The Seventh Cholera Pandemic

There are two biotypes of the cholera vibrio—the classical *Vibrio
cholerae* which was responsible for the first six cholera pandemics, and
the El Tor vibrio, officially known as *Vibrio eltor*, which is responsible
for the present seventh pandemic. Both these biotypes fall into three
immunological types, or serotypes—Inaba, Ogawa and, rarely, Hikojima.
As the designation implies, the two biotypes, although they have much
in common in their immunological make-up, have different physiologies
and therefore different life-styles and different epidemiologies. The El
Tor biotype can frequently infect without causing disease, the ratio of
the number of inapparent infections to actual cases of cholera being
about 100 to 1, compared with a ratio of 10 to 1 with the classical
vibrio [12]. Moreover, the El Tor has a much greater capacity to survive
in the environment [117]. These two factors make it possible for it to
disseminate through a community without being recognized [446] and
it is likely that they are the factors that made it possible for an El Tor
cholera pandemic to take over from the classical vibrio in places where
it had hitherto reigned, to spread throughout a larger area of the world
and to persist in a way that the classical vibrio was never able to do.
Although the El Tor case rate may be lower than that of the classical

20. He need not have been so hasty. A year later, at the Second Conference on
cholera in May 1885, he was able to report on successful experimental cholera infection
in animals [235].

vibrio, there appear to be no significant differences between the clinical and biochemical manifestations caused by the two biotypes in the same populations at the same time.

Vibrio eltor gets its name from the quarantine station established in 1886 at El Tor, on the Sinai peninsula, where the organism was discovered by Gotschlick in the bodies of dead pilgrims returning from Mecca. The pilgrims had no symptoms of cholera before death. It differed from the classical vibrio in two respects: it produced a haemolysin which dissolved red blood cells and it appeared not to cause real cholera, but only a mild variant called "para-cholera". In 1937, it appeared in the Celebes, where it caused an epidemic of cholera-like disease in which the case-infection rate was low, but the fatality-case rate at least as high as that of the classical vibrio, 50 to 60 percent. In 1961, El Tor defied all ideas about its being of a non-epidemic nature and set out on the seventh cholera pandemic, spreading rapidly through Indonesia to China and the Philippines and thence eventually to India and East Pakistan, the Middle East, Southern Europe, and East and West Africa, where its own characteristics and the local conditions make it likely that it will stay [127].

With all the properties that render it so adaptable to travelling, why did El Tor not set off on its pandemic sooner? Selwyn suggests that when it lost its haemolysin in 1961, it lost its innocence as well [395], but Finkelstein has pointed out that when epidemic cholera first broke out in the Philippines in 1961 the El Tor vibrio strains were markedly haemolytic and lost the property only later [127]. The year 1961 stands to the seventh cholera pandemic as 1817 stands to the first. We are unable to say whether El Tor underwent a change about that time or not, because although we know something about its life-style now, we know very little about it before it became so notorious.

II

The Long-Delayed Discovery of Cholera Toxin

1. The Instrument of the Disease: The Idea of Microbial Poisoning

By what instrument does the cholera vibrio bring about severe diarrhoea in the person it infects? The causes of the harmful effects of most infectious diseases are not yet understood. The ability of a microbe to grow in the body of the host is not the same thing as its capacity to produce disease, for there is no intrinsic reason why harm should arise from the mere presence (after multiplication) of a very small weight of invading microbes in the body of a patient—from a few millionths of a gram in tetanus to a tenth of a gram at most in anthrax. The idea that the transmissible external agents of disease, whatever they were, should be poisons was a natural one, and as often as not these agents themselves were actually referred to as "poisons".[1] With the coming of the germ theory of infectious diseases, the idea of poisoning was carried on in the suggestion that the germs produced poisons. Thus, in 1886, Watson Cheyne, discussing the recently established germ theory, expressed a view that is still widely held today, although there is little hard evidence for it in most infectious diseases:

> How the bacteria act in the production of the disease is also a question on which but little has been done. Their mode of action is possibly different in different instances. Probably the most general mode of action is by the production of poisonous chemical substances, which act locally on the affected part, thus setting up local appearances, and are also absorbed into the system and cause fever, the general disturbance of the various organs, and the fatal result [454].

1. A word which Howard-Jones could have added to his list of terms—"virus", "germ", "animalcule", "microphyte", "seed", "fungus", "insect", "miasm"—that were used interchangeably [210].

Like most of his contemporaries, Watson Cheyne believed that these "poisonous chemical substances" were the cadaveric alkaloids, or "ptomaines", of Selmi which were thought to arise from the putrefaction of proteinaceous materials in the body [394]. The idea of disease had been linked for a long time with putrefaction [74], and the idea of putrefaction of proteinaceous material had always gone hand in hand with fermentation of carbohydrates since both were associated with germs of one sort or another. It did not matter whether the germs caused the putrescence or were produced by it. Studies on the production of poisonous substances by putrefactive processes were started in earnest toward the end of the eighteenth century and culminated 100 years later in the work of Brieger, who isolated a number of feebly toxic ptomaines (putrescine, cadaverine, etc.) from putrefying meat and human cadavers [37]. The ptomaine doctrine was generally accepted in its time and had such powerful adherents as Robert Koch, who stated firmly of the cholera bacilli that "we can only explain their action by supposing that they generate poisons belonging to the group of ptomaines, which are absorbed, and then act on the entire organism [235]". But this can perhaps be regarded as the last serious invocation of the ptomaine doctrine, for it effectively collapsed after another two or three years,[2] not only for want of supporting evidence but also because of the discovery of three powerful bacterial toxins—those of diphtheria, tetanus and botulism—that were definitely not small-molecular ptomaines, but large, "ferment-like" protein molecules. Up to this stage, there had been no real evidence of any poison being produced by any pathogenic microbe under the conditions of a natural disease, and the idea of a bacterial poison had had no real basis—it was simply a notion that easily sprang to mind and filled the vacuum that existed for want of any other explanation for the harmful effects of infectious diseases. And except for the few diseases to be discussed, this vacuum persists today.

Since the discovery of diphtheria, tetanus and botulinum toxins, it has been shown that many other pathogenic bacteria produce toxins, but the fact that a pathogenic organism produces a particular toxin does not necessarily mean that the toxin plays an important part in producing the harmful effects of the infectious disease. In cases other than diphtheria, tetanus, botulism and cholera (and some other diarrhoeal diseases),

---

2. Isolated pockets of resistance held out for a long time, and the word "ptomaine" still strikes terror in the breasts of laymen. Recently, putrescine has enjoyed a revival in an entirely different sphere—it belongs to a group of polyamines that are ubiquitous in normal animal tissues and occur in higher concentration in cancer tissues [244, 413].

there is no good reason for concluding that any toxin produced does, or does not, cause harm in the course of the disease.[3]

2. Exotoxins and Endotoxins

There are two types of bacterial toxins, exotoxins and endotoxins, so named originally because it was believed that, respectively, they were secreted by Gram-positive organisms into the culture medium, or contained within the cell substance of Gram-negative organisms. This distinction is no longer so clear, but there are more important differences, shown in Table 2.1.

The toxins relevant to the diseases discussed in this essay are all the more toxic, more individualistic, more enzyme-like, more simply constituted exotoxins, but cholera endotoxin must, alas, also be discussed since it was an irrelevant nuisance, a very large red herring, in the history of cholera toxin for nearly 70 years.

Diphtheria, tetanus and botulinum toxins were all hypothesized about the same time as cholera toxin, and their existence was demonstrated within a few years of their being hypothesized; but cholera toxin was not discovered for 75 years. The object of this chapter is to discuss that long delay, but before proceeding with it, let us for comparison consider the hypothesization and discovery of the toxins of diphtheria, tetanus and botulism.

3. The Quickly Discovered Toxins

Diphtheria Toxin

Diphtheria is an acute infectious disease caused by the Gram-positive *Corynebacterium diphtheriae*. In the majority of cases, the growth of the organism is localised at the site of infection on the mucosal surfaces of the upper respiratory passages, where it causes a primary lesion in the form of superficial ulceration, covered by a membrane consisting of a coherent mass of bacteria, together with necrotic epithelium, phagocytes and fibrin, firmly attached to the underlying tissues. Occasionally, this membrane threatens life by blocking the respiratory

---

3. It is true that the staphylococcus produces two exotoxins which cause harm in the course of disease, but they are unimportant, and not the cause of the fatal effects of some staphylococcal infections. The red rash of scarlet fever is due to a toxin that frightens the mother more than it hurts the child. The epidermolytic toxin of scarlet fever can produce a most distressing and uncomfortable peeling off of the skin of infants, but it is a rare condition and when it occurs it is short-lived and never fatal [432].

Table 2.1
Differences between bacterial exotoxins and endotoxins

Property	Exotoxins	Endotoxins
Parent organisms	Gram-positive Gram-negative	Gram-negative
Within or without parent organism	within and without	within
Chemical nature	simple protein	protein-lipid-polysaccharide
Stability to heating	labile	stable
Detoxification by formaldehyde	detoxified	not detoxified
Neutralisation by homologous antibody	complete	partial
Biological activity	individual to toxin	same for all toxins
Toxicity compared with strychnine as 1	100 to 1,000,000	0.1

passage. However, the most serious lesion in diphtheria is not this local mechanical one, but a distant biochemical one, which in humans occurs particularly in the heart and the peripheral nerves, which remain sterile. In experimental guinea pigs, the kidneys and adrenal glands are affected and there is also marked pleural effusion. These distant effects are due to a toxin carried to the affected organ by the bloodstream from the site of the local lesion. The heart muscle, especially, suffers damage and it is usually this that is the cause of death in humans.

Diphtheria toxin is a bipartite protein toxin (as cholera toxin also turned out to be), that is, it is a protein consisting of two parts—A and B—joined together by easily cleavable peptide bonds and disulphide bonds. Part B binds to receptor sites (as yet not identified) on the membranes of susceptible cells and in so doing facilitates the passage of part A through the membrane to the interior of the cell. Part A is an enzyme that blocks protein synthesis in the cell by preventing elongation of polypeptides [80]. This inhibition of protein synthesis causes necrotizing of tissues and thus the break-down of heart muscle and damage to other organs.

People who survive diphtheria are generally immune to it, or at least to its worst effects, for life, largely because they have gained immunity to the toxin. Diphtheria can easily be prevented by actively immunizing those at risk (mainly infants) with diphtheria toxoid, which is the toxin rendered non-toxic by treatment with formaldehyde (see Table 2.1) without destroying its capacity to stimulate the production of antibodies.

In 1878, Robert Koch laid down as one of his criteria or so-called "postulates" for regarding a particular bacterium as the cause of a particular disease the condition that *"the bacteria must be demonstrated without exception in such proportions with respect to their number and their distribution that the symptoms of the disease in question can be completely explained"* (Koch's emphasis) [231]. The next year, Koch was joined at the Kaiserlichen Deutschen Gesundheitsamt in Berlin by an assistant, Friedrich Loeffler, nine years his junior. One supposes that in the presumably authoritarian atmosphere of the Imperial German Health Office at that time Loeffler must have stood in awe of his superior. But if that was so, it did not, when he cautiously[4] proposed that Klebs's[5] bacillus was the causative organism of diptheria, deter him from stating a conclusion that ran contrary to the part of Koch's postulate referring to the distribution of suspected bacteria. He had found that when inoculations of the bacillus were made through the skin or mucous membrane of guinea pigs they fell easy victims and died with the usual symptoms of diphtheria, including haemorrhages throughout the body, pleural effusion, lobular consolidation of the lungs and inflammation of the adrenal glands. But all these organs were sterile—the bacilli remained restricted to the site of inoculation. Loeffler concluded that death was not due to the spreading of the bacillus throughout the body, but to the spreading of a poison produced at the site of inoculation by the bacterium that remained restricted to this site. The symptoms produced at a distance from this site were not to be explained, as Koch had specified, by a distribution of the bacterium,

---

4. His caution was due to other considerations: absence of paralysis in animals that had been inoculated with the bacillus and had sickened but survived; the presence of a bacillus identical to Klebs's in the mouth of a healthy infant; failure to find the bacillus in certain typical cases of diptheria [229].

5. Poor Klebs! He "was one of the first in every advance in bacteriology but had the misfortune to miss almost every discovery that has turned out to be correct" [40].

but rather by the distribution of its product, the soluble diphtherial chemical poison [253].[6]

In 1887, and again in 1888, Loeffler attempted to isolate this poison and claimed that he had succeeded in doing so [254], but his evidence does not support him. In October 1887, he grew a number of cultures of the diphtheria bacillus for three days, by which time the cultures were still acid, but none was toxic. He attacked the problem again in the summer of 1888, this time being guided by his conclusion that the bacterial poison resembled the recently studied proteinaceous poison, abrin, that occurs in the seeds of the tropical Jequirity vine, *Abrus precatorius* [274], since both poisons acted similarly on the mucous membranes of men and animals and both were inactivated by heating at 60° to 70° C.[7] Since the Jequirity poison was a "kind of enzyme", soluble in water and glycerine and insoluble in alcohol, Loeffler added glycerine to four- or five-day-old cultures, then precipitated the glycerine extracts by the addition of five volumes of alcohol. After standing in alcohol for 24 hours, the precipitate was filtered off, again mixed with alcohol, and acidified. Large amounts (100 to 200 mg) of the material thus precipitated were injected subcutaneously into guinea pigs. These hapless animals "bristled up their hair and raised themselves on their feet, uttering loud cries". No doubt they were cries of protest, for they were suffering in vain, not from diphtheria toxin, but from what in laboratories nowadays is called "crud". Loeffler's four- or five-day-old acid cultures were unlikely to have contained more than traces of diphtheria toxin, and such toxin as they might have contained would not have survived that prolonged treatment with five volumes of alcohol. Loeffler himself noted that the Jequirity poison was active, not in hundreds, but in hundredths of milligrams.

Where Loeffler failed, Roux and Yersin succeeded in the same year. They succeeded because they used old alkaline cultures of the diphtheria bacillus rather than young acid cultures. Moreover, they filtered these

---

6. The word "toxin" was hardly used (if at all) until von Behring invented the word "antitoxic" in 1890 [443], although Bretonneau, who was the first to differentiate and name diphtheria, used the word "toxaemia" in 1855 in referring to a terrible visitation of Angina Maligna (i.e. diphtheria) in Tours in 1825 [278]. But he was referring generally to the effects produced by the agent of the disease and not specifically suggesting that this agent produced a toxin.

7. Loeffler's comparison of diphtheria toxin with abrin was much later to prove far more appropriate than he could possibly have imagined. It is now known that both poisons are very similar not only in molecular structure (being bipartite proteins, one part binding to the surface of susceptible animals' cells, thereby permitting the entry of the other, enzymically active, part into the cell), but also in mode of action at the molecular level (in each case, the enzymically active component of the toxin blocks protein synthesis). See Olsnes [314].

cultures through porcelain filters and showed that these germ-free filtrates were toxic, thus demonstrating for the first time the presence of a bacterial exotoxin. Enormous doses (35 ml) of filtrates from 7-day-old cultures were needed to kill guinea pigs, but only 0.125 ml of a 30-day-old culture filtrate (by now alkaline) was needed for a lethal dose. When the toxin was precipitated from such a filtrate with calcium chloride, the lethal dose was 0.4 mg. The lesions in animals succumbing to diphtheria toxin (that is, the induration at the point of injection, the haemorrhagic congestion of the kidneys and adrenal glands, and the pleural effusion) were the same as those observed in the natural disease and in animals inoculated with the bacillus. As Loeffler had already observed, the toxin was destroyed by gentle heating and therefore comparable with an enzyme. Credit for the first demonstration of a bacterial toxin must go to Roux and Yersin [379], but Loeffler deserves a very good share of it. It was he who first suggested that such a toxin must exist, and he would probably have demonstrated its existence himself had he used 30-day cultures of the diphtheria bacillus rather than 4- to 5-day-old cultures. He used young cultures because, when he injected the bacillus into guinea pigs, the organisms were at their most active at four to five days; he did not realize that the toxin was formed much later in artificial cultures.

Tetanus Toxin

Tetanus is an ancient disease resulting from infection by the Gram-positive *Clostridium tetani* of wounds that are often so slight as to be undetectable post mortem. It is endemic, but never epidemic, in all countries because the spore of the tetanus bacillus is always present in greater or lesser degree in all soil. The incidence varies according to people's sanitary habits and the richness of the soil in spores. The world death rate, which possibly amounts to two million a year [434], is by far the highest in the underdeveloped tropical countries of Asia, Africa and South America. Most of the victims are new-born babies who die of *tetanus neonatorum*, or umbilical tetanus, due to infection of the newly severed umbilical cord.[8]

Tetanus is a terrifying disease of spastic paralysis, resulting from opposing muscles pulling against each other. It generally starts with restlessness, muscular irritability and twitching, then with stiffness of the neck muscles, and difficulty in opening the mouth and feeding. Muscular spasm quickly increases, first causing difficulty in swallowing,

---

8. In the mid-nineteenth century so many newborn babies died of tetanus on the island of St. Kilda, 110 miles west of the Scottish mainland, that a woman rarely provided clothing for her baby until 8 days had passed [408].

then spreading to the main muscles; the abdominal muscles become board-like, the back arches, the neck muscles are rigid and the jaw is locked. Convulsions then begin to take place under the slightest stimulus (a light switched on, the bed-clothes twitched), and the whole body is contorted in a major spasm resulting from violent contraction of all the muscles—the spine is strongly arched, the jaws tightly clenched in a fearsome grin (*risis sardonicus*), and spasms of the larynx impede respiration. The patient is fully conscious, sweating profusely, exhausted from continuous muscular activity, and in dreadful pain. When the spasm relaxes, he lies in awful apprehension of the next spasm which will certainly come. Death is due to exhaustion, heart failure or collapse of the lungs.

This violent spastic paralysis is very similar to that brought about by strychnine, and is due to an amount of tetanus toxin which may be as small (if a pound of man is as susceptible as a pound of experimental mice) as one thirty-millionth of a gram. The toxin appears, like diphtheria toxin, to be a bipartite toxin, that is to say, it is a protein consisting of two parts, one twice the size of the other, joined together by easily cleavable bonds. The two parts are inactive singly, but when joined together again the reconstituted protein is fully toxic. The larger part binds to the tetanus toxin receptor in nervous tissue, which has been identified as a ganglioside [276, 429] similar, except for a detail, to the one that is the receptor for cholera toxin (see p. 261). The toxin acts, by a means not yet understood, by preventing the output of transmitter substance from nerve endings, mainly in the central nervous system, but also in the peripheral and autonomic nervous systems. It is its action on the central nervous system that results in the muscular spasms mentioned above. The toxin blocks the release of transmitter substance from the inhibitory interneurones in the spinal cord which normally allow movement by causing one muscle to relax while the opposing one pulls—the consequence is that both muscles pull against each other and rigidity or spasm ensues [432].

Unlike the diphtheria patient, the tetanus patient who survives has no immunity to the disease. The reason is that the lethal dose of tetanus toxin is far smaller (a million times?) than the dose that immunizes. Artificial immunization with tetanus toxoid is highly effective.

The credit for the discovery of the tetanus bacillus, and for the hypothesization of tetanus toxin, must go to Arthur Nicolaier. As a 22-year-old medical student at Gottingen, Nicolaier worked for his doctoral thesis on the production of tetanus-like symptoms in experimental animals following, after an incubation period, the injection of samples of earth. Post mortem, the animals showed surprisingly little change,[9] except for a very small amount of pus at the site of inoculation. The pus contained micrococci and various kinds of bacilli among which invariably, and often in overwhelming masses, were fine slender bacilli, a little longer but hardly thicker than the bacillus of Koch's mouse septicaemia. These could not be found anywhere away from the site of inoculation. Samples of heated earth produced no effect, thus ruling out a poison in the earth, but sieved clear extracts of unheated earth also produced tetanus symptoms. Inoculation of pus from animals that had died from the injection of earth also produced tetanus,[10] with a much reduced incubation time. Nicolaier was unable to prepare a pure culture of his "feine schlanke Bacillen", as demanded by Koch's recently expressed postulates, but nevertheless ventured the assertion that "in spite of the not completely satisfactory results of the microscopic examinations the thought cannot be dismissed that one has to do here with an infectious tetanus brought about by microorganisms".

Nicolaier concluded that the inability of the tetanus bacillus to spread and multiply in the body must mean that the organism produced a poison that was similar in its action to strychnine. He stated that he was busy with investigations to confirm this hypothesis [307]. All he needed to do was to test the effect of a germ-free culture filtrate, but if he did so, he did not report it.

Brieger, up to these times the acknowledged master of bacterial poisons, inevitably claimed to have isolated not only one, but two (and later four) varieties of the tetanus poison, tetanin and tetanotoxin, which, he averred, produced typical tetanus symptoms within 20 minutes of injection into experimental animals [37]. (Real tetanus toxin, even when 50,000 lethal doses are injected, cannot evoke symptoms in less than an hour.) Kitasato started work on tetanus under Koch and was the first to achieve the difficult task of isolating the tetanus bacillus in pure culture. He produced tetanus with it [227] and was evidently impressed by Brieger's "meisterhaften Experimentaluntersuchung", for he and Weyl set out to repeat his work with their pure cultures. In order to isolate tetanin, the culture was subjected to procedures guaranteed to destroy any protein, such as heating for some hours at 60° C in dilute hydrochloric

9. Although the manifestations of tetanus ante mortem are violent and terrifying, post mortem there is nothing to see with the naked eye or the microscope. No organ, no tissue is damaged, and a skilled pathologist, not having seen the patient alive, would probably not be able to determine the cause of death.

10. About the same time, Carle and Rattone showed that human tetanus could be transferred to rabbits by inoculating them with the pus from the site of infection [45].

acid, treatment with a great excess of alcohol, precipitation with platinum chloride, repeated precipitation with ether, etc. It needed large doses to produce any effect in experimental animals, and that was hardly notable. For example, a medium-sized guinea pig received 525 mg (half a gram!) of tetanin hydrochloride subcutaneously; after 10 minutes, there was a strong secretion from the nose and mouth, the animal sat motionless for 30 minutes, then got better and survived.

The experience with tetanotoxin was much the same, and Kitasato came to the conclusion, as a result of his observations on the toxicity of liquid tetanus cultures, that the tetanus bacillus must produce a substance of much greater toxicity. He made no mention of tests with cell-free culture filtrates [228].

The ubiquitous Brieger, in papers concerned mainly with diphtheria poison, but with several others as well, now revised his views somewhat and produced two more tetanus toxins, a "hydrochloric acid toxin" and a proteinaceous ("toxalbumen") "spasmotoxin" that produced cramp in animals [38]. With the latter, Brieger had at least come nearer—but not near enough to—something like the truth. In fact, far simpler and better work was being done at the same time in Italy and in Denmark. Tizzoni and Catani[11] had set out to investigate whether the action of the tetanus bacillus could be explained by the production of a poison. They showed that sterile filtered cultures in very small amount (part of a drop) brought about exactly the same picture of tetanus in rabbits as the inoculation of virulent cultures. Thus, six years after Nicolaier's hypothesization, they showed clearly that the tetanus bacillus produced a toxin. When they used Brieger's method for isolating toxalbumen, which involved frequent precipitation with acidified alcohol, their material was completely lacking in toxicity. But they were able to get a highly toxic dry material by a procedure that is still sound practice today with active proteins, i.e., dialysis to remove small-molecular impurities, and then drying in a vacuum, or precipitation with ammonium sulphate. They considered that tetanus toxin was a protein, something in the nature of an enzyme. They also came to the important conclusion that it acted directly on the nervous system [417, 418].

Faber, who is often credited with the first demonstration of tetanus toxin, independently reported more or less the same experiments as Tizzoni and Catani a month later and came to the same clearly stated simple conclusions about the nature of tetanus toxin [114].

At the end of that year, 1890, Emil von Behring and Kitasato published their very important paper "Ueber das Zustandekommen der Diphtherie-

---

11. Dr. Giuseppina Catani—was she the first woman to publish (in 1890) in a regular scientific journal?

Immunität und der Tetanus-Immunität bei Thieren" in the *Deutsche medizinische Wochenschrift* [443], in which they reported that rabbits and mice treated with diphtheria and tetanus toxins detoxified by treatment with iodine trichloride did not succumb to the subsequent injection of many otherwise lethal doses of these toxins. This immunity was due to the appearance in the blood serum of these animals of specific antibodies (or "antitoxins", as von Behring called them in a footnote) which neutralized the toxicity of the toxins.[12]

Botulinum Toxin[13]

In diphtheria, the multiplication of the germ is limited to a small area around the site of infection, which generally takes the form of a membrane in the throat; in tetanus, the bridgehead is even smaller and frequently is so small as to be undetectable; in the body of a botulism patient, there is no growth at all of the germ, which may well be separated from its victim in space and in time. For botulism is generally not an infectious disease, but a poisoning resulting from the ingestion of food on which *Clostridium botulinum* has grown and produced a toxin as lethal as tetanus toxin. Recently, it has been found perhaps to be responsible for some hitherto inexplicable deaths of infants, whose as yet not acid stomachs fail to protect them from ingested spores of the bacillus [5]. Botulism is a rare disease, especially in Great Britain, where the last serious outbreak took place in 1922 at Loch Maree in Scotland, when eight people died after eating sandwiches of infected duck paste [247], and where in 1979 two people died of infected tinned salmon.

The manifestations of botulism generally appear 12 to 36 hours after ingestion of the toxin, but the period of delay could be as short as 2 hours or as long as 2 weeks. Illness begins with fatigue, weakness, headache and dizziness. The disease is a general flaccid paralysis, i.e., an inability to move any muscle, compared with the spastic paralysis of tetanus where all the muscles are pulling at the same time. The patient remains mentally clear throughout the course of the illness and suffers no physical pain, except for the headache. There is no fever. Paralysis of the cranial nerves leads to dilation and side-to-side move-

12. Armand Gautier was carried away by the magical powers of tetanus antiserum. In his 1896 monograph *Les Toxines Microbiennes et Animales* [154], he states that "une quintilionème" of a cubic centimetre (i.e., 10^{-18} cc) of tetanus antiserum would protect a mouse against a lethal dose of toxin, or one drop of serum would protect 10 "trillion" (i.e., 10 million million) men. At this rate, that drop of serum would protect 2,000 times the present human population of the world.

13. Consistency demands that it should be called botulism toxin, but this is what it is usually called.

ments of the pupils of the eyes, drooping of the upper eyelid, squint, and double vision. The face becomes expressionless (compare the sardonic smile of tetanus); chewing, swallowing and speaking become difficult; and the tongue is uncontrolled. The neck muscles no longer support the head and the limbs become progressively weaker. Breathing becomes difficult, and the patient dies within 2 to 10 days, from paralysis of the respiratory muscles, obstruction of the airways and attendant infection of the lungs.

The toxin that produces these effects is a protein that varies in molecular size according to the immunological type of the organism producing it. A very small proportion of the ingested toxin is absorbed from the gut and acts parenterally on the motor nervous system. Like tetanus toxin, it blocks the output of transmitter substance from nerve endings, but in this case only from the endings of motor nerves where they make a junction with the muscles. This makes it impossible for the muscles to receive nervous impulses and consequently the patient is unable to move any muscle and goes into a state of flaccid paralysis.

There was no interval of time between the hypothesization and the discovery of botulinum toxin, since the relation between the cause and effect of botulism had always been clear. The disease had been known as sausage poisoning and was clearly quite different from the infectious diseases transmitted directly or indirectly from one patient to another by an external agent. It was called sausage poisoning because it often developed from the consumption of badly smoked sausages (mainly in south Germany) in the nineteenth century. When van Ermengem started investigating the famous disaster that took place in December 1895 in the Belgian village of Ellezelles, where 20 people suffered acute poisoning and 3 died after eating a preserved ham at a funeral feast, he realized that the ham poisoning was the same as sausage poisoning. Tiny volumes (a thousandth of a cubic centimetre) of watery macerations of the ham produced all the symptoms of sausage poisoning when injected parenterally into experimental animals. The ham was not decomposed, but was infected, and van Ermengem isolated a pure culture of the infecting organism as an anaerobic spore-bearing rod-shaped bacillus to which he gave the name *Bacillus botulinus*,[14] and so the disease came to be called botulism. In the same investigation, he grew the bacillus in artificial culture and showed that if sterile germ-free filtrates of the

---

14. From the Latin *botulus*, a sausage, or rather a black pudding. In Russia and Japan, where the disease more often results from the consumption of infected fish, it is sometimes called ichthyism, and in North America, where cases result from eating improperly canned vegetables, there was a fortunately abortive attempt to name it taricheutolachanism. (See Dolman [104]).

culture were injected parenterally into animals, all the characteristic symptoms of botulism could be reproduced. Thus, he had discovered botulinum toxin and showed that it was extremely toxic. He calculated that 50 mg of the organic matter in a culture filtrate would kill 100,000 kg of rabbit, or 0.035 mg would kill a man.[15] The poison was considerably more toxic than any ptomaine, and its chemical properties were entirely different, too, being like those of the recently discovered diphtheria and tetanus toxins [421, 422]. A third bacterial toxin had been discovered within eight years.

4. Cholera Toxin

The Hypothesization of Cholera Toxin

For diphtheria, the time interval between the hypothesization of the toxin and the demonstration of its existence was four years; for tetanus it was six years; for botulism there was no interval. But for cholera, the delay was 75 years—from 1884, when Robert Koch suggested a cholera poison, to 1959, when S. N. De found it. The idea that cholera was a poisoning was not entirely new, as others had groped in the darkness towards something like this many years earlier; at least they had realized that cholera was a disease that differed from other communicable diseases. William Scot, in a report in 1824 to the Madras Medical Board, noted that

> When medical aid is clearly administered, and when the constitution is otherwise healthy, the recovery from an attack of cholera is so wonderfully rapid, as perhaps to be decisive of the disease being unconnected with any organic lesion. In natives of this country, especially, in whom there is ordinarily little tendency to inflammatory actions, the recovery from cholera is generally so speedy and perfect, that it is only to be compared to recovery from syncope, colic and diseases of similar nature. . . [390].

John Snow observed 30 years later in London:

> A consideration of the pathology of cholera is capable of indicating to us the manner in which the disease is communicated. If it were ushered in by a fever, or any general constitutional disorder, then we would be furnished with no clue to the way in which the morbid poison enters the system; whether, for instance, by the alimentary tract, by the lungs, or in some other manner, but we should be left to determine this point by circumstances

---

15. Today we know that pure botulinum (or tetanus) toxin is about 1,000 times more toxic, i.e., 500 mg would kill a million tons of living matter.

unconnected with the pathology of the disease. But from all that I have been able to learn of cholera, both from my own observation and the descriptions of others, I conclude that cholera invariably commences with the affection of the alimentary canal. The disease often proceeds with so little feeling of general illness that the patient does not consider himself in danger, or even apply for advice, till the malady is far advanced [403].

Snow refers to a "morbid poison", but he and other early investigators could not crystallize their ideas, because the germ theory of disease had not yet been spelled out. It could not have occurred to them to think of a "poison" producing a poison.

Snow also made an observation that was uncannily prescient of, and contrary to, an argument to be disastrously advanced nearly 30 years later by Koch, and it is central to the present discussion:

If any further proof were wanting than those above stated, that all the symptoms attending cholera, except those connected with the alimentary canal, *depend simply on the physical alteration of the blood, and not on any cholera poison circulating in the system*, it would only be necessary to allude to the effects of a weak saline solution injected into the veins in the stage of collapse. The shrunken skin becomes filled out, and loses its coldness and lividity; the countenance assumes a natural aspect; the patient is able to sit up, and for a time seems well.[16] *If the symptoms were caused by a poison circulating in the blood, and depressing the action of the heart, it is impossible that they would thus be suspended by an injection of warm water, holding a little carbonate of soda in solution* [our emphasis].

After Robert Koch had discussed the part played by the comma bacillus at the First Conference on the Cholera Question in Berlin on 26 July 1884, he addressed himself to the problem of how the bacillus was able to cause the disease when, as he had observed, it remained confined to the lumen of the intestine and did not spread into the blood or tissues, or even to the mesenteric glands. We have seen how his junior assistant at the Imperial Health Office, Loeffler, had already considered a similar problem when he observed that organs at a distance from the restricted site of infection by the diphtheria bacillus were affected but remained sterile, and had suggested in December 1883 that the diphtheria bacillus produced a poison that spread about the body. Whether Koch was influenced by his young colleague's hypothesis he

16. We shall see later that the reason why the patient only "for a time seems well" was that the intravenous injection of saline solution was stopped because the diarrhoea recommenced. If the infusion had been continued, the diarrhoea would eventually have stopped and the patient would have recovered.

did not say, but he also did propose, six months later at the Berlin conference, that the cholera bacillus produced a poison. In doing so, he repeated the arguments of the ineffable Brieger, namely, that in their growth bacteria not only used up matter, but also produced matter of a different kind, and some of these products of bacterial decomposition were poisonous. In support of this suggestion, he stated that he was in possession of "certain facts", both of which, in the light of present knowledge, would seem to be irrelevant. The first was that when he cultivated the comma bacilli in gelatin containing a large number of red blood corpuscles, the red cells in the neighbourhood of the bacterial colonies disappeared. Cholera toxin does not lyse red blood cells— perhaps they were lysed by the haemolysin produced by some strains of the cholera vibrio independently of toxin. The second fact was that animals could die from consuming inanimate material apparently derived from the cholera bacillus. In India, a Dr. Richards of Gulundo had fed pigs on large quantities of human cholera dejecta and they had died. When the intestinal contents of one of these pigs were fed to a second pig, it did not die. Koch argued that if the first pigs had died of a cholera infection, then this infection should have been passed to the second pig and it should also have died; the cholera dejecta fed to the first set of pigs therefore contained a poison. The first pigs might well not have died of cholera infection, but whether they died of cholera toxin is open to question. They died of convulsions within 15 minutes of the repast, symptoms which are not persuasive of poisoning by cholera toxin, either in the natural disease or in experimental intoxication. Cholera toxin does not produce convulsions when introduced into experimental animals either parenterally or enterally, and it elicits diarrhoea (with no convulsions) in experimental animals and human volunteers after administration by mouth. In any case, when it produces an effect, it takes some hours to do so, not a few minutes.

History has proved that Koch was correct in hypothesizing the existence of a cholera poison. But it took 75 years for this proof to come, and we shall see that Koch himself was to a large extent to blame for the delay. We shall also see that an inherent difficulty was to make the ultimate demonstration of cholera toxin much more difficult than the demonstration of diphtheria, tetanus and botulism toxins, but if Koch had not blundered—gratuitously—in the very beginning, with all the massive weight of his authority, cholera toxin would have been demonstrated sooner. It matters little that Koch assumed that his cholera poison was a ptomaine—he can hardly be blamed for that—but what does matter is that he insisted, in the face of all the glaring evidence to the contrary, that the cholera poison acted systemically and not locally.

Koch's Blunder

By the time Koch gave his report to the first cholera conference, he had examined the bodies of nearly 100 victims of cholera and in all of them had demonstrated the presence of the comma bacilli: "the investigation has not only proved that they were present, but, as I have already indicated, they always stand in direct relation to the cholera process itself. For where the true cholera process causes the most marked changes in the intestine, namely the lower half of the small intestine, they were found most numerously. . .". Here, the organism was complying with Koch's "postulate" that the presence of the bacteria in the disease must be proved, and that their distribution must afford a complete explanation of the symptoms exhibited. Later in his Berlin discourse, he restated this condition: "and what I specially lay stress upon, the occurrence of the pathogenic bacteria must correspond to the pathological changes in the body, and to the course of the disease". But in spite of this insistence on the local action of the cholera germ, Koch went on, astonishingly, to assert that the main action of his hypothetical poison was not local but systemic:

> The action of the poison shows itself, partly directly in the destruction of the epithelium, and in more severe cases of the superficial layers of the mucous membrane, partly indirectly when it is absorbed and acts on the entire organism, but especially on the circulating system, which is brought to a state of paralysis. In my opinion the group of symptoms in a regular attack of cholera, usually thought to be the consequence of the loss of water and thickening of the blood, should in reality be considered as poisoning. For it not infrequently happens that, even though a comparatively small quantity of fluid has been lost during life through vomiting and diarrhoea, the intestine will be found to contain only little fluid after death. If death occurs in the stage of cholera poisoning the post mortem appearances correspond to these cases in which the intestinal mucous membrane is very little changed, and the intestinal contents consist of a pure culture of the comma bacilli.

To Koch, the direct effect of cholera infection on the intestine, and the consequent dehydration, so prominent in by far the most cases of the disease, apparently was negligible. The important effect of the poison was the systemic, "paralytic" effect on the circulating system. As to the direct effect of the poison on the intestine, Koch went on to state: "On the other hand, if this stage of systemic intoxication is prolonged, or if it is survived, then the consequences of the necrosis of the epithelium and the mucous membrane make themselves evident". The consequences he mentioned were capillary haemorrhage in the mucous membrane, and decomposition of the albuminous fluid, with formation of secondary poisonous substances under the influence of "Faulnissbacterien" [233, 234].

Koch simply could not see what others had seen so clearly 53 and 30 years previously. In 1831, Hermann stated "das die Absorptions-fähigkeit des Darmakanals wahrend der Cholera absolut ertodtet seyn muss", and consequently the blood thickened because it lost fluid and did not regain it and so ceased to circulate. In 1854, John Snow observed that the disease was an "affection of the alimentary canal" resulting in the exudation into the intestine of watery fluid derived from the blood and that the consequent thickening of the blood was responsible for the symptoms of cholera. He calculated that the loss of 5 imperial pints (2.8 l) of water from the blood would be enough to bring about a state of collapse and anticipated modern practise in the intravenous rehydration of patients by stating that the volume of fluid injected should keep pace with that loss. After Snow's death in 1858, Filippo Pacini argued that the cholera organisms attached to the most superficial part of the mucous membrane of the small intestines, thereby causing the loss of water by which cholera declares itself. He calculated that once a critical portion (about one-thirteenth) of the surface of the small intestine was affected, secretion of water into the lumen would exceed absorption from it, and fluid would accumulate in the gut. The "prox-imate" cause of cholera was the loss of three to five pounds of water (about half of Snow's figure) from the blood [324].

Cholera toxin was also hypothesized by the leaders of the French Cholera Commission, 10 days after the Berlin meeting, and they made the same assertion about its systemic—rather than local—action. The French Academy of Medicine had also been discussing the cholera question, at a series of 16 weekly meetings. At the seventh of these, on 5 August 1884, Isadore Straus and Emile Roux reported on their investigations of the cholera outbreak at Toulon, continuing their in-vestigations started in Egypt in the previous year at the same time as Koch. They stated:

> If the comma bacillus is the real cause of cholera, then, since it resides nowhere but in the intestinal contents, at least in the rapid cases, and does not appreciably invade the intestinal mucous membrane, it must be accepted that, to produce such rapid and intense effects, it secretes a soluble ferment, a ptomaine, some sort of extremely energetic poison, which *absorbed* [emphasis added] provokes the symptoms of cholera. Therefore attempts must be made to extract from pure cultures of the bacillus a soluble poison which will reproduce in animals symptoms analogous to those seen in cholera patients [410].

Presumably, the word "absorbed" implied what Koch had asserted 10 days earlier—that the toxin acted systemically.

At the second conference the next year (1885), Koch restated his poison hypothesis: "As I have previously mentioned to you, since the cholera bacilli do not pass into the blood we can only explain their action by supposing that they generate poisonous substances belonging to the group of ptomaines, which are absorbed and then act on the entire organism". He then said that he had tried directly to demonstrate these poisonous substances, but with no success [235].

When Koch referred to cases of cholera with very little fluid loss, he may have been thinking of cholera *sicca*. There is (or evidently used to be—it is hardly mentioned today) a rare and particularly severe form of the disease that can kill within an hour. The disease in this form is known as cholera *sicca* because there is little or no diarrhoea, only a very rapid accumulation within the intestinal tract of a volume of fluid not large enough to demand discharge. It is also known by another name, which may be considered more appropriate, cholera *siderans*, from the Latin *sideror*, "I am struck by a planet". Witness James Jameson's account of a manifestation of the disease that killed 700 men of a division of 5,000 Bengal Troops in the spring of 1781 at Ganjam: "It assailed them with almost inconceivable fury. Men in perfect health dropt down by dozens; and those even less severely affected were generally dead, or past recovery, within less than an hour" [214]. A group of British soldiers, perhaps not long out of Britain, on a forced march under the Indian sun, probably wearing red serge uniforms, might simply have dropped dead of heat stroke, but the expression "Bengal Troops" would undoubtedly have meant more hardened native troops; and cholera had been prevalent in the region for some time before they arrived (see p. 5), and there was purging and vomiting among those who fell ill. There are many accounts of sudden prostration and death from cholera with very little fluid loss, apparently not enough to cause severe dehydration [360, 372]. If the victims do not die of dehydration, what do they die of? They die probably because an overwhelming accumulation of the cholera bacillus (which is capable of very rapid growth) in the gut rapidly produces a large amount of toxin that suddenly extracts about 2 litres of water from the blood. This happens so fast that there is no time for the dehydrated blood to draw more water from the tissues; consequently, there is a sudden fall in blood volume and therefore a fall in blood pressure that is lethal. The underlying cause of this is still the same as that of the ordinary form of the disease, i.e., action of cholera toxin on the epithelial cells of the small intestine.

It is hardly credible that Koch should have ignored the great majority of cases of cholera and concentrated on the rare instances of cholera *siderans*. Attempts at history are supposed to delve for motives, but perhaps Koch just tossed off his idea of systemic action without much thought. Others, like Hermann, O'Shaughnessy, Snow and Pacini, had been wise before the event, but Koch did what he did, and in so doing took "a long step backwards"—half a century backwards, to the time when many physicians believed that cholera was primarily a cardiovascular affection, and, indeed, the name *cardiogmus vitalis epidemicus* had been suggested for cholera [see 210]. Koch's insistence on the systemic action of cholera delayed the search for a proper animal model for testing the local action of cholera toxin, and this delay gave time for irrelevant theories on the nature of cholera toxin to be elaborated. The universal preoccupation with these theories deflected people's minds from the real problem, and since the fruits of their labours with the unreal problems were inevitably meagre, and, to tell the truth, boring, there was little inducement for fresh minds to take up the real problem of cholera toxin.

The Years in the Wilderness

Pollitzer's important monograph on cholera contains a conscientious account of the search for cholera toxin during the 75 years after the First Conference on the Cholera Question in 1884. It is, to use an expression favoured in another context by that trenchant medical historian Norman Howard-Jones (personal communication), "a can of worms". To state this is not impolitely to criticize the redoubtable Pollitzer, but economically to summarize the long drawn-out confusion that followed the Berlin conference.

Cholera is different from the other exotoxinoses that were soon to be known in the years after the Berlin conference—diphtheria, tetanus and botulism. Parenteral administration of these toxins leads to symptoms that mimic the natural disease, but parenteral administration of the true cholera exotoxin does not lead to the mimicry of cholera; in fact, it produces symptoms by this route only when administered in large doses, and then the symptoms (which can include death) can be described only as general debility. Only when presented enterally does cholera exotoxin, even in very small doses, mimic the disease by causing diarrhoea. If Koch had not decreed that the cholera poison acted systemically, those seeking it in cholera culture filtrates (where the poison would be if it were soluble, like the mythical ptomaines or like diphtheria or tetanus toxins) would presumably have wanted to concentrate their efforts enterally, that is, on the intestinal epithelium. But how could they have done this? By feeding cholera filtrates, or by introducing them into the intestine with syringes or tubes, and looking for signs of fluid accumulation or diarrhoea? As we shall see, it is likely that experiments on these lines could have been successful if properly carried out, but only if the culture filtrates contained cholera exotoxin, which they might well not have, because the cholera bacillus needs the right culture conditions to produce exotoxin, and these are attained only if appropriate measures are taken. But such difficulties were not faced—they were not even encountered—because attention was diverted from the intestinal tract from the very beginning, and from culture filtrates very soon after. The first tests for the poison were studies of the effects of parenterally administered material. Toxicity was, unfortunately, observed, and therefore every conceivable preparation—young, old, heated, dried, chemically treated cholera cultures, their filtrates and their bacterial cells, or extracts of them—was injected by every conceivable parenteral route—intravenous, intraperitoneal, subcutaneous, intramuscular and more—into an astonishing array of animals. The reader who wishes to know more about this work should read Chapters 4 and 6 of Pollitzer. They make dreadfully confusing reading, and it would be carrying a sense of duty to the point of obsession now to cover all the ground again, since all this effort was to little avail. The wrong material was administered by the wrong route by the wrong people, and practically every experiment was worthless as far as cholera was concerned. The innumerable effects observed threw absolutely no light on the question of the existence of cholera toxin, let alone its nature, and had no relation to the symptoms of the natural disease of cholera. Only one or two investigators seem to have been bothered by the fact, which surely must have been obvious, that they were not mimicking the natural disease. How could anyone have imagined that the effects they were seeing were due to cholera toxin? We shall see that in most cases they were, indeed, not due to cholera toxin, which is an exotoxin, but to something quite different—cholera endotoxin. The only good that came of this work was the discovery of the bacterial endotoxins which, although of little relevance to cholera toxin, are of great importance for other reasons to the group of Gram-negative enteric bacteria, including cholera, typhoid and dysentery bacilli and *Escherichia coli*.

The confusion started immediately with Nicati and Rietsch's studies during the cholera epidemic in Marseille in 1884 [305, 306]. When they injected filtrates of 8-hour cholera cultures intravenously into dogs, they found no effects. This is what we would expect even if the filtrates had actually contained exotoxin, because of its low parenteral toxicity. But when they injected filtrates of week-old cultures, they observed respiratory difficulties, attempts to vomit, and paralysis of the extremities. With hindsight, we can now conclude that the non-toxic young cell-free culture filtrates may or may not have contained exotoxin, whereas the bacterial cells in the week-old cultures had probably autolyzed and shed their endotoxins into the culture medium, and thus rendered the culture filtrates toxic. It was Cantani who, with poisonous fungi in mind, first suggested that the cholera bacilli themselves were toxic and proved this by showing that heat-killed bacilli killed dogs when injected intraperitoneally or intravenously. He suggested that this showed that the cholera poison was responsible for anatomical changes in the intestinal mucosa which led to the diarrhoea (thus relieving the poison of this responsibility, which should have pleased Koch). He believed the cell poison was responsible for the weakening of heart activity, the cyanosis and the collapse, but that these effects of the poison were aggravated by the thickening of the blood. He suggested that cholera should be treated on two fronts: that the bacilli should be washed out of the gut with a powerful jet of tannic acid solution ("Enteroklyse") and the poison should be washed out of the blood by subcutaneous injection of warm saline solution ("Hypodermoklyse"), which would also rehydrate the patient [44].

Cantani's idea of a bacterial cell toxin was confirmed and vigorously developed by Pfeiffer, who made many important observations on endotoxins. He, too, found that whole cultures of the cholera bacillus, whether living or killed by boiling, were toxic when injected parenterally into guinea pigs, whereas cell-free filtrates of unheated cultures were completely non-toxic. Thus, the cell bodies appeared to contain a heat-stable poison, whereas the fluid medium of unheated bacteria contained no toxin (or no toxin detectable on parenteral injection!). He further showed that filtrates of boiled cultures were as toxic as whole cultures, thus demonstrating that the poison was released from the cells by heating. He came to the conclusion that "the primary cholera toxin stands in a very close relationship with the bacterial bodies, perhaps forming an integral component of them". Pfeiffer made several further observations that are of the greatest importance to the bacteriology and immunology of Gram-negative enteric organisms. He showed that other organisms in this group, such as the typhoid bacilli, contained similar "Bakterienzelltoxinen", that their antibodies did not neutralize their toxicity (unlike the recently discovered antitoxic antibodies of diphtheria and tetanus toxins, and of the plant poisons ricin and abrin), but that they did cause species-specific immune lysis of the organisms. In other words, antibody to the cell toxin was antibacterial (or bactericidal), rather than antitoxic. This was a new and important concept in the new science of immunity[17] [330].

---

17. From 1892 to 1896 Richard Pfeiffer was working in the Institut für Infektionskrankheiten in Berlin, of which Koch was the director. He is generally—and justifiably—credited with the discovery of the endotoxins [see 280, 464]. The authors just cited also give Pfeiffer

Pfeiffer and Wassermann in 1893 did at least note that the natural disease of cholera in humans was something wholly different from the "Infection und Intoxication gemischte Process" induced in guinea pigs by the intraperitoneal administration of cholera bacteria. They thought that the cholera infection induced in guinea pigs by mouth according to Koch's method (see below) was much closer to the natural disease [332]. This was a good beginning, but no benefit accrued; a few years later, Pfeiffer was able to reconcile the symptoms evoked in guinea pigs by intraperitoneal injection of endotoxin preparations with the symptoms seen in man in the natural disease. He considered—"mich anlehnend an die classischen Arbeiten Robert Koch's"—that cholera was an infectious process that took place on the intestinal epithelium, exactly as did that of the influenza germ on the epithelium of the air passages. The vibrios multiplied in the intestine between the epithelial cells and damaged them (see Cantani, above). This damage to the epithelium, he said, was an invariable phenomenon in severe cholera.[18] While the intact intestinal epithelium was a sure protective wall against the absorption of cholera poison brought into the intestinal tract, the broken-down intestinal mucosa was unable to resist the attack of the comma bacilli. The bacterial cell toxins were absorbed and a situation arose that was similar to that in the peritoneal cavity of guinea pigs injected intraperitoneally with cholera cell toxins. The absorbed toxin then produced the symptoms of intoxication seen in the so-called algid (or collapse) stage of cholera, where the pulse fails and the face assumes the choleraic expression—features pinched, eye-balls sunken, lids half-closed and pupils contracted. Like most workers at the time, Pfeiffer seems to have had no interest in the cause of the most characteristic symptom of cholera—the terrible diarrhoea [331, 332].

The structure of the bacterial endotoxins and their major properties were elucidated by Boivin and Mesrobeanu 40 years after they were discovered by Pfeiffer, and the cholera endotoxin was the first one they studied. They showed that the endotoxins, which they extracted from the organisms with cold tricholoracetic acid, accounted for all the toxicity of the organisms and were identical with the dominant somatic antigens (the O antigens) of the organisms. These proved to have a constitution hitherto unknown, in that they were complexes of different types of

the credit for the word "Endotoxine", but in none of the papers referred to by them does the term appear. Pfeiffer used expressions such as "intracellularen Toxine", intracellularen Bakterientoxine", "Bakterienkorpertoxine", and "Bakterienzelltoxine". A search by the present authors for the origins of the words "exotoxin" and "endotoxin" has failed.

18. See discussion on desquamation in the next section.

molecules. At first, they were thought to consist of polysaccharide and phospholipid molecules, but later it was shown that they also contained a protein component [32, 33]. This elucidation of the nature of the endotoxins established their scientific respectability and further entrenched the almost unquestioned conviction that the cholera poison was an endotoxin. Topley and Wilson, undisputed leaders of contemporary medical bacteriology, had stated with massive authority in the first edition (1929) of their "The Principles of Bacteriology and Immunity" that "no true exotoxin is formed by [*Vibrio cholerae*] but disintegrated bodies of the bacilli are very toxic to animals" [420]. In the second edition (1936), they declared more firmly:

> We may conclude that the cholera vibrio does not secrete a true soluble exotoxin, but it contains endotoxins which are liberated on the autolysis of the bacilli in culture or on the active disintegration by the cells of the animal body. The analogy that it presents with the meningococcus—another organism that undergoes autolysis—is very close, though the cholera vibrio is far more toxic.

This statement was repeated in the third edition (1946); a little toned down in the fourth (1955) and fifth (1964) editions,[19] by which time the existence of cholera exotoxin had been established but was known only to a few; and finally abandoned in the sixth edition (1975), by which time the acceptance of cholera exotoxin was wide-spread.

The most ardent of the proponents of the Boivin polymolecular endotoxin as the cholera toxin was William Burrows [42], who laboured with cholera endotoxin for more than two decades, but finally accepted the finding in 1959 that the cholera bacillus produced an exotoxin that reproduced the disease when administered enterally to experimental animals (see below). However, he continued as late as 1968 to cloud the issue by clinging to the notion that there were further cholera toxins that were relevant to the disease, viz: type 1 toxins, the Boivin endotoxins; type 2 toxins, that fell into two subgroups: "the choleragenic toxins[20] which produce cholera-like disease in experimental animals, and the toxins whose activity is demonstrable in other systems, e.g., by intradermal inoculation and in mammalian cell cultures"; and type 3 toxins,

19. "It is doubtful whether any of the vibrios produces a true soluble exotoxin—and there is reason to believe that the toxicity of old cultures of vibrios . . . depends on the liberation of endotoxins".

20. Note the plural noun. Presumably, one of these choleragenic toxins was the cholera exotoxin discovered nine years previously.

small-molecular heat-stable substances that produced various effects in the laboratory (but whose relevance to the disease was not explained) [43].

In the year that saw the eventual discovery of cholera exotoxin, Pollitzer, who was himself firmly committed to the endotoxin, summarized the ideas that had been suggested for the role of cholera toxin. The richness of their variety reflects the confusion that reigned. The cholera syndrome was due to: (1) Nitrite poisoning. (2) Cholera endotoxin being absorbed into the bloodstream through an intestinal epithelium damaged by desquamation and producing hypothermia, paralysis of the circulation and muscular debility. (3) The endotoxin acting locally on the capillary blood vessels of the intestinal mucosa and increasing their permeability—with consequent outpouring of blood plasma into the lumen of the intestine. (4) Anaphylactic or allergic phenomena brought about by break-down products of other temporary inhabitants of the intestine (*E. coli,* staphylococcus, etc.) passing through mucous membrane damaged by the cholera vibrio. (5) The action of histamine. (6) Last, but definitely, one would hope, not least, direct local action resulting in dehydration with consequent effects on the circulation of the blood.

Pollitzer himself was on the side of local action—local action, that is, of endotoxin. But he uttered a warning: "overshadowed though it is by the spectacular manifestations due to dehydration and its sequelae, a direct (i.e., systemic) role of the toxin in the causation of the general cholera syndrome should not and cannot be disregarded".

Perhaps the most amazing aspect of the 60 years wasted on cholera endotoxin is that nobody seemed seriously to have considered whether endotoxin would actually exert any systemic toxicity in the one and only location where it would be delivered in the course of the disease, namely, the intestinal tract. This was collective culpable negligence, for, in fact, endotoxins are not toxic in the intestinal tract. The lower end of the human intestinal tract is normally colonized by large numbers of harmless, arguably helpful, organisms, mainly endotoxin-containing Gram-negative bacteria. They eventually make up a quarter or a third of the faeces, which means that the intestinal tract is daily exposed to about a gram of endotoxin, equivalent to at least 5,000 mouse intravenous lethal doses. Yet no harm is done.[21]

The toxicity of cholera endotoxin was examined by every conceivable

21. Jacob Fine, a distinguished Boston surgeon, conscientiously dismayed at the loss of some of his patients from surgical shock after faultless surgery, blamed these endotoxins in the gut. He argued that they were slowly absorbed from the normal gut into the blood, and were in the normal course of events detoxified as soon as they got there; but if a person were subjected to trauma from surgery or some other cause, the detoxification process broke down and shock from endotoxin poisoning followed [126].

parenteral route, but never by the enteral route; and nobody seems to have asked whether the cholera bacilli would liberate their endotoxins fast enough, or whether the liberated endotoxins, which in their native state are very large, complex molecules, would be absorbed from the gut at all, let alone fast enough to exert systemic effect in the very rapid course of the disease.

Pfeiffer averred that the intestinal epithelium had to be broken down before the endotoxin could be absorbed (p. 53). His assumption of a broken-down intestinal epithelium in cholera, though unjustified, is understandable, because at that time it was believed by many that the epithelium was stripped in cholera. This idea was not generally accepted, and was found in the end to be false, as will be seen in the next section.

In fact, the evidence for the absorption of endotoxin from the gut is far from persuasive [35] and the evidence against it is convincing [25]. Moreover, there is clear direct evidence that endotoxin is not toxic enterally: for example, daily feeding of large amounts of heat-killed cholera bacilli over 4 weeks to human volunteers produced no ill effects [145]; and intravenous injection of 3 µg (micrograms) of endotoxin killed mice, whereas 10 mg of endotoxin, more than 3,000 times as much, had no effect when introduced enterally, even when the intestinal epithelium was damaged by treatment with chemicals or X-rays [25].

The Revival and Extinction of Desquamation

The question of desquamation, or stripping, or flaying, of the intestinal epithelium was another diversion that obscured the debate on the pathogenesis of cholera and the role of the toxin. Desquamation was considered as the cause of the prodigious loss of fluid across denuded intestinal villi by Virchow [442]; as a mere by-product of the action of the cholera poison by Koch; as a prerequisite for the absorption and subsequent systemic action of the endotoxin by Pfeiffer; and both as a cause of fluid loss and prerequisite for the systemic action of endotoxin [261]. Virchow's view on desquamation was subsequently supported by Fraenkel, who had performed many autopsies during the cholera outbreak in Hamburg in 1892 [143]. Virchow was "The Father of Modern Pathology", and a member of the Prussian Lower House and of the Reichstag to boot, so his views presumably were treated with respect. In the opening words of his address to the first cholera conference in 1884, with Virchow himself in the chair, Koch discussed the desquamation hypothesis, but it is difficult to make out whether he was for it or against. Mentioning the difficulties he had expected to meet in tracing the "virus" of cholera, he said:

To be sure the investigation did not meet with such difficulties in this direction as in another, where I expected it the least. I had pictured to myself the pathological conditions entirely according to the descriptions in the textbooks, namely that the intestine in cholera would show peculiarly little change, and that it would be filled with a material like rice water. I had almost forgotten the result of the autopsies which I had formerly seen, so that I was unable to correct my erroneous views from them. Therefore I was at first somewhat surprised and uncertain when I saw something quite different in the intestine. In the first postmortem examinations it almost at once became apparent that in an overwhelming majority of cases remarkably deep and striking changes existed in the intestine; other cases again showed changes less serious; and lastly, I came across cases which corresponded in some measure to the type described in the textbooks. But it required time, and a number of postmortem examinations as well, before I succeeded in forming a correct general idea, and in properly estimating all the different changes that came before me.

Later in his discourse he seemed to accept desquamation; we have already remarked that when he hypothesized a poison, he endowed it with the dual properties of destroying the epithelium, and even the upper layers of the mucous membrane, and of acting systemically after absorption.

At the second sitting of the first cholera conference 3 days later, Virchow led the discussion on Koch's paper by posing 16 questions, none of which raised the question of desquamation; nor was the question brought up by anybody else in the course of the discussion.

We have also remarked that Pfeiffer took the view that his endotoxin was not effective until the epithelium had been broken down to allow absorption of the endotoxin. The epithelial cells were said to be destroyed by the cholera bacilli, but there was no clear idea how the bacilli brought this about. Koch believed his poison did it; Cantani and Pfeiffer vaguely left it to the bacilli; nobody seemed to have a firm suggestion.

There was opposition to the desquamation hypothesis. Cohnheim[22] firmly rejected it: "there cannot, in my opinion, be a doubt that the entire desquamation of the epithelium is nothing but the result of maceration". He based this claim on the observation by many workers on many patients in many hospitals in the 1866 cholera epidemic that there were no epithelial cells in the watery stools. He argued that if

22. Cohnheim was also an apparently lone voice against Koch's hypothesis of systemic intoxication, and argued, as had Pacini and Snow and their predecessors, that the syndrome of cholera was due only to dehydration: "It is equally unnecessary to show specially that the fluid evacuations really form the central point of the entire disease; for, as already pointed out, it is these which bring about that extreme inspissation of the blood which in the severest cases finally puts an end to the circulation and in this way destroys life".

before. As Carpenter points out [60], earlier well-controlled studies by his colleague Chaudhuri with orally administered antibiotics (chloromycetin and terramycin) [70, 94] had shown that the vibrio was rapidly eliminated but the death rate was not affected. But at that time, intravenous rehydration was still comparatively ineffective: "since survival is determined by the adequacy of water and electrolyte replacement therapy, it is now clear that mortality figures alone cannot provide an accurate assessment of the efficacy of antibiotic therapy in cholera" [60]. Tetracycline by itself will not save lives in cholera, but it will help the physician to do so by halving the volume of replacement fluid and the time of hospitalization needed. This, in countries where cholera can occur on a massive scale, and where money is scarce, is an immeasurable boon.

3. Coping with Crises

At the end of December 1963, the holy hair of the Prophet Muhammad was reported missing from the shrine where it was kept in Srinagar, and after nine days' search it was found, on 4 January 1964. But the incident led to demonstrations in Moslem Pakistan and to anti-Hindu riots in Khulna, Dacca and Narayanganj in East Pakistan [195]. About 10,000 Hindus took shelter, herded together in several cotton and jute mills. Three or four days later, cholera broke out among them, and the PSCRL was asked to help deal with it. Conditions in the overcrowded refugee camp were terrible. The Dacca magistrates were told that it was impossible to deal with the situation in the mills, and that the only way was to transfer the patients to hospitals. It was decided to send one-third of the patients to the Mitford Hospital, one-third to the hospital in Narayanganj and one-third to the PSCRL. Thus, 100 patients were transferred on trucks in one movement to the 20-bed PSCRL ward, which was supplemented by tents put up on the grounds of the laboratory by the Pakistan army. It was soon found that it was impossible, with so many patients, to keep pace with remembering which patient should have had 2 litres of saline, which needed 1 litre of bicarbonate, and which one needed maintenance fluid. Gordon therefore suggested that all the patients should be treated from the start with the 5:4:1 maintenance solution. It was logistically impossible to import all the transfusion solution that was needed, and too expensive, so the bottles were reused and the solution was made in a "factory" by the indefatigable pharmacist, Bazhur Rahman. Bottles of water containing 5 g NaCl and 1 g KCl per litre distilled were sterilized by autoclaving, and the appropriate amount of $NaHCO_3$, 4 g for every litre (clean, but not sterilized because of its heat sensitivity), was placed in a phial attached to the neck of the bottle, and dissolved in the fluid when needed.[8] Each patient received one capsule of tetracycline every four hours, which halved the burden which otherwise might not have been sustainable.

Within 48 hours, all but two of the patients were discharged from the PSCRL. The death rate had been zero; in the Mitford Hospital, 27 percent of the patients died; in the Narayanganj hospital, 47 percent of the patients died. Benenson showed these figures to the Director of Health Service in Dacca and suggested that the PSCRL should take charge of all cases of diarrhoea in the city. The invitation was accepted.

4. Clinical Assessment of Patients

Laboratory tests of blood specific gravity as a measure of degree of dehydration of a patient, and therefore of the volume of replacement fluid he would need, suited Phillips very well. The test was, in its more practicable form, his invention; it was, to a laboratory man like him, the natural thing to do; it was, in his eyes, more objective than clinical assessment of the patient's condition; and he maintained it was quicker to carry out. He and his NAMRU-2 colleagues lost no opportunity to preach this doctrine [445]. But his enthusiasm was not shared by the more clinically oriented physicians at the JHCMRT and the PSCRL. They used Phillips's method initially, but soon came to prefer judging degree of dehydration and hydration by looking at and feeling the patient and assessing the turgor of his skin; the degree of consciousness by talking to him; his blood pressure by feeling his central and peripheral pulses; the state of his heart by auscultation of the chest. This quick assessment is particularly necessary when patients suddenly purge and go into hypovolaemic shock. Moreover, clinical tests can detect dangerous conditions that cannot be revealed by laboratory tests, and could not await them even if they existed. Kussmaul's respiration and basal râles are a sign of dangerous acidosis and the threat of pulmonary oedema that calls for the immediate infusion of alkali. Laboratory tests require a high ratio of physicians to patients, such as prevailed when NAMRU-2 was working in Bangkok and the Philippines and other countries in the Far East, and where the patients were not so ill, but in the crowded wards of Dacca and Calcutta they were not possible, even if they had been considered desirable.

There was another reason why the PSCRL came to rely on physical

8. Benenson had another reason for preparing his own solutions and not using imported materials. It was part of the PSCRL's mission to develop a method of treating cholera that could be used in any hospital in Pakistan. All the chemicals were bought in the local market in Dacca and only the bottles and the administration kits were imported.

signs rather than laboratory tests for determining a patient's condition and how to treat him. As has already been mentioned, it was part of the laboratory's mission to teach Pakistani physicians how to cope with cholera with the means at their disposal. That is also why Benenson would not have air conditioning in the cholera ward, and why he insisted on making his own infusion fluids from materials that were locally available, and why the laboratory used only one infusion fluid to treat all cases of cholera, regardless of the age of the patient.

5. El Tor Cholera

Vibrio eltor arrived in East Pakistan and West Bengal shortly after the Americans. It appears to have reached Dacca in 1963, and then reached Calcutta in April 1964, possibly on boats travelling from East Pakistan. It does not seem to have had a common source of entry to Dacca, since Barua and Mukherjee isolated it from eight patients at all the points of the compass around Calcutta [13]. Cases of El Tor (Ogawa strain) cholera were studied at JHCMRT during their third year, in the spring of 1964, at the same time as they were carrying out their studies on the evaluation of tetracycline. The El Tor disease that they saw did not differ in any way from classical cholera. The patients were just as ill, their stool electrolytes were exactly the same, they were rehydrated in the same way, and they responded to treatment in the same way [446]. This is not to say, however, that the epidemiology of the El Tor disease is the same is that of the classical vibrio. A greater proportion of El Tor patients had a milder disease than the classical vibrio patients, but the severity of the disease in patients seen at JHCMRT was the same, regardless of the infective agent, because only severely ill patients were admitted to the study ward.

6. *Escherichia coli* Diarrhoea and Other Diarrhoeas

At the same time as the JHCMRT workers were studying El Tor cholera and evaluating tetracycline, they were also studying cases of severe diarrhoea that were not due to either the classical or the El Tor vibrio, or indeed to any vibrio. Very soon after their arrival in Calcutta, during preliminary studies between November 1962 and March 1963, Carpenter and Sack had observed that among sporadic cases of clinically diagnosed cholera only 50 percent of the patients could be proved bacteriologically to be infected with cholera vibrios. They distinguished thus between cases of true cholera and non-choleraic diarrhoea; later, non-choleraic disease came to be called non-vibrio cholera, NVC, to be distinguished from non-cholera vibrios, NCVs, that were being investigated at about the same time at PSCRL in Dacca. We shall dispose of these NCVs first and then no longer concern ourselves with them. The NCVs are the same as NAGs, or nonagglutinable vibrios, i.e., vibrios that are related to the classical and El Tor vibrios, but not closely enough to agglutinate in the presence of antisera (0 group 1) that agglutinate the vibrios associated with epidemic cholera [127]. Interest was aroused in these organisms when workers at PSCRL found that they predominated in the stools of some patients suffering relatively mild diarrhoea and producing antibodies to the NCVs [265]. However, the duration of the diarrhoea, the volume of fluid excreted and the volume of rehydration fluid required for treatment could not be compared with those of patients suffering from moderate to severe cholera due to *Vibrio cholerae* or *Vibrio eltor*; nor can the diseases due to NCVs or NAGs be compared with the non-vibrio cholera (NVC) observed by JHCMRT, to which we will now return.

Having made the preliminary studies in 1962–1963 that revealed that only 50 percent of patients with severe diarrhoea could be proved to be infected with cholera vibrios, the JHCMRT group returned to the subject in March to June 1964, when an unusual epidemic of acute non-vibrio diarrhoeal disease, closely simulating cholera, occurred in Calcutta, during the period which was the usual time for the annual cholera epidemic. Bacteriological studies made on 145 consecutive patients with acute diarrhoeal disease and low blood pressure admitted to the Calcutta Infectious Disease Hospital showed that 86 percent of these patients were not suffering from infections with *Vibrio cholerae*, although, like the El Tor patients, they were just as sick, and as sick in the same way, as classical cholera patients, except that tetracycline had no demonstrable effect on them, and that in a few cases the hypotension was far out of proportion to the severity of saline depletion [49, 51].

Later, in the cholera season of 1968 in Calcutta, JHCMRT workers, notably S. L. Gorbach, J. G. Banwell and R. B. Sack, succeeded in identifying the organism that was causing this non-vibrio cholera. Seventeen patients admitted to the Infectious Disease Hospital with severe diarrhoeal disease, but from whom no known enteric pathogenic bacteria could be isolated, were studied by having tubes inserted through the mouth into the small bowel. By this means, it was possible to take samples and show that the small bowels of most of these patients were colonized by *Escherichia coli*, an organism hitherto considered to be a harmless colonizer of the human large bowel [8, 165, 401]. These studies suggested that the *E. coli* may have produced an enterotoxin which caused the diarrhoea, and the suggestion was later confirmed by JHCMRT, when it was shown that strains of *E. coli* isolated from patients with non-vibrio cholera do in fact produce an enterotoxin similar in some respects to cholera enterotoxin [384].[9]

At first, the *E. coli* enterotoxin appeared to differ from cholera toxin in several ways, and to resemble it only in so far as it induced fluid accumulation in ligated ileal loops of rabbits. For one thing, it is not an exotoxin-like cholera toxin (nor is it a tedious lipopolysaccharide endotoxin, as discussed in Chapter 2!) but is an intracellular toxin [76, 361]. It appeared not to be reactive in the skin by the Craig test. However, Ruth Rappaport (who prepared the glutaraldehyde cholera toxoid for the field trials; Chapter 8) showed that the *E. coli* toxin was produced by the organism as an inert protoxin that could be activated by the proteolytic enzyme trypsin [365]. The protoxin was active in the rabbit ileal loop which contains trypsin, but in the skin there is no trypsin and therefore no activity. But if the protoxin was treated with trypsin, it was then reactive in the skin like cholera toxin. At first, *E. coli* toxin appeared to be far more complex, and far less active, than cholera toxin. All sorts of attempts were made to purify it, and the products thus obtained were all different from each other, varying in molecular weight from 10^4 to greater than 10^6. When the toxin was finally isolated by Finkelstein, after 10 years of struggle, it appeared to be almost, but not quite, identical with cholera toxin in its molecular structure and its biological activity (see Chapter 10). *E. coli* toxin also binds to the cholera toxin receptor in all cell membranes, the neuraminidase-stable monosialosyl ganglioside GM_1 see Chapter 10), but apparently not so avidly [76, 204, 346]. Finally, *E. coli* toxin and cholera toxin are immunologically related, i.e., antitoxin to one will neutralize the other [113].

Finkelstein has speculated on the possibility that *E. coli* may have received its toxin gene from the cholera vibrio. In the vibrio, the toxin might have survival value by increasing the number of vibrios disseminated into the environment, so increasing the likelihood of their infecting other humans, the only known natural host of the organism. *E. coli* survives more easily in nature and therefore does not really need its enterotoxin for survival. Its acquisition of the toxin gene may have been a genetically recent accidental event.

The immunological relationship of cholera and *E. coli* toxins may possibly have a useful application. Enterotoxic *E. coli* strains are not only the most frequent causes of travellers' diarrhoea [166], but are also important as a cause of endemic infantile diarrhoea world-wide [183]. If an effective means of active cholera antitoxic immunization can be

9. In fact, Smith and Gyles had already shown that *E. coli* produced heat-labile and heat-stable enterotoxins [400].

developed, perhaps such as is hoped for for Texas Star (see Chapter 8), then it could also be effective against enterotoxinogenic *E. coli*. What is probably more important than the possibility of active antitoxic immunization is the fact that the methods of intravenous and oral (Chapter 9) rehydration that have been developed for the treatment of cholera patients are equally applicable to *E. coli* diarrhoeas, indeed, to all dehydrating diarrhoeas all over the world, whatever their cause.

Besides the heat-labile cholera toxin–resembling toxin, *E. coli* also produces a heat-stable diarrhoeagenic toxin [113, 400], and some strains of *E. coli* that produce neither toxin are still capable of producing diarrhoea [250].

The diarrhoeagenic capacity of *E. coli* was in fact observed in Calcutta several years before the JHCMRT arrived there. S. N. De had observed that strains of *E. coli* isolated from cases of gastroenteritis caused fluid accumulation in his newly rediscovered intestinal loops [97]. Perhaps it was that that inspired Kenneth Goodner, who, according to his fellow Inner Circle member Theodore Woodward,

> must be given full credit for the perceptive observation of the significance of *Escherichia coli* as a causative agent of human diarrheas when the cholera vibrio was reborn. K. G. said simply to a group of experimental physiologists and clinical microbiologists, "Don't forget to put *E. coli* in the intestinal loop". This was his kind of catalytic thinking. My faltering memory places the approximate data of this prophecy in about 1960, during the formative years of the Dacca program [465].

But De's paper had been published in a well-known and respected journal, the *Journal of Pathology and Bacteriology*, in 1956, for all to read, whether they were in Dacca, Calcutta or Philadelphia.

Enterotoxinogenic *E. coli* are a common cause of diarrhoea, especially in children under two years of age, in other developing countries besides India and Bangladesh (e.g., Brazil, Peru, Mexico, Kenya, Morocco). In a recent study in Bangladesh it was found to be the most frequent pathogen in adults with diarrhoea, the rate of hospitalized cases being 8.1 per 1000—the highest of all enteropathogens [460]. But *E. coli* is not the only organism besides the cholera vibrio that causes diarrhoea. The dysentery bacillus causes much diarrhoea in children in Bangladesh, so much so that the Teknaf Dysentery Project was established in late 1974 in the southeastern tip of Bangladesh between the Bay of Bengal and Burma to study the epidemiology of the disease and to discover methods of intervention and therapy. It was originally financed by the United Nations Children's Emergency Fund (UNICEF), but it is at present run by the successor to the PSCRL, the ICDDR/B (Chapter 11) [162].

Other important infectious agents causing diarrhoea world-wide, especially in children, are viruses, in particular rotaviruses. The cholera and *E. coli* diarrhoeas have it in common that it may be possible to immunize them by a single immunizing agent (Chapter 8); all dehydrating diarrhoeas, whatever the agent that causes them, are curable by rehydration, and now more simply and far more cheaply by rehydration by mouth rather than by vein (Chapter 9).

VII

The U.S.-Japan Cooperative Medical Science Program

On 12 and 13 January 1965, President Lyndon B. Johnson and Prime Minister Eisaku Sato met in Washington to "exchange views on the current situation and matters of mutual interest to the United States and Japan". The major purpose of the meeting, from President Johnson's point of view, was to attempt to resolve the problem of the industrious Japanese exporting too much and importing too little. From this perspective, the meeting was a failure, but to ensure that at least some agreement could emerge from it, President Johnson asked Colin MacLeod, who was at the time Deputy Director of the White House Office of Science and Technology, to suggest a suitable topic for mutual cooperation. Unconfirmable legend has it that MacLeod was instructed to come up with his suggestion by breakfast time the next morning and was incarcerated all night in a room in the White House. The suggestion that emerged the next morning, and was accepted by both parties, was reported in the Joint Communiqué as follows:

> The President and the Prime Minister, mindful of the many areas of human health which are of great concern to all the peoples of Asia, agreed to undertake a greatly expanded program of cooperation in medical science with respect to such diseases as malaria, cholera, schistosomiasis, tuberculosis, and stomach cancer, in addition to cooperative efforts on problems of air pollution and pesticides. As a first step to implement the agreement they agreed to convene a conference of the foremost medical scientists from the United States and Japan to look at the details of the new program for discussion with other governments concerned.

President Johnson had found something to export to the East, but not for any material gain; however, the scientific community of the United States was going to benefit from this incentive, and from the research grants that were going to be awarded under the wing of the new

147

program. The upshot of the Joint Communiqué and the subsequent joint planning conference in April 1965 was the foundation of the U.S.-Japan Cooperative Medical Science Program (U.S.-Japan CMSP), with MacLeod as Chairman of the U.S. Delegation[1] (appointed by the Secretary of State) and Toshio Kurokawa, Director of the Cancer Institute Hospital in Tokyo, as the Chairman of the Japanese Delegation. The U.S. side was under the aegis of the Department of State (Bureau of Ocean and International Environmental and Scientific Affairs), and was initially placed under the purview of, and funded by, the Office of International Research, then part of the Office of the Director of NIH. The Japanese side was under the Planning Section of the Public Health Bureau of the Ministry of Health and Foreign Affairs. In July 1968, the U.S. side of the program was transferred to the Geographic Medicine Branch of the NIAID and John R. Seal, Chairman of the NIH Cholera Advisory Committee, became program officer of that Cholera Panel. He was succeeded by Carl Miller in 1970. In March 1973, the Cholera Advisory Committee was abolished and its place in effect taken by the U.S. Cholera Panel of the CMSP. The first Chairmen of the Cholera Panels were C.C.J. Carpenter (to be succeeded in 1972 by John P. Craig and in 1977 by Nathaniel F. Pierce) and Hideo Fukumi of the National Institute of Health in Tokyo.

Today, after 15 years, the U.S.-Japan CMSP still flourishes. Perhaps, in part, the success may be attributed to the strong direction provided to the panels by the Joint Committee. The cholera panel, and all the other panels, soon developed mutually agreed guide-lines which focused the research effort and provided for maximum collaboration. Ever since the year of their foundation, the U.S. and Japan cholera panels have held joint annual conferences alternately in the United States and Japan, at Honolulu, Hakone, Palo Alto, Untzen, Williamsburg, Hakone, Woods Hole, Aso and Tokyo, Grand Canyon, Kyoto, New Orleans, Sapporo, Atlanta, Tokyo, and NIH. These meetings have been useful in an unquantifiable way, and their greatest value from the U.S. point of view has been that they have sustained the good feeling that has always existed among American cholera workers since the sixties, fired by the interesting and exciting scientific and medical developments that were taking place. They intensified the collaborative research effort, and became the international forum for discussion of diarrhoeal diseases. It must be granted that most of the developments discussed were due to

---

1. See the United States–Japan Cooperative Medical Sciences Program, Five Year Reports 1965–1970, 1970–1975, 1975–1980, Washington, D.C., Department of State Publications 8598 (1971), 8864 (1976), 9127 (1980). These publications were written by the staff of the NIAID.

the Americans, probably because the amount of money expended by the Americans for grants and contracts greatly exceeded that of the Japanese, due to marked differences between the two countries in the methods of financing projects. However, there can be no doubt that the Japanese contribution was also most important.

Most important to the American workers were the research grants and contracts awarded to them for cholera and diarrhoeal disease research by the U.S. Cholera Panel. During the first decade, it distributed 58 grants and contracts for nearly an equal number (61) of projects, while the Japanese Cholera panel distributed a similar number (55) of grants for more than double that number (126) of projects. The third five-year report lists 89 publications by the Japanese and 266 by the Americans during the years 1975–1980, in addition to the *Proceedings of the Annual Joint Symposia.*[2]

2. Obtainable from the National Institute of Allergy and Infectious Diseases, NIH, Bethesda, Maryland 20205.

VIII

Attempts to Prevent Cholera

1. Antibacterial Immunization

In terms of epidemic control the CRL has firmly established that currently available cholera vaccines are useless.

Editorial in first number
of the International Centre
for Diarrhoeal Disease Research/Bangladesh
newsletter, *Glimpse*, January 1979

Early Vaccine[1] Trials

Pasteur was greatly impressed by the phenomenon of immunity that followed attacks of smallpox, and by the efficacy of variolation and of Jenner's vaccination. He was the first, through his work on fowl cholera,[2] anthrax, swine erysipelas and rabies between 1880 and 1888, to draw attention to the possibilities of similar prophylactic immunization against the newly discovered infectious diseases by inoculation with attenuated or killed causal organisms. When the French and German cholera commissions made their reports halfway through this period, it was natural that the possibility of prophylactic inoculation against the disease should soon be considered.

Pollitzer asserts (p. 284): "Modern writers are nevertheless unanimous in stating that Férran (1885), though acting rather injudiciously, deserves credit for having first demonstrated the possibility of actively induced immunity against cholera" [119]. The word "nevertheless" was apropos the conclusion that no satisfactory results had been derived from Férran's method (injection of cultures—apparently highly impure—obtained from cholera patients during the epidemic in Spain in 1884); the word "injudiciously" referred to the fact that Férran's injections "often pro-

---

1. We are dealing with words that have strayed a long way from their etymological origins—vaccines no longer have any connection with cows; nor does inoculation with eyes (i.e., plant buds); nor toxins with bows and arrows.

2. A pasteurellosis, nothing to do with the Asiatic cholera that concerns us.

duced severe, according to some observers occasionally even fatal, reactions" in man. (Topley and Wilson reported that Férran's work was suppressed by the government [420].) This was the sorry beginning to a dismal tale that is no better in the telling now than it was then. We know how to cure cholera, but our attempts effectively to prevent it have been far from successful.

Pasteur himself, according to his Russian pupil Gamaleia,[3] had struggled in vain for five years against "cruel obstacles" to apply his "experimental method", which had seemed to be so successful with other infectious diseases, to prophylaxis against cholera, and had been obliged to leave this disease for his pupils to work on in the future [149]. Gamaleia was one of these. He inoculated pigeons with an ordinary (therefore non-virulent) culture of the cholera vibrio and showed that they became refractory to the lethal effect of cultures that had been made highly virulent by passage through guinea pigs and pigeons. If such virulent cultures were completely sterilized by heating at 120° C for 20 minutes, they could be shown to contain a substance that was toxic to guinea pigs, but to which the guinea pig could be made refractory by previous injections of sublethal doses of the same material. This refractory state arose within a day [150]. Pasteur was greatly impressed with the work, so much so that he asked the President of the Academy of Sciences of Paris to submit Gamaleia's paper to the Commission for the Prix Bréant for the best paper of the year on cholera [see 149]. This Commission had missed two important opportunities when it failed to award the prize either to Pacini or to Snow, who had both offered papers in 1856. At any rate, it did not compound its errors by awarding the prize to Gamaleia, for his work had little to do with prophylactic immunization against cholera. The "virulence" with which he was concerned was the ability of the organisms (whether alive or sterilized) to produce ill effects on parenteral administration to animals. These ill effects, which are not seen in the natural disease, were probably due to endotoxin, a conclusion supported by his observation that the refractory state induced by his "chemical vaccine" (i.e., the heat-killed cultures) appeared within a day of administration. (This is not to say that administration of cholera endotoxin cannot produce antibacterial immunity of limited value to the prevention of the disease; see below).

Gamaleia went back to Odessa, and Pasteur read his paper to the Academy of Sciences in Paris. He stated that he had had a letter from Gamaleia offering to determine the tolerable dose of his vaccine on himself in the presence of a Commission of the Academy, and to undertake a journey in the countries ravaged by cholera to prove the

3. The foremost microbiological research institute in Moscow is named after him.

efficacy of his method. There do not appear to be any reports of such a mission, but another Russian pupil of Pasteur's, W. M. Haffkine, did carry out a remarkable number of trials in India, some of them very extensive [184–188]. He worked in the Laboratoire de Microbie Technique in the Pasteur Institute between 1889 and 1893, developing his technique of cholera vaccination on lines used by Pasteur for prevention of rabies. The principle was first to immunize the subject with a vaccine made weak (by cultivation under continuous aeration at 39° C) in order to withstand an injection given five days later of a strong vaccine made of organisms whose virulence had been enhanced by intraperitoneal passage through guinea pigs. Haffkine tested his vaccines on himself and 60 other human volunteers to satisfy himself as to their innocuity.

In 1892, Pasteur made an offer on Haffkine's behalf through Prince Alexander of Oldenburg to the Russian government to try out his vaccine in the then cholera-stricken provinces of Russia. But the Russians had heard about Férran's trials in Spain and refused the offer. Haffkine then selected Siam as the first country for a trial of his vaccine (anticipating the Inner Circle's liking for that country?), but on the advice of Lord Dufferin, the British Ambassador in Paris and formerly Viceroy of India, and after consultation with scientific authorities in England, he chose Bengal as the first and most important of the countries affected by cholera. Haffkine had obviously made a good impression in the corridors of power. The Russian Ambassador in Paris, Baron de Staal, wrote on his behalf to the Secretary of State for India, the Earl of Rosebery, to ask for a letter of introduction to the Governor General of India in Council and Viceroy, Lord Elgin, and for special authority to enable him to visit freely in all parts of India where garrisons were stationed. The Principal Medical Officer of Her Majesty's Forces in India instructed all District Principal Officers to smooth Haffkine's path.[4]

Haffkine was unable to start his trials in Bengal as he had—for good reasons—intended, because at first there were no volunteers in Bengal. He started, therefore, between April 1893 and March 1894, in the North West Provinces, Oudh and the Punjab, where the inhabitants were the first to come forward and submit themselves to inoculation. In these areas he inoculated 22,703 people. Between March 1894 and August 1895 it became possible to direct his operations to those parts of the country where cholera prevailed, the endemic areas of lower Bengal and Assam. He injected 19,473 people during this period. The next year he injected a further 30,000 people in Bengal and in the Bombay

---

4. Compare this British acceptance of Haffkine (who became a British subject in 1899) with Lutzker's allegation that he was badly treated by the British, and not accepted by the Indian Medical Service because he was "an outsider—and a Jew" [262].

area, making a total of 72,176 people inoculated, of whom about two-thirds received 2 inoculations (the weak and the strong vaccines) and one-third only the weak vaccine. These inoculations were done in the Calcutta bustees, in military camps, in gaols and on tea estates. Sometimes inoculations had to be made during an epidemic; at other times, the epidemic occurred more than a year after inoculation.

Ill health forced Haffkine to return to Europe, but he was satisfied with the results of his trials, even though there was much still to be done. He believed that prophylactic immunization against cholera was feasible, although he did not know how long the immunity would last. He returned to Europe in a blaze of glory; his satisfaction with his vaccine was shared not only by Koch himself, who pronounced that the demonstration of the vaccine had been complete, but by the British scientists consulted by Lord Hamilton, Secretary of State for India, who conveyed these views to Lord Elgin, Viceroy of India, and to Lord Sandhurst, Governor of the Presidency of Bombay. Queen Victoria conferred the Order of the Indian Empire (C.I.E.) on him in 1897.[5]

Haffkine's data were later analysed by the redoubtable statisticians Greenwood and Yule, whose calculations Chi^2 and P for eight of Haffkine's trials are shown in Table 8.1 [181]. It will be seen that in only three of the trials was the value of Chi^2 higher than 6, that is, the probability (P) of the difference in the attack rates between the inoculated and uninoculated groups being due to chance was less than 1 in 10,000. They came to the conclusion that the results of these three trials established "a presumption in favour" of Haffkine's vaccine. They could perhaps have anticipated an additional conclusion which, as we shall see below, was arrived at more than 70 years later: that it is easier to immunize the inhabitants of cholera endemic areas than people coming from elsewhere. Table 8.1 shows further that the three positive results were obtained with indigenous people (and that the two inconclusive results with indigenous people were obtained when inoculations

5. Haffkine was one of those who, on the nomination of the Académie des Sciences of Paris, won the Prix Bréant for cholera in 1909. He was also much concerned with plague, for which he developed a vaccine. In 1899, he was appointed first director of the newly founded Plague Research Laboratory in Bombay, which he left under a cloud in 1904, having been censured for a batch of apparently contaminated plague vaccine that caused 19 deaths from tetanus in the Punjab in October 1902. In 1907, he was exonerated, largely as a result of the efforts of Sir Ronald Ross, it having been shown that the incriminated batch of vaccine was contaminated only when the bottle was opened in the Punjab. The restoration of his good name culminated in 1925, 10 years after his retirement from service in Calcutta, with the renaming of the laboratory in Bombay as the Haffkine Institute.

Table 8.1
Protection afforded by Haffkine's vaccines

Vaccine Trial	Total Number involved	Percent attacked uninoculated x	Percent attacked inoculated y	Percent Effect-[f] iveness	Chi^2 [g]	p [g]
Calcutta bustees, 1894-6[a]	818	12	1	92	29.70	0.0001
East Lancers Regiment, 1894[b]	773	19	14	26	2.04	0.5652
British Troops, Cawnpore, 1894[c]	872	2.4	0	100	1.83	0.6113
Manchester Regiment, 1894[c]	922	0.8	0	100	1.60	0.6639
Gya Jail, 1894[d]	410	10	4	60	5.90	0.1176
Durbhanga Jail, 1896[d]	209	11.1	4.6	59	3.18	0.3682
Margherita Coolies, 1895[d]	343	3	2	33	37.92	0.0001
Cachar coolies 1895-6[e]	12,327	3	0.5	83	111.92	0.0001

a) Exposed 5-416 days after inoculation, b) Exposed 14 months after inoculation, c) Exposed 13 months after inoculation, d) Inoculations during epidemic, e) Time of inoculation not stated, f) % reduction in attack rate, i.e. 100 (x-y)/x, calculated by W. E. van H., g) Calculated by Greenwood and Yule, Proc. Roy Soc. Med. 8, part 2, 113, 1915.

were made during epidemics), whereas all three trials with British troops gave inconclusive results.

In spite of his apparent success, Haffkine came to the conclusion that it was not feasible to maintain his living vaccines in the field, and proposed the use of his "strong" vaccine, killed by heating at 50° C and preserved in 0.5 percent phenol. Kolle, in 1896, was the first to prepare such a vaccine and it was first tested out on a large scale in Japan in 1904, but with inconclusive results [237]. But in the sanitary corps of the Grecian Army, inoculated before the disease broke out in the Balkan war of 1914, it was significantly (P = 0.0001) 76 percent effective [181]. It may be significant that in the inconclusive Japanese trials, only a single injection was given, whereas in the Balkan trials two inoculations were given. Unlike Haffkine's trials, this suggests that people from non-endemic areas can be immunized against cholera. Haffkine does not state whether his inoculated British troops received more than one inoculation, and since about two-thirds of his subjects did not, they may not have. In that case, another conclusion might perhaps be drawn from this early work—that although people in a non-endemic area cannot be immunized by a single inoculation they may be immunized by two inoculations.

Sir Leonard Rogers reported in 1930 an unpremeditated trial of cholera vaccine under "controlled conditions equivalent to a laboratory test". He states that C. A. Bentley recorded that during a severe outbreak of cholera, Hindus submitted to inoculation and the disease ceased among them, but continued among uninoculated Muhammadans. The Muhammadan males were then inoculated and the disease promptly ceased among them, but continued among the uninoculated females, and ceased among them only when they too were inoculated. This, stated Rogers, was "a double control which leaves no doubt regarding the protective value of vaccine". Later, he stated that the protection lasted only about six months [373].

When the Cholera Research Advisory Team made its recommendations in August 1959 for the programme to be undertaken by the Cholera Research Laboratory, they included careful field trials of cholera vaccine, because in their opinion the efficacy of cholera vaccines had by no means been established, in spite of the millions of inoculations made since Haffkine's time, and the apparently encouraging results obtained in the past. For example, when the Inaugural Conference on Cholera was held in Dacca in December 1960[6], Luang Binbakya Bidyabhed (Dr. Pyn), Undersecretary of State in the Thailand Ministry of Public Health, reported that during the 1958–1959 outbreaks in his country, nearly 20 million inoculations were given, yet all he could say about the efficacy of the vaccine was, "so it looks as though there might be some relation between the vaccine and the disease after all". Similar reports were received from Japan, the Philippines, Indochina and Pakistan. There was a vague idea that cholera vaccine was of some good, but not enough to warrant complacency. The reason for this uncertainty was that up to that time none of the cholera vaccine trials had been properly controlled. The inoculated and control groups were often widely unequal in size, and unevenly exposed to infection; the trials were generally carried out in the face of epidemics already begun; the control groups were not administered placebos; there was inadequate laboratory confirmation of the disease in either group, so that many other diarrhoeal diseases, such as bacillary dysentery, could be mistaken for cholera. The very extensiveness of the trials, in numbers involved and area

6. When Phillips changed flights in Bangkok on his way from Taipei to this meeting, it emerged that his cholera vaccination was out of date and he was not allowed to proceed further until he had had another injection, despite his protests that they were no good.

covered, far from being an advantage was a disadvantage because it made comprehensive case-finding impossible and therefore etiological diagnoses were done only on small samples.

At the same inaugural conference in Dacca, Colin MacLeod laid down the conditions for adequate field trials of vaccines, as follows: (1) The field trial should take place in an accessible area where the disease is endemic, so that long-term continuous studies can be carried out. In this way, detailed knowledge of the population can be obtained with respect to the disease, especially of previous infection with cholera, which would be necessary for interpreting the effect of vaccination. (2) There must be laboratory facilities for the etiological diagnosis of cholera that is, bacteriological isolation and identification of the organism, and serological studies on cases and contacts. (3) It must be borne in mind that circumstances that favour cholera also favour the spread of other enteric infections, including dysentery and typhoid bacteria, and enteric viruses, and that all these infections can be commonly concurrent. Analysis of cholera vaccine efficacy must be based on proved cases of cholera only, severe and mild, in vaccinated and control groups. (4) Trials must be properly randomized and double blind, with the control groups receiving a comparable non-cholera vaccine, such as typhoid, paratyphoid A and B (TAB). (5) The vaccines must be administered at intervals to give maximum response; for example, a series of three doses, spaced at intervals of four to six weeks should be given, with the last dose a month before the outbreak of the epidemic. (We shall see that this very important proviso, which exploits the secondary immune response, was not carried out in the first PSCRL vaccine trials.) In order to understand the behaviour of the disease in vaccinated and control groups, serological studies should be carried out in samples of both groups, and in family contacts without overt disease. (7) Mass trials are unlikely to provide as much value as concentrated studies carried out continuously on relatively limited groups during epidemics, and between them.

Matlab Thana Trials [7]

With these provisos presumably in mind (except perhaps for the fifth) Benenson and Oseasohn and their colleagues started this first cholera vaccine trial in the field facility they had set up in Matlab thana. The cholera vaccine they used was one that had originally been selected for a proposed field trial in the Philippines shortly after the outbreak

7. See references 17, 18, 19, 20, 285, 286, 316, 334, 335.

of cholera there in the autumn of 1961,[8] presumably because the laboratory at Dacca was not yet ready for a field trial. Smadel, as chairman of the Cholera Advisory Committee, had asked D. A. Henderson (then of the CDC in Atlanta, now dean of the School of Hygiene and Public Health of Johns Hopkins University) to visit the Philippines to determine whether a field trial of cholera vaccine would be feasible in that area.[9] Henderson and P. Joseph made the visit and reviewed the previous visitations of cholera in 1902–1908, 1923–1926 and 1930–1934. After some weeks in the area, they concluded that it was unlikely that there would be a sufficient number of cases in the right place to justify a field trial. The Lederle and Lilly cholera vaccines that had already been sent to the Philippines were kept in storage there and later shipped to Dacca. The Lederle preparation (now called CRL) was used in Dacca. It was made from a mixture of Ogawa and Inaba serotypes of classical vibrios (isolated in India in 1941), grown on solid agar, phenol killed, suspended in 0.5 percent phenol to a concentration of 2.5 to 5×10^{10} organisms per ml, and applied in doses of 0.4 to 0.5 ml. It had an exceptionally high potency as determined by the only criterion available at the time, but whose relevance to the natural disease of cholera is not obvious, i.e., the ability to induce resistance in experimental animals to the lethal (non-cholera) effects of parenterally injected live vibrios. By this criterion it was about 30 and 40 times as active respectively as a standard reference vaccine in protecting against challenge with Inaba and Ogawa vibrios [116].

As a placebo for injecting into control subjects, a typhoid/paratyphoid A/paratyphoid B vaccine was used.[10] The cholera and typhoid vaccines were labelled A and B, coded by one observer who did not reveal their identity until the end of the trial.

The immunizations, single injections, mainly by jet gun, were done during six weeks beginning 1 November 1963 by a team proceeding along the rivers by houseboat. Out of the total population of 27,639 in the 23 villages, 14,059 (51 percent) volunteers took part in the trial, 61.7 percent of them being in the 5–14 years age group. People with even numbers on their cards received preparation A; those with odd numbers received preparation B. Each recipient's card recorded his name, age, sex, village, vaccine trial number, and date of inoculation. On the back of each card, there was a notice in Bengali asking that the study team be notified promptly in case of diarrhoea, and that the patient

---

8. This was an outbreak of the El Tor vibrio—the beginning of the seventh cholera pandemic.

9. There is no record of this in the minutes of the Cholera Advisory Committee.

10. In later years, tetanus toxoid was substituted for TAB as a placebo.

FIGURE 8.1. Christening of the motor vessel *Joseph E. Smadel* used in river transport of staff and supplies to cholera field hospital at Matlab Bazaar. Lower deck, left to right, unidentified, A.K.M. Fahimuddin, unidentified, Colin MacLeod, Theodore Woodward, Abram Benenson, unidentified. Upper deck, left to right, Robert Phillips, A.K.M. Abdul Wahed, and Robert Cruikshank.

come at once to central field hospital at Matlab Bazaar for medical care if he had any symptoms resembling those of cholera.[11] Patients with cholera received tetracycline and intravenous fluids when necessary. For case-finding, the 23 villages were divided into 3 groups, each of which was supervised by an experienced field worker with graduate training in social sciences, assisted by seven field workers and a midwife (dai) resident in each village. Families were visited twice weekly for inquiries about diarrhoeal disease and to encourage prompt use of the field hospital in case of illness. Whenever a new episode of diarrhoea occurred, details were entered in a simple report form, and a faecal sample was collected and sent to Dacca within 24 hours for bacteriological examination by Monsur's methods. Diarrhoeal disease was classified in four categories: (1) no interference with usual duties; (2) inability to

11. In time, many of the people living in the surveillance area became so attached to their cards that they framed them and hung them on the walls of their houses.

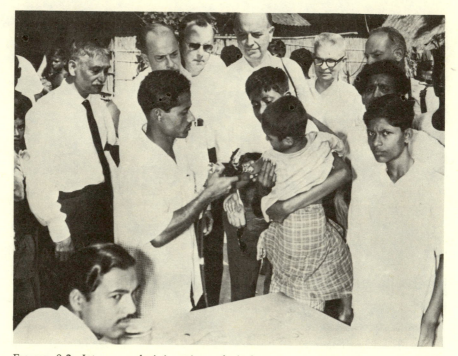

FIGURE 8.2. Jet gun administration of cholera vaccine, Matlab Bazaar, 1964. Onlookers, left to right, A.K.M. Abdul Wahed, Colin MacLeod, Clifford Pease, Alexander Langmuir, Robert Phillips, and Abram Benenson.

perform usual duties; (3) inability to walk; (4) inability to respond. During the first six months of the trial, in cases of subjects with diarrhoea in categories (3) or (4), faecal samples were collected from vaccinated contacts who were asked about diarrhoea for two (later four) consecutive days.

Thus were laid the plans for the first really carefully controlled trial of cholera vaccine trial under ideal circumstances. Six of MacLeod's seven specifications (see above) for an adequate trial were met. The one specification that was not met was that a series of three doses of vaccine should be administered at intervals of four to six weeks. There appears to have been no consideration, or at least published discussion, of this very important point. The trial was designed to answer three questions: (1) Can parenterally injected vaccine prevent cholera? (2) If so, for how long? (3) Does vaccine prevent inapparent infection among family contacts of persons with cholera?

The first results of the trial were promising. During the first year, the incidence of cholera was significantly lower in the group receiving

FIGURE 8.3. Cholera patient being carried to field hospital at Matlab Bazaar from rural village.

vaccine B, and when the code was broken this proved to be the cholera vaccine, CRL. The incidence of cholera among the controls was 6.1 per 1000; among those receiving cholera vaccine it was 1.7 per 1000. Thus, the vaccine was $100 \ (0.61 - 0.17)/ \ 0.61 \ = \ 72$ percent effective (see footnote f, Table 8.1). The answer to the first question was "yes, or 72 percent yes"; the answer to the second question needed more time. After 19 months, it seemed to be "about 2 years," since the vaccine was still 62 percent effective, but not statistically significantly so. But these reasonably (by a narrow margin) favourable answers were never again obtained. When the same CRL vaccine was tested again in 1964 in 35 villages adjacent to the 33 villages of the previous year, it was initially as effective as it had been before, but after 19 months its effectiveness had fallen to a statistically insignificant value of about 30 percent. In vaccine trials at the same time in the Negros Occidental Province of the Philippines (where the cholera epidemics were due to the Ogawa serotype of the El Tor biotype), moderately significant immunity to cholera did not last more than two or three months.

The fact that the 1963 trial in Matlab thana had shown that whole-cell cholera vaccine could confer significant protection against cholera raised the question whether one or more specific antigens in these cells

FIGURE 8.4. Police barge houseboat first used as field hospital and for staff housing at Matlab Bazaar, in 1964. Speedboat ambulances in foreground.

might be responsible for this protection. A specific antigen in the form of a lipopolysaccharide, in other words, the somatic antigen, or endotoxin, of the Ogawa serotype had been prepared by Watanabe and Verwey [453] and was tested in the field in Matlab thana in 1964 at the same time as the second trial of the CRL vaccine. Cholera in the ensuing season was mainly due to the Inaba serotype of the classical cholera vibrio (in the previous season it had been the Ogawa serotype), but the Ogawa antigen did produce some immunity. It was 80 percent effective in subjects over 10 years old, but only 32 percent effective in those younger. In the second cholera season, it had no detectable effect.

There was a third question to be answered: Does vaccine prevent inapparent (i.e., asymptomatic) infection among family contacts of cholera patients? In other words, does vaccination help to reduce the spread of cholera? The answer to this question also was not encouraging. Both in East Pakistan and in the Philippines, the number of asymptomatic vaccinated family contacts of cholera patients excreting cholera vibrios was only slightly smaller than those of unvaccinated contacts.

Two further vaccine trials were carried out in the Matlab thana area in 1966–67 and 1968–69, in different hands. In 1965, W. H. Mosley

Figure 8.5. Dr. Mizamur Rahman (center) takes carboys of diarrhoea medicine to first aid stations in Matlab cholera surveillance area in speedboat ambulance. Note "country" boat dwelling at left.

came from the Center for Communicable Diseases in Atlanta to succeed Oseasohn as head of the epidemiology division, and in December 1965 Phillips came from his command of NAMRU-2 in Taipei to succeed Benenson as Director of the PSCRL.

It soon became apparent that among the control groups in East Pakistan, the incidence of cholera was greatest in the youngest age group—those under 4 years. Thus, in the 1964–65 cholera season, for example, the attack rate per thousand was 12 for the 0–4 year age group, 4 for the 10–15 age group, and 2 for the 30–40 age group. This was the inverse of the titre of antibacterial (both Ogawa and Inaba) antibodies in the blood samples taken from these groups. In both cholera- and control-vaccinated groups, as the age went up, so did the antibacterial titre, and with each doubling of the antibody titre the cholera case rate was halved. Thus, it became clear that vaccination studies in an epidemic were being confused by a mixture of haves and have-nots—the older ones with preexisting immunity resulting from previous exposure to cholera (not necessarily always resulting in overt disease), and therefore easier to immunize further by vaccination; and the younger ones without such experience and therefore immunologically innocent, and therefore with the added handicap of being not only more susceptible but less immunizable.

In the Philippines in 1964, where cholera was still a relatively new disease, the differences in susceptibility to disease and ease of immunizability were not so marked between infants and their seniors. Because cholera, and immunity to it, was thus so clearly more a problem of children and babies than of adults, later studies in Matlab thana were restricted to children under 15 years of age [283, 284, 287, 288].

In the trials up to this stage, the effect of only a single injection of vaccine was tested. In active immunization, it is the well-established practise to employ at least two injections of the immunizing agent, the spacing between the two usually being four to six weeks. This is because it is a fact of life that when the low antibody levels that are produced after one injection begin to fall, a second injection is followed by a vigorous response. This is why MacLeod had recommended that in any cholera vaccine trial the vaccine should be administered a month before the expected oubreak of the epidemic. In the 1966 trials in Matlab thana, the effects of one and two doses of cholera vaccine, spaced 25–35 days, were compared in children under 14 years of age. The result that might be expected was found: In the age group 0–4 years a single dose was, as before, ineffective: two doses evoked 67 percent effective immunity. In the age group 5–14 years, immunity was evoked whether one or two injections had been given (79 percent and 61 percent effective, respectively).

Up to this stage, mixed vaccines from both the Ogawa and Inaba serotypes had been tested in Matlab thana. In the 1968 trials, the effects of single injections of separate monovalent Ogawa and Inaba vaccines, and of a purified Inaba lipopolysaccharide preparation, were tested. During the first cholera season that followed these inoculations three months later, practically all cases were due to the Inaba serotype of *Vibrio cholerae*. Both the Inaba vaccine and lipopolysaccharide give excellent protection (95 percent effective) in the first season, but the Ogawa vaccine was ineffective against the Inaba cholera. The conclusion was drawn that vaccine-induced immunity to cholera depended on the development of serotype-specific immunity. But later trials seem to suggest something different: Although Ogawa vaccine produced high titres of anti-Inaba antibodies in young children (0–5 years), it did not protect them, yet did afford some protection (48 percent) in the 5–14 year group. What was protecting them?

On the other hand, protection does not seem to be specific as to the biotype of the organism, i.e., whether the classical *Vibrio cholerae* or

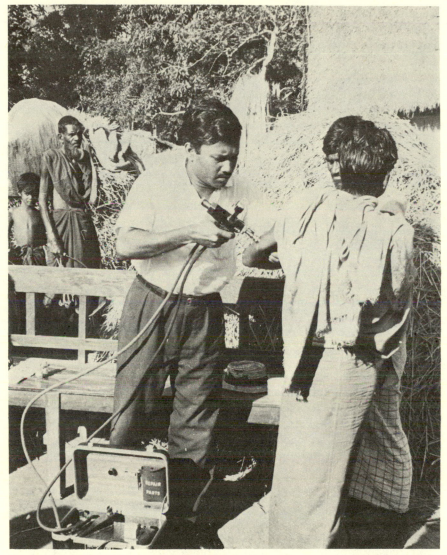

FIGURE 8.6. Dr. A.K.M. Jamiul Alam vaccinating volunteer at village in Matlab, 1964.

the *Vibrio eltor* is concerned. Studies in the Philippines in 1970, where the predominant organism was biotype El Tor, serotype Ogawa, showed that there was no difference in the protection afforded by monovalent El Tor Inaba and Ogawa and classical Inaba and Ogawa vaccines [336].

An enormous amount of very careful work was done on cholera

FIGURE 8.7. New hospital at Matlab Bazaar. Speedboat ambulance in foreground.

vaccination in East Pakistan (and in the Philippines) by many highly competent investigators on a large population of volunteers under ideal conditions over six years, but the only conclusion that has emerged is that older people in cholera-endemic areas have some immunity to cholera[12] and that immunity can be boosted, but to not much more than 50 percent efficacy, and, unless reinforced annually, this effect does not last more than about two to three months. The first vaccine, CRL, to be administered in Matlab thana was the only one to evoke immunity lasting at least two years, but this had never been repeated.

Although the population of a cholera-endemic area could be partially protected by repeated injections of cholera vaccines, this would not be effective as an epidemic control measure. Mosley compared the cost benefits of prevention of cholera by vaccination of the whole population with treatment only of patients, by intravenous and oral (see Chapter 9) rehydration at the field hospital in Matlab Bazaar. During the year 1 July 1969 to 30 June 1970, this hospital, serving a population of

12. Not always enough to prevent them from having recurrent attacks of cholera in successive seasons; see below.

750,000 people, treated 1,743 cases of cholera with a loss of only 4 patients (0.2 percent fatality rate). The cost of this operation, including the 14 speedboat ambulances, was $60,000, or $34 per case (and this does not take into consideration the 6,432 cases of non-cholera diarrhoea successfully treated during the same period). Immunization of the same population at $0.06 a head would cost a little less ($45,000), but would it do any good [283]?

In reality, with only two to three months' protection afforded by the vaccine, and with the limited manpower available, vaccination in the Indian subcontinent is generally withheld until the start of an epidemic, and then restricted to family contacts of cholera patients. But this is entirely ineffective. The PSCRL investigators showed that there was no difference in the attack rates between family contacts receiving and not receiving cholera vaccine [405]. Calculations based on the experience over 6 years with the 23 villages in Matlab thana showed that even if the injection of the entire population were started within 1 day of the index case of cholera, immunization would be impracticable and ineffective. With half the cholera cases taking place within the first week of the index case, and with induced protection taking 5 days to develop, and then being only 50 percent effective, and with it taking 2 weeks to inoculate 500 people, only 12.5 percent of potential cases of cholera can be prevented. But experience shows that, in fact, it was more likely that there would be a delay of two weeks from the index case in starting the inoculations, in which case only 5 percent of potential cases of cholera would be prevented [406]. Thus it was concluded: "Short of hiring sufficient personnel to vaccinate the entire country or endemic area every 3–4 months, something which no country, not even a wealthy industrial one, can afford, there is no obvious method for transforming the vaccination campaign into an effective public health programme". The lesson to be drawn was that "public health officials would do well to concentrate their limited resources on providing therapy centres and gradually upgrading sanitation while awaiting development of better cholera vaccines" [406].

Can there be such a "better cholera vaccine"? Up to now we have been considering immunization against the bacterium, by means of vaccines made by growing the bacteria on a solid or in a liquid medium, harvesting, washing and killing them. But in gathering and washing them, have we thrown away the baby with the bath water? Cholera, as we have seen in chapter 2, is a toxinosis, and, indeed, an *exo*toxinosis. It produces all its harmful effects by means of a toxin which it secretes into its culture medium. This toxin-containing culture medium is discarded when the bacteria are filtered off and washed in the preparation of the vaccines we have considered until now. But should we not retrieve the toxin and immunize against it? Tetanus and diphtheria are also exotoxinoses, and they have been practically completely eliminated in countries where active immunization against their exotoxins is practised. The immunization is very simple, and completely effective, and needs only occasional boosting, if at all. But this immunization is against the toxin—it has probably never occurred to anybody to prepare vaccines from washed tetanus or diphtheria bacilli. So why do we continue to immunize against cholera bacilli? Should we not be immunizing against cholera toxin? The answer is not so simple, as we shall now see.

2. Antitoxic Immunization

The Recognition of Cholera Toxin

When Phillips investigated the phenomenon of cholera in Egypt in 1947, he came to the conclusion that there was no cholera toxin, but, as we have already seen, it was a logical conclusion. Koch's doctrine of the systemic action of the cholera poison still prevailed, and since NAMRU-3 saw no systemic effects in their patients, they concluded there was no toxin. When NAMRU-2 encountered cholera eleven years later in Bangkok (before De's paper on cholera exotoxin had appeared), Phillips concluded in effect that the cholera vibrio did produce an extracellular poison that acted not systemically, but locally on the epithelial cells of the gut. As a result of their observations on the loss of electrolytes in cholera patients, NAMRU-2 postulated that these could be explained by a defect in the reabsorptive capacity of the intestinal mucosal cells caused by "*V. comma* or its products" [456]. Phillips replaced the last two words with "cholera toxin" the next year at the inauguration of the PSCRL, and suggested that the toxin partially or completely blocked the "sodium pump" which regulates the concentration of sodium ions in cells [455]. At the same conference, he reported on experiments in which he had measured the electrical current flowing across a membrane in the form of pieces of frog skin forming a semi-permeable barrier between two halves of a suitable apparatus (the Ussing chamber). Under appropriate conditions, the sodium ion is the only ion flowing across such a membrane, and in so doing it creates an electrical current. He found that cholera culture filtrates, and the stool of cholera patients (presumed to contain cholera toxin), abolished this current, and he inferred that the passage of sodium ions, that is, the action of the sodium pump, had been affected [211].[13] Phillips came near the truth—

13. Similar results were found at the same time by the Fuhrmans at Stanford University, but their cholera preparation was heat-stable and they concluded that they were dealing with endotoxin, whereas the NAMRU-2 preparation was heat-labile, like exotoxin [146].

Vibrio cholerae does cause diarrhoea through the agency of a toxin, and, as we shall see, the toxin does act on mucosal cells, as he suggested, and it does affect the passage of ions in and out of these cells—but he did not come near enough, because the toxin does not block the sodium pump, or at least only partially.

We have seen that in the meantime, in 1959, S. N. De of Calcutta very clearly demonstrated the existence in cholera culture filtrates of an exotoxin that mimicked the symptom of cholera that was responsible for all the ill effects of the disease, namely, the outpouring of fluid into the gut. In other words, cholera, like diphtheria and tetanus, was an exotoxinosis. But the significance of De's discovery was not immediately grasped, and his historical paper went unnoticed for some years, even, apparently, in the PSCRL. Cholera toxin may have been discovered in 1959, but its existence was not recognized until five years later, through the work of R. A. Finkelstein at WRAIR in Washington, and of J. P. Craig at the PSCRL. Finkelstein's paper in the *Journal of Infectious Diseases* was received by the editor in October 1963 (before Craig had started his work) and was published in June 1964; Craig's paper in *Nature* was published in August 1965; both investigators reported their findings at the second SEATO Cholera Research Symposium in Honolulu in January 1965, the report of which was published at an unspecified time later. Finkelstein thus has every right to claim priority (and, as we shall see, greater relevance of his work to the disease), yet it was Craig's work that was first recognized and exploited by the cholera establishment (the word is not intended in a derogatory sense) in America. This was perhaps due to three factors: Craig's work was done at the PSCRL, the institution of the establishment's making; it was simpler to assay the toxin and the antitoxin—to put it through the toxinologists' hoops—by the means that Craig had devised; Finkelstein in his younger days was highly endowed with ability, but with more than his fair share of self-assuredness, and this may have abraded his well-established elders.

Finkelstein's "Choleragen"

Richard Finkelstein was no new-comer to the cholera field by the time he came to work on the toxin in 1963. Except for a three-year virological interlude, he had worked on cholera ever since he became a graduate student of Charles Lankford's in the early fifties at the University of Texas in Austin, where, as we have seen in Chapter 3, he developed a synthetic medium for the culture of the cholera vibrio. In 1958, after the virological interlude, he joined the staff of WRAIR in Washington as a civilian to work under S. B. Formal in the Division of Communicable Disease and Immunology. When he arrived there, he was greeted by A. S. Benenson, then Director of the Division, with the news that there was cholera in Bangkok, and was told that if he were willing to return to the cholera field he would be sent to Bangkok with the WRAIR team that went there. But in the event he was not sent to Bangkok, in spite of having resumed work on the cholera vibrio. He worked on several aspects of the organism in several places. Much of this work is still quoted today. It will not be discussed here in detail since that has already been ably done by Finkelstein himself in an admirable review [127] containing all the references. He started in WRAIR by taking part in the development of a technique for the rapid recognition of the vibrio with fluorescent antibodies, and then in studies on the virulence of the vibrio and its endotoxin for the chick embryo. Realizing eventually that this had nothing to do with cholera, he turned to N. K. Dutta's newly published work on the infant rabbit as a model for cholera studies (see below). In 1960–61, he "fooled around" rather unsuccessfully with this technique for some time (because he was introducing the vibrios into the stomach rather than the small intestine). Then, when cholera broke out in Hongkong in 1961, he turned to developing a haemagglutination test on the vibrio as a measure of its ability to adhere to the walls of the gut, which is an important aspect of its capacity for virulence. In the autumn of 1961, when NAMRU-2 went to the Philippines to deal with the outbreak of cholera, the Army also sent a team of four, including Finkelstein. He worked in the Bureau of Research and Laboratories in Manila evaluating the fluorescent antibody technique and developing a vibriocidal test for determining antibodies to the vibrio. He then travelled to India, and worked on haemagglutination with S. T. Mukerjee in the Indian Institute for Biochemistry in Calcutta. He also visited the Haffkine Institute in Bombay, where Dutta was Director, and saw a demonstration of his technique of inducing diarrhoea in the suckling rabbit by feeding or intestinal inoculation of the cholera vibrio or its products. This reinforced his previous belief that the suckling rabbit was a useful model for studying cholera. When he returned to WRAIR, he resumed his studies on the infant rabbit, which received further impetus from a visit to WRAIR by Dutta at Burrows's instigation and by Formal's invitation in the autumn of 1962. Formal, as we have seen (Chapter 2), had been interested in De's ligated ileal loop model but had been discouraged because although he had got positive results in the loop with whole cultures of the vibrio he had not got them with culture filtrates, as De had done, and furthermore De had stated that, unless precautions were taken, falsely positive results were sometimes obtained with non-toxic material. For these reasons, Finkelstein was not impressed with De's work. That is understandable; what is regrettable is that to this day, when De's observations have been amply confirmed and their fundamental importance fully acknowledged, Finkelstein still insists on pooh-poohing them. While Dutta was in Formal's laboratory, he, Formal, Finkelstein, H. T. Norris and H. Sprinz carried out a collaborative experiment which was reported in a communication of less than 200 words [310]. Its main import, which was that diarrhoea is not caused by endotoxin, does not seem to have struck its authors. They introduced intact cholera vibrios, an ultrasonic lysate of the vibrios, a cell-free extract of the lysate, and endotoxin, intraintestinally into suckling rabbits, and all the preparations except the endotoxin induced diarrhoea.

In 1963, Finkelstein set about his classically important work which was to lead to the purification and crystallization of the diarrhoea-inducing cholera exotoxin, to which he gave the name "choleragen" [133]. He did this work with the *Vibrio cholerae* Inaba serotype strain 569B supplied by Dutta—the strain originally used for the Haffkine vaccine and now universally used for cholera toxin production.[14] He started with a filtrate of ultrasonically disrupted organisms grown in a peptone medium. This is curious, since Formal maintains that "while Dutta's toxin was a sterile whole cell lysate, Finkelstein kept insisting that it was present also in culture supernatants".[15] Indeed, he soon redirected his attention to culture supernatants. "It was considered that the active principle might be elaborated by the cell during growth and be found in good amount in the culture medium", he stated in his paper [133], as if De never existed. Yet he refers to De's "encouraging results—with enterotoxic filtrates of 5% peptone-water cultures", but dismisses them in the introduction since they proved to "not be entirely reproducible" (S. B. Formal, personal communication, 1979). When Finkelstein grew the 569B strain on a brain-heart infusion broth, he found that instead of feeding rabbits with multiple doses of concentrated suspensions of the vibrio as Dutta had had to do, he could reproduce cholera with a single dose of culture filtrate, even diluted filtrate. He then tried growing his cultures on the synthetic medium he had devised under Lankford's guidance 7 years earlier in Austin, Texas [129], and found that although the organism grew well the culture filtrates failed to produce diarrhoea; but when he supplemented the synthetic medium with 10 g of casamino acids, i.e., hydrolysed casein, per litre, thus developing his "syncase" medium, highly choleragenic culture filtrates were obtained. It was at this time that Finkelstein indulged in his liking

14. Dutta did not actually take part in this work, but Formal insisted that his name be included since he had taught the WRAIR group how to assay the toxin in the infant rabbit.

15. Personal communication, 1979.

for coining names, and he christened the active principle of his syncase-grown cultures "choleragen"—not because he was sure it induced cholera, but, strangely, "because, at the time, we were uncertain of its relevance to cholera in man [127]". For a brief while, he chased two wild geese, a large-molecular one named "procholeragen A" and a small-molecular one named "procholeragen B" which were necessary together to constitute "choleragen", but it turned out the B goose was merely a buffer that protected the A goose from destruction by the acidity of the stomach. In more complex media, this protection was provided by the high concentrations of protein that were present.

Shortly after the work on choleragen was completed, cholera broke out again in Bangkok in the summer of 1963 and Finkelstein was ordered to proceed to the Thailand-SEATO Medical Research Laboratory, the American component of which was operated by WRAIR (Chapter 4), to help cope with the disease. But the order was not ratified until the end of November and by the time he got to Bangkok at the end of 1963, the cholera had abated, but had flared up in Vietnam, so after a few days he moved on to Saigon, where he worked at the Pasteur Institute on the haemagglutination test which became the quickest and most reliable test for distinguishing between the classical biotype of the cholera vibrio and the newly emerging El Tor biotype. Finkelstein did not stay in Bangkok for long on his way back to Washington, but while he was there he did an important experiment in collaboration with Chanyo Benyajati, who had worked with Phillips and with the WRAIR group in Bangkok in 1959, and knew how to deal with cholera patients. Finkelstein wanted to test the relevance of his choleragen, which for all he knew produced diarrhoea only in suckling rabbits, to the disease in man. He and Benyajati wanted to feed his syncase choleragen to humans. They did not believe there would be any serious risk involved since the worst that could happen was that the subject would get diarrhoea, and if he got dehydrated he could easily be rehydrated. So two human volunteers (who thoroughly understood the implications of the test) were given the choleragen through a tube into the small intestine. One of them had half the dose that would induce diarrhoea in a rabbit and had one loose stool; the other had four times that amount of choleragen and produced 18 litres of diarrhoeal stools. He was properly treated and affirmed afterwards that he had never felt better in his life. Finkelstein dared not put his name on the paper [24] that was subsequently published for fear of getting into trouble with the Army.

After a brief interlude back in Washington, Finkelstein returned to the laboratory in Bangkok in the summer of 1964 for a more prolonged spell of duty, as deputy chief of bacteriology. There, in collaboration

with P. Atthasampunna, he started work on the production and purification of choleragen that was eventually to lead to its complete
purification, but they were obliged to proceed in an amateurish way
because they "were isolated from any input of modern technology".

Finkelstein did not get the promotion he expected to get to the
headship of the bacteriology division of the laboratory in Bangkok, and
had other reasons for dissatisfaction, and so, after three years, he decided
to leave the Army and take up an appointment in the Department of
Microbiology of the Southwestern Medical School in Dallas, Texas, in
1967. There he intended to proceed to the purification of choleragen,
and for this purpose sought the help of a competent biochemist, Joseph
J. LoSpalluto of the Department of Biochemistry. Between the two of
them, they succeeded by the beginning of 1969 in purifying the toxin
to a state of apparent complete purity, or to use a biochemist's expression,
homogeneity, or a physical chemist's, kinetic unity [131]. This in itself
was triumph of considerable importance, but with it came a discovery
of almost equal importance, since (1) it was later to throw a strong
light on the structure and mode action of the toxin at the molecular
level, as we shall see in Chapter 10; and (2) there is a possibility that
it may play a part in the future in immunizing against cholera, as we
shall see later in this chapter. This was the discovery of choleragenoid,
a substance nearly identical with choleragen but rather smaller in
molecular size and biologically inert. The discovery came about because
the output of the purification process was being monitored in two
ways—by measuring its toxicity and its ability to precipitate with specific
antitoxin. In the end, they found one fraction of pure protein that was
toxic and precipitated with antitoxin, which was choleragen; and another
fraction of pure protein which was not toxic but still precipitated with
the same antitoxin—which was choleragenoid, which Finkelstein considered a natural toxoid, biologically inert but immunologically very
nearly identical with the toxin. In fact, as we shall see, it turned out
not to be a modified toxin, as most artificially prepared toxoids are,
but the larger, and inert, part of the cholera toxin molecule. Finkelstein
and LoSpalluto suggested that choleragenoid might be the precursor of
choleragen, and, it should be noted, already at this stage made the
suggestion: "If choleragenoid is a precursor of choleragen, it might be
possible to isolate a stable mutant, which one might predict would be
incapable of causing cholera, and which could potentially provide the
ideal immunizing agent—a living, attenuated vibrio, capable of multiplication in the gut and stimulation both of antibacterial and antitoxic
immunity at the important local level." We shall see that the dream
of finding such a mutant vibrio producing choleragenoid but not chol-

eragen was to come true, but whether the rest of the dream will come true is still a question.

Henceforth, we shall employ the word choleragen as little as possible, preferring the words cholera toxin, but there is at present no substitute for the word "choleragenoid".

Craig's "Skin Toxin"

In April 1963, J. P. Craig, at the Department of Microbiology and Immunology of the Downstate Medical Center of the State University of New York in Brooklyn, was approached by Smadel[16] who, in his capacity as Chairman of the Cholera Advisory Committee, offered him the two-year post as epidemiologist to succeed Stockard at the PSCRL in Dacca.[17] Craig was unable to take two years' leave from his appointment in Brooklyn, so Smadel arranged (through Benenson, who was on home leave from Dacca) for him to apply to NIH for a one-year research fellowship. Craig set about learning about cholera by visiting nearly all of the few laboratories in the United States then working on the problem, namely those of Burrows, Goodner and Margaret Pittman (who was in charge of the control of vaccines to be used in field trials), but, in spite of De, nobody suggested that cholera was a toxinosis. Craig was toxin-minded, having recently worked with A. A. Miles at the Lister Institute in London on the iota toxin of *Clostridium welchii*, which causes changes in the permeability of capillaries in the skin. These changes in vascular permeability can be measured by a technique that is simple and convenient and allows many estimations of the toxin's activity to be carried out at the same time. Since this technique came to be much used by cholera workers, it is worth a brief description now. Small volumes (0.1 ml) of the toxin are injected into the skin of the shaved or depilated backs of rabbits or guinea pigs, and after a latent period of about 1.5 hours an area of redness (erythema) and hardness (induration) begins to develop in the skin at the site of injection. This induration reaches its maximum at 6 to 18 hours, and declines in 18 to 30 hours. If a dye, such as Pontamine Sky Blue, is injected intravenously near the peak time of induration, the area of induration is soon coloured blue, the area of blueing being a measure of the concentration of toxin injected. It is comparatively easy to make 144 injections in the back of one rabbit. Since Pontamine Sky Blue is

16. With whom he had worked on haemorrhagic fever in 1952 in the U.S. Army laboratory in Korea.

17. Craig's innocence of cholera at that time was such that he thought Smadel meant Dakar in Senegal, but Smadel considered this an advantage, since he wanted someone with new ideas. In the event, Stockard was succeeded by Oseasohn.

fixed to plasma protein, particularly the albumin, it follows that the accumulation of dye at the site of injection signifies an induced permeability in the vessels of the capiallary endothelium not only to water, but also to such large molecules as protein.

Craig therefore drew up a research proposal which included, among others, the search for a vascular permeability factor in cholera stools and culture filtrates, that is, a factor which caused the walls (the endothelium) of blood vessels to become permeable to fluid. He had concluded (as had others, including De) that the fluid accumulation in cholera might be due to increased permeability of the capillaries serving the villi of the small intestine. If the permeability of these capillaries was changed by a product of the cholera vibrio, the permeability of other blood vessels might also be changed, and amongst these might be the capillaries in the skin. His choice of rabbit or guinea pig skin was only coincidental with Phillips's choice of frog skin, and his motives quite different. His first thought was to look for a capillary permeability-inducing toxin in the stools of cholera patients (as had Phillips) rather than in cholera filtrates, because it might be possible that such a factor might be produced *in vivo* in the course of the natural disease, and not *in vitro* in a laboratory culture.

Craig's research proposal (which Smadel, who was dying, never saw) was accepted, and he arrived in Dacca in early January 1964, to be plunged immediately into the first severe cholera epidemic that faced the PSCRL, the epidemic which, as we have seen in Chapter 4, followed the anti-Hindu rioting. This was his first exposure to the disease. There was no question of his being able to do any laboratory bench work and he spent his first month in Dacca riding ambulance, bringing the most severely affected patients into the cholera ward. But he did at least take advantage of this opportunity to make a collection (with the help of Sister Torrance) of rice-water stools from severely ill patients and store them at $-70°$ C for later investigations.

The first stool sample he injected into the skin of a guinea pig[18] was obtained from an elderly patient who had been purging 20 litres of stool a day. It produced marked induration of the skin, and when Pontamine Sky Blue was injected the dye appeared in the area of induration. Stools from 13 out of 20 bacteriologically confirmed cases of cholera produced similar "blueing" reactions, with the induration and erythema beginning 6 to 8 hours after injection, reaching its peak in 18 to 24 hours, receding somewhat by 48 hours, but persisting for 4 to 5 days. No such reactions were observed with stools from 33

18. At that time, the laboratory animal house was not yet breeding guinea pigs and they had to be gathered from all the pet shops in Dacca.

patients with acute diarrhoea with no demonstrable cholera vibrios. When cholera organisms taken from rectal swabs of patients were cultivated by De's method (which Craig was now aware of), skin capillary permeability factor (PF) could be demonstrated in the culture filtrates. Sera taken from convalescent patients, or from rabbits immunized with culture filtrates containing PF, neutralized the PF activity of cholera stools or culture filtrates. The cholera vascular permeability factor could be titrated against antiserum exactly like any typical bacterial exotoxin [81, 82, 83].[19]

But was this toxin the toxin that was responsible for diarrhoea? Craig was well aware that the cholera exudate, as was shown by Snow in London in 1856, by Phillips in Cairo in 1947 and by Gordon in Bangkok in 1958, contained little or no protein, yet the exudate induced by PF from skin capillaries was rich in protein. He therefore had to postulate that when permeability was induced in the capillaries of the intestinal villi, the protein had somehow to be filtered out by the epithelial cells before the exudate reached the lumen of the gut.

The question of the identity of Craig's PF and De's and Finkelstein's diarrhoea-producing toxin was approached with caution when it was first demonstrated, and 5 years later there were still claims that they were not identical [e.g., 172]. However, the question was settled in 1970 when Mosley and his colleagues [282] at the PSCRL, following a suggestion of W. E. van Heyningen as visiting consultant to the Technical Committee, showed that the two activities were due to the same antigen; in other words, the PF and the diarrhoea-producing toxin were the same. When the capacities of a number of samples of antisera from convalescent patients and immunized animals to neutralize samples of toxin were tested, the same answers were obtained whether De's ileal loop test or Craig's skin test was used as indicator of excess of toxin over antitoxin. This meant that both activities must be due to the same antigen, because it was inconceivable that many antisera, from

19. As long ago as 1932, Yu and Chen claimed that cholera culture filtrates produced a "skin reaction" (not described) in humans and rabbits to which humans vaccinated three years previously were immune [467]. The factor producing this reaction is unlikely to have been Craig's PF, since it was stable to heating at 80° C for 1 hour, whereas PF is destroyed by heating at 56° C for 30 minutes. This obscure, vague and irrelevant Chinese paper was later to be spotted by a sharp-eyed but not sufficiently informed official at NIH who on this ground refused permission for the chairman of the Cholera Advisory Committee to apply for patent to exploit Craig's discovery. Basu Mallik and Ganguli showed, shortly before Craig, that cholera stool filtrates injected into the skin would produce a "blueing reaction [14]". But their effect was not that observed by Craig because it was produced also by non-cholera stools, and the increased permeability was produced immediately, rather than after a period of 6 to 8 hours. It is a common non-specific effect [see 81].

several species of animals immunized in different ways, would all have identical ratios of antibodies to two different antigens [430].

But although "skin toxin" was the same thing as the "loop toxin", it did not follow that the toxin was promoting the same reaction in the gut in the natural disease as it was when it was introduced artificially into the skin in the laboratory. The rather farfetched idea of induced leakage of plasma from villus capillaries, followed by the epithelial cells filtering out the plasma protein, was ruled out in 1968 when Carpenter and Greenough at Johns Hopkins University showed that toxin-induced fluid loss was independent of blood flow in the superior mesenteric arteries supplying the gut [54]. As will be seen in Chapter 10, the fact is that cholera toxin can act on any animal cell to which it is exhibited. When exhibited to endothelial cells of skin capillaries of guinea pigs or rabbits by scientists in laboratories it will act on them, and in doing so it will cause the capillaries to leak blood plasma. But this does not happen in nature. As we shall see, in the case of the natural disease, cholera toxin acts on the epithelial cells lining the crypts between the microvilli of the small intestine and causes them to pour out chloride and bicarbonate ions, and with these ions flows the protein-free *milieu intérieur*.

Although the skin test for cholera toxin had nothing to do with cholera, it had a great deal to do with advancing research on cholera. It put cholera research in the hands of the biochemists, because it provided a simple, fairly rapid, fairly reliable and fairly accurate method for measuring cholera toxin and its antitoxin, and thus made it possible for many people who had no appetite or aptitude for the surgical manoeuvres of De's ileal loop tests, or the feeding of toxin to Dutta's infant rabbits, to do research on cholera. More than anything, it brought research on cholera toxin in its early days into laboratories in the United States and elsewhere.

The Cholera Advisory Committee and Cholera Toxin

We have already remarked that it was to a large extent Craig's work at the PSCRL in Dacca that first concentrated the minds of the Cholera Advisory Committee in Bethesda on cholera toxin. The awakening and quickening of interest in cholera toxin, and the accelerating crescendo in its enthusiastic development, can be followed in the minutes of the Cholera Advisory Committee that met once or twice a year from 4 May 1960 to 13 March 1972.[20] But there was a lag period before an awareness

---

20. Smadel took the chair at two meetings in 1960. There are no minutes of meetings in 1961 or 1962, but it does not follow that there were no meetings. Smadel had no taste for the details of bureaucracy and may not have bothered about minutes. After his

of toxin was manifest. Up to the time of the third (?) meeting in August 1963, the nearest reference to any suggestion of toxin was from MacLeod, who listed among the aims of the PSCRL the determination of "what factors of the organism account for its pathogenicity". It is surprising that such an experienced and enthusiastic toxinologist as MacLeod should not have referred to De's clear demonstration four years previously of an enterotoxin causing fluid accumulation in the gut, or to Phillips's postulation at the inaugural conference in Dacca in 1960 of "a defect in the reabsorptive capacity of the intestinal mucosal cells [caused] by cholera toxin". There is no mention of toxin in the minutes of the meeting in February 1964. When the second SEATO Cholera Research Symposium was held in Honolulu on 24 to 29 January 1965, Craig gave a paper on the "skin toxin", Schafer on the "ligated loop toxin" and Finkelstein on the "infant rabbit toxin". Fired by these papers and by earlier reports, MacLeod made a clear and explicit statement on the role of cholera toxin in the disease, comparing it with two other exotoxinoses, diphtheria and scarlet fever.[21] At a meeting held at the time of the Honolulu Symposium, the Cholera Advisory Committee approved an application from Craig for a research grant to continue with his work on the skin permeability factor. So it was through Craig's work that official cognizance of a possible cholera exotoxin was first taken by the U.S. cholera establishment and recorded in its minutes. By the time of the meeting in October 1965, interest in cholera toxin was definitely stirring. Carpenter reported that at the meeting of the Cholera Panel of the U.S.-Japan Cooperative Medical Science Program held earlier that month (also in Honolulu), emphasis had been placed on the need to study the toxin causing the disturbance in cholera, to elucidate its mechanism, and to determine its immunogenic properties. Despite this reference to the possible immunogenic properties of cholera

---

death in 1963, Clifford Pease was chairman from August 1963 to September 1965, when he left the NIH for the Population Council. He was succeeded by John R. Seal, who up to that time had represented the Navy on the committee in his capacity of Captain in the Medical Corps, and was now Scientific Director of the NIAID. Recently (18 September 1981), at a party at NIH to mark his retirement from the Deputy Directorship of NIAID, it was revealed that his translocation from the Navy to the NIH had been arranged by members of the Inner Circle, including James Shannon, Director of NIH, because they were anxious to have him as Chairman of the Cholera Advisory Committee. He presided until March 1973, when the Cholera Advisory Committee was abolished and its functions taken over by the U.S. Cholera Panel of the U.S.-Japan Cooperative Medical Science Program (Chapter 7).

21. Not that scarlet fever toxin is lethal—it causes a red rash that looks alarming but is of little consequence. He should rather have mentioned tetanus.

toxin, the Cholera Advisory Committee itself, in discussing future plans, did not turn to cholera toxin. But the subject was taken up vigorously and forthrightly by the Director of the National Institutes of Health, James A. Shannon. Shannon, though ultimately responsible for the Cholera Advisory Committee, was not a member of it, but he made it his business to attend as many of its meetings as he was able. There were a number of representatives of AID present, and Shannon made an important statement for their benefit. Much of this concerned the funding of the activities of the PSCRL by the State Department,[22] but this is what he had to say about cholera toxin:

One thing I would like for you to discuss this afternoon—is whether you really want to hit this for all it is worth. I think that the big lead that is available to you now that was not available a year ago is the fairly well documented presence of one or two isolatable toxins upon which may be based the physiological disturbance. Now if this is demonstrated it leads to the possibility of mounting a development program based primarily in industry rather than in the university, and if you really feel that the data upon which these judgments are based are hard, then I think that you ought to be talking about $200,000 or $300,000 in the way of industrial contracts to really go after this. Now if this is a problem that this group doesn't take up, I will take it up with the Japanese-American Medical Science Program. I really think you may have a problem here not too different from the problem of diphtheria, where it makes little difference how widely the Klebsiella [i.e., the diphtheria bacillus] is distributed in nature as long as one has solid immunity as a result of diphtheria toxoid. The disease that we know as diphtheria is unimportant. It could well be that cholera is susceptible to a somewhat similar challenge, but this will not take place within the frame of reference of the present program. . . . If it can be shown that the noxious effects of the organism are transmitted by one or another, or both, . . . of the toxins that are purported to have been demonstrated these past 12 to 15 months, then the complex antigenic structure of the whole organism becomes of lesser importance and one gets at the toxin that produces the result. This I would really appreciate your giving pretty serious consideration.

At the next meeting of the Cholera Advisory Committee in April

---

22. E.g., "I would hope that the State Department would continue to expend the small amount of money they have in the Program, if for no other reason than to credit unto themselves an accomplishment that in a very concrete way is much greater here, in the medical field, than they are able to fund in many of their other activities—I think it is in their self interest to buy, for a fairly cheap price, a considerable amount of prestige for themselves".

1966, there was much discussion of cholera toxin, toxoid and antitoxin. Craig gave an account of his findings of antitoxic activity in the serum of convalescent patients. Col. Tigertt of WRAIR reported on Finkelstein's findings, and Carpenter reported on his success in inducing cholera in dogs at Johns Hopkins University. This was the beginning of the very important contribution the group at Johns Hopkins were to make to the physiology of the cholera problem. Carpenter had arranged to test the effect of Craig's toxin in the animal model and it was agreed that in view of its potential importance this work should proceed as rapidly as possible to get data on the role of toxin in the cholera syndrome, and whether active and passive protection against the disease could be obtained by the use of toxoid and antitoxin respectively. Large amounts of toxin would be needed for this work, and the toxin would have to be purified in order to define it biochemically and standardize its dosage. Shannon repeated what he had said at the previous meeting, namely, that the large-scale production of toxin could be carried out only by a commercial firm with experience in the field. The Chairman of the Committee, Seal, was asked to investigate the possibility of obtaining a large amount of Craig toxin by contract with a commercial firm, and of the firm's undertaking the purification of the toxin, and the preparation of a potent toxoid. It was also agreed that Carpenter should arrange for a Symposium on the Pathophysiology of Cholera to bring the information on cholera toxins and antitoxins up to date. It was to be held in association with the next meeting of the committee. The committee was about to become deeply involved in cholera toxin, and the scene was being set for an explosion in knowledge of cholera and cholera toxin.

Carpenter's workshop in the Pathophysiology of Cholera was held at the Johns Hopkins Medical School on 7 and 8 December 1966. The participants were limited to 15 people actually known to be working with toxins. The only observers were 8 members of the staffs of the Johns Hopkins University and the University of Maryland Medical Schools who were especially invited by Carpenter because of present or planned collaboration in studies at Johns Hopkins, and the 10 members of the Cholera Advisory Committee, for whose enlightenment the meeting was held. In order for the presentation and discussion of work in progress to be uninhibited, no record of the workshop was made. It was an important meeting. Among others, Craig and Finkelstein gave accounts of the preparation, characteristics and immunology of their toxin preparations, the Johns Hopkins group reported on their dog models and Phillips and Watten from NAMRU-2 discussed the human pathophysiology of cholera. The part that cholera toxin played in the disease was now firmly established.

At the meeting of the Cholera Advisory Committee on the day after the workshop, it was decided to procure from commercial sources not only a large (1500 litres of culture filtrate) batch of toxin made according to Craig's specifications as had been agreed at the previous meeting, but a similar batch made according to Finkelstein's specifications.[23] The Chairman of the Committee also wanted a discussion on the "timetable and requirements for further work on toxins to bring it to field trials in Dacca", in order to provide AID and NIH with a guide-line for future funding of the Cholera Research Program. This appears to be the first record of any intention of the Cholera Advisory Committee to test the role of toxin in immunization against cholera, but no doubt there had been unrecorded discussions of such intention. It was decided that much more work on experimental animals would be needed for a further understanding of the action of the toxin and the protective value of toxoid against challenge with toxin and living vibrios. When enough information had been collected, Theodore Woodward and his group at the University of Maryland would test toxicity and antitoxin response in man. If materials could be developed that could safely be administered to many people in doses sufficient to provide definite antitoxin responses, then field trials could be carried out. The committee members were satisfied that the present information, such as had been presented the previous two days at the workshop, was promising enough to call for all possible speed in bringing the toxin to a final test in man; and since the PSCRL in Dacca was the only place where critical field trials could be conducted, it must be preserved until the work was completed. It would need at least two to three years for the animal work and biochemical studies, and another year for studies in human volunteers in the United States before the material could be taken to a foreign country, and at least three years would be needed for field tests on an increasing scale. The SEATO Cholera Research Program and the PSCRL in Dacca had been established with short-range goals, and its continuance was renewable at three-year intervals. It was therefore agreed to recommend to SEATO, AID, the Government of Pakistan and NIH that the PSCRL, "as the single known site where the now promising leads for a more effective control of cholera could be brought to fruition", should continue until at least 1973 or 1975.

---

23. Goodner was anxious that Craig and Finkelstein should not think they were being taken over, but was assured by Seal that Craig was being consulted on procurement contracts, and that Finkelstein was looking forward to receiving large amounts of his material. Finkelstein had been concerned that the WRAIR should not lose interest in preparing a large quantity of his "choleragen" and the committee was assured by the Director of the WRAIR, Col. W. D. Tigertt, that the Army had every intention of making a large quantity of choleragen available.

It was an important meeting, and it ended with the Cholera Advisory Committee in an ebullient mood. Kenneth Goodner,[24] of the original Inner Circle of 1958, introduced several resolutions that were unanimously adopted: placing it on record that "this has been one of the most pleasant meetings this Committee has ever had"; recording its opinion that the Dacca laboratory, and Phillips's direction of it, was "one of the most glorious stories of American enterprise anywhere in the world"; regretting the fact that this was the first meeting "of this unique Committee" that Dr. James Shannon had missed, and assuring him that it had been carried on "in its usual vigorous fashion with the intense interest which is so characteristic of its meetings in the past"; and finally, and characteristically, sending "its love to Doris Parkinson".[25]

The feeling expressed in these resolutions was to continue to imbue cholera research for the next half-dozen years. The original Inner Circle had greatly expanded, and its average age had gone down, but it continued to consist of competent people who liked and respected each other, who were fired by enthusiasm, not only for the scientific and medical problems of cholera, but also for its humanitarian aspects, and—let us not overlook it—its Eastern glamour. There was little self-interest. There was a feeling of comradeship in arms that quickened the pulse of anyone joining this band of enthusiasts, and made cholera research the most pleasant and rewarding occupation that any scientist could hope for. It was, to repeat Goodner's words, a most glorious story of American enterprise. Later, when cholera toxin came to be used in all kinds of biochemical research unconnected with the disease (see Chapter 10), the feeling was less comradely, more competitive.

The Development of a Toxoid

When the Cholera Advisory Committee met again, in September 1967, it was reported that contracts had been awarded to Wyeth Laboratories, Philadelphia, for the production of 1500 litres of Craig toxin, and to Merck, Sharpe and Dohme for a similar amount of Finkelstein toxin, the products to be available early in 1968. Although the primary purpose of the large batches of toxin was for research by contractors on the purification and the determination of the immunogenicity of the toxin, it was agreed that reasonable quantities of them should be made available to any scientifically competent applicant. This distribution of samples of toxin was, in fact, done in succeeding years, thus putting cholera toxin (in the form of freeze-dried culture filtrate)

24. It was his last meeting, for he died on 30 August 1967.
25. The surpassing executive secretary of the Cholera Advisory Committee, who had been prevented by illness from attending the meeting.

in the hands of many people who might otherwise not have the means of getting it, and so widening the circle of interest. But when the NIH solicited contracts for research development on the toxin, and the responses were reviewed by the U.S. panel of the U.S.-Japan CMSP, none of them were in the end judged to be suitable. However, the large-scale purification of "choleragen" had, in fact, been started by Finkelstein at WRAIR and eventually accomplished in his department at the Southwestern Medical School in Dallas, as we have seen.

At the meeting of the Cholera Advisory Committee[26] a year later, in October 1968, there was still little progress to report on the preparation of any immunizing agent directed towards antitoxic immunity to cholera. The need was discussed for an antigen that would stimulate significant levels of antitoxin in the circulation, or the gut, or both. The minutes record that "Dr. Verwey[27] noted that efforts to purify cholera toxin seemed to be going ahead at the expense of learning whether it played any role in protection against cholera. In fact, an impure product would probably be superior to a pure product as an antigen". There is no record of whether he amplified these wise words, but they went apparently unheeded, because the Committee then went on to discuss the "critical need" for an antigen which stimulated the production of antitoxic antibody without stimulating production of antibacterial antibodies at the same time, i.e., a highly purified antigen. Such an antigen would be needed in quantity for field tests "since the important question was whether it would prevent the clinical disease". The wisdom of using a highly purified toxin antigen was questioned again shortly afterwards at the meeting of the Technical Committee of the PSCRL in Dacca in December 1968. This meeting was attended by W. E. van Heyningen[28] of the University of Oxford, a cholera neophyte. As a toxinologist, he simplistically saw the problem of immunization against cholera only as a toxinological problem. In his innocence, he was impatient at any further discussion of trials of whole cell vaccines, and

26. Whose membership had increased on 1 July 1968 to include all members of the cholera panel of the U.S.-Japan CMSP (Benenson, Gordon, Oseasohn and Feeley). All cholera research was now centred in the National Institute of Allergy and Infectious Diseases, of which the Chairman, J. R. Seal, was then Director of Intramural Research.

27. Of the University of Texas Medical Branch, Galveston, a member of the Cholera Advisory Committee, and later Director of the Cholera Research Laboratory in Dacca from 1974 to 1977.

28. He had worked on bacterial toxins since 1940, and heard of cholera toxin for the first time in December 1967 from Craig when visiting his department in Brooklyn. At MacLeod's suggestion, he was invited by Phillips to visit the laboratory in Dacca in February 1968, and was subsequently invited to attend the meetings of the Technical Committee in Dacca and the Cholera Advisory Committee as a consultant on toxins.

urged immediate toxoid trials, not realizing how much this was already on the minds of the Cholera Advisory Committee. There was no need for an elaborate toxoid preparation; all that needed to be done, he thought, was to treat a cholera culture filtrate with formaldehyde, as had originally been done with tetanus and diphtheria, and inject it into volunteers. His compatriot, Sir James Howie,[29] a member of the technical committee, went further and suggested leaving out the filtration step and treating the whole culture with formaldehyde, making an "ana-culture", as is done with some veterinary preparations, thus combining antitoxic and antibacterial immunization. Tests with highly purified toxoid were "a Ph.D. exercise" that could be carried out later, if combined antibacterial and antitoxic immunization should prove to be effective enough to warrant further investigation. MacLeod argued for a highly purified toxoid preparation, and his argument is best expressed in the words he used the next year at a Workshop in Cholera Immunology in Williamsburg, Virginia, sponsored by the U.S.-Japan CMSP:

> One school of thought holds that we shouldn't fiddle around with obtaining purified toxoid preparations but should proceed as soon as possible to test crude preparations of toxoid in combination with the best possible whole bacterial vaccines. . . . The argument goes that combination is bound to be better than either one alone and that the answer would probably be sufficient to satisfy public health needs. Others of us hold the viewpoint that unless we settle once and for all the protective effect of purified toxoid, essentially free of somatic components, we will be on unsure ground indefinitely and will be forced to employ empirical mixtures that will never be satisfactory and will lead to scientific uncertainties and large costs in the future.

But van Heyningen was not so much concerned with the advantage of adding bacterial antigen to the toxin antigen as with the dangers of using highly purified antigen. He had learned while working on gas gangrene toxins in the Wellcome Physiological Research Laboratories[30] during the war that while highly purified antigens might still stimulate the production of antibodies, these antibodies tended to be "non-avid". A non-avid antitoxin would not combine strongly with the toxin, and so would have a reduced capacity to protect against a toxinosis. There was no published evidence to support this view, perhaps because no experiments had actually been done specifically to test it, but nevertheless

29. Director of the British Public Health Service.
30. Still under the erroneous impression that U.S. scientists were dragging their feet, he suggested in an aside to Howie that they get the Wellcome Laboratories to make a toxin preparation, to be tried out under the British Medical Research Council in India. See footnote 33, p. 186.

this was the strong impression (if not the conviction) among experienced practical immunologists concerned with the production and control of immunizing bacterial antigens, such as A. T. Glenny of the Wellcome Physiological Research Laboratories and Sir Percival Hartley, Director of the Bureau of Biological Standards in London.

The Technical Committee recommended "that work on the diarrhoea-producing toxin be pushed forward with all possible vigour both in PSCRL and in laboratories in the United States and elsewhere, and that toxoid (alone or in combination with bacterial antigens) should be developed for field trial use in 1970". They suggested that a number of toxinologists be invited to the next meeting of the Cholera Advisory Committee to review the cholera problem and assist in efforts towards the development of such a toxoid. The meeting was held in March 1969 and it included the toxinologists A. M. Pappenheimer (diphtheria), C. Lamanna (botulism), K. Miller (tetanus), C. Hardegree (tetanus), and W. E. van Heyningen (gas gangrene, dysentery, tetanus).

W. H. Mosley reported on determinations of the antitoxin content of the sera of cholera patients in East Pakistan. As might reasonably be expected, the sera of diarrhoea patients were low in antibacterial and antitoxic antibodies on admission, and both these titres rose in patients convalescent with cholera diarrhoea, and did not rise in non-cholera diarrhoea. But the antitoxin titres of sera of children with cholera tended on admission to be equal to, or even higher than, those of convalescent adults. These data could be interpreted as undermining the importance of circulating antitoxin in resistance to cholera, but the Committee were not discouraged—there was at least one other toxic state, tetanus, where enough toxoid artificially introduced provided good immunity, whereas the natural disease provided none.[31]

A subcommittee was set up under W. F. Verwey to define the course of action the Committee should take in producing a toxin or toxoid for field trials,[32] to determine whether parenterally induced antitoxic immunity would be better—and especially, more long-lasting—in preventing cholera than the conventional whole cell vaccines. It had to be pure enough, that is, free enough of somatic antigens, not to produce any antibacterial immunity, and enough was needed to give two doses to 15,000 children, and it had to be produced soon because the duration

31. The immunizing dose of tetanus toxin is more than a million times the lethal dose!

32. At this stage, March 1969, Finkelstein's work on cholera toxin had not yet received the recognition that was due it; Verwey thought that a purification procedure designed by S. H. Richardson of the Bowman Gray School of Medicine was the first to give promise of yielding pure toxin in quantity.

of the field test facility at Matlab Bazaar might be limited. Van Heyningen reported that he had interested the Wellcome Research Laboratories in London, which had had a great deal of experience in the large-scale production of toxins and toxoids, in the production of a cholera toxoid. They had offered to develop and provide, free of charge, a sufficient amount of sufficiently purified toxin that would be toxoided with formaldehyde.[33] Such a product would, of course, have to conform to U.S. regulations, and be tested in U.S. nationals, before it could be tested in the field under U.S. auspices. It would also need the endorsement of the PSCRL Technical Committee and the Clinical Investigation Committee. Even then, it could not be guaranteed at this stage whether the British preparation would be tested in the field.

The Director of NIH, James Shannon, had lost some of the enthusiasm he had displayed at the meeting in October 1965. The whole program was in difficulty, he said, because of financial constraints being imposed on the government, and the reluctance of U.S. industry to enter into the field with their own resources, and because it was becoming increasingly difficult to move a product towards large-scale evaluation in human populations. He thought the interest in Great Britain, as shown by the Wellcome Laboratories, might be helpful in support of seeking funds to continue the work. Moreover, he had not found the data presented at this meeting adequate to justify the enthusiasm of the committee and thought more data were needed fully to justify the need for funds to continue the effort.

This meeting of the Cholera Advisory Committee was memorable for something unconnected with immunization against cholera. W. B. Greenough (who had returned from PSCRL four years previously to the Johns Hopkins University) reported on the newly discovered method of detecting the action of the toxin *in vitro*. This was the toxin-stimulated release of glycerol from fat cells, apparently due to the stimulation by the toxin of the cyclic-AMP (the "second messenger") system. This was the beginning of a tremendous growth of scientific interest in cholera toxin, much of it with little or no connection with the actual disease of cholera (see Chapter 10).

An important Workshop on the Immunology of Cholera was held in Williamsburg, Virginia, on 25 and 26 September 1969 under the sponsorship of the U.S.-Japan CMSP. A number of papers were given

33. On his return from the meeting of the Technical Committee in Dacca in December 1968, van Heyningen had asked the Wellcome Research Laboratories if they would produce the toxoid if he could persuade the British Ministry of Overseas Development or the Medical Research Council to pay for it. The Wellcome Research Laboratories agreed to prepare the toxoid, but stipulated that it would be free of charge.

on the production of cholera toxin, including that of Richardson, mentioned in footnote 32 on p. 185, but by far the most important in its consequences was that of Finkelstein and LoSpalluto [132], concerned not only with "choleragen" but also the biologically inert "choleragenoid" immunologically closely related to, but not identical with, choleragen.

The workshop in Williamsburg left Colin MacLeod (and many others) with what he appropriately called "a gut feeling" that pure antitoxic immunity was likely to be effective. He believed further that the outpouring of fluid into the gut that was caused by toxin was not only the primary manifestation of the disease, but also a source of nutrient that encouraged more growth of the vibrio in the gut, and so the production of more toxin (a suggestion supported by the experimental evidence of Carpenter and Greenough) [54]. To MacLeod, the most reasonable explanation for the spontaneous recovery from cholera (within a week or less of infection) was the development of antitoxic immunity in the course of the disease,[34] and he restated the suggestion that administration of sufficient toxoid would be a more effective way of inducing immunity than the natural disease.

The Cholera Advisory Committee met again in October 1969, shortly after the Williamsburg workshop, with the entire object of drawing up specific instructions as to the toxin or toxoid product to be developed under commercial contract for field trial in East Pakistan in 1971. Verwey's subcommittee on toxoids had met in April and concluded that there should not be any particular problems in the large-scale production of crude toxin, and that methods of purification had been devised. The possibility was discussed of using a crude preparation of toxoid in Dacca in 1971 as a stopgap if purified material could not be made available in time. There were many steps involved in processing a contract for the development of an immunizing agent and therefore the utmost speed and co-ordination of effort would be needed to get a toxoid preparation ready for trial in the field in late 1971. To determine the duration as well as the degree of protection, at least three years following the initial vaccination would have to be allowed, and a minimum of 50,000 volunteers would be needed to test each preparation. Thus, with the present study population of 220,000 people in Matlab thana, three toxoid preparations and one placebo could be tested. The idea of testing

34. It is more likely that antibacterial rather than antitoxic immunity resulting from infection is responsible for spontaneous recovery from cholera. Antibacterial antibodies clear the gut of the vibrio, and antitoxic antibodies may neutralize any free toxin produced, but they cannot reverse the action of toxin that has already poisoned epithelial cells. Recovery therefore depends on the natural shedding of epithelial cells which takes place within a week, by which time the vibrios have been eliminated by antibacterial antibodies. Poisoned cells are then replaced by fresh normal cells (see Chapter 9).

crude toxoid had apparently not yet been rejected, since it was suggested that the simultaneous testing of both highly purified and crude toxoid should be done on this occasion because it was unlikely that the PSCRL could be supported by AID at its present level beyond 1975. The Chairman, Seal, noted that he and MacLeod felt that efforts to produce crude and pure products should proceed simultaneously and that they should be tested simultaneously, but if this were not possible, the pure product should have priority. The main point was not to lose the opportunity to determine the role of antitoxin in man. In any event, unfortunately, no comparison was ever made of the efficacy of crude and purified toxoid preparations.

The Cholera Advisory Committee did not meet again until a year later, in October 1970, but in the meantime Verwey's subcommittee on toxoids had met five times. A contract for the production of toxoid had been awarded to Wyeth Laboratories of Philadelphia, and a pilot batch had been prepared for laboratory tests, and for studies in human volunteers in Texas, by Verwey and his group in the Ramsay Unit of the Texas State Prison System, and by William Hornick, University of Maryland, at his facility at the Maryland House of Correction in Jessup. The Wyeth toxoid, lot 00101, had been prepared by Ruth Rappaport by purifying the toxin by a modification of the method of Finkelstein and LoSpalluto until its content of somatic antigen had been reduced to 0.6 percent of that of standard whole-cell vaccine [362–364]. This purified material was then detoxified by treatment with the usual toxoiding agent, formaldehyde.

R. O. Thomson of the Wellcome Research Laboratories reported difficulties they were encountering with the stability and non-specific toxicity of their purified preparations. It had become clear that the original starting date for field trials in 1971 was not going to be attained, but it was hoped that an approved toxoid could "be put in Dr. Mosley's hands during the summer of 1971 with the objective of conduct of major field trials during the winter of 1972–73".

But by the time the Cholera Advisory Committee met again on 25–26 June 1971, Mosley and the rest of the Americans had been evacuated from the laboratory in Dacca, and were not to return for some time, because war had broken out between East and West Pakistan, resulting in the transformation of East Pakistan into the People's Republic of Bangladesh on 16 December 1971 (see Chapter 11). But the war in Bangladesh did not noticeably delay field trials of toxoid. At the meeting in June 1971, Verwey reported on trials with the Wyeth 00101 batch of toxoid on American volunteers. It was disappointing: The material stimulated production of unwanted antibacterial antibodies ranging in value from about an eight to equal to the average adult Pakistani titre, and the wanted antitoxic antibodies were produced in concentrations which were not impressive. They were similar to those observed in convalescent cholera patients, and such naturally acquired levels of antitoxin were not necessarily protective. It had been hoped to attain much higher levels by artificial immunization. There was a further problem, namely, that the formalinisation of the toxoid tended to reverse, and therefore the preparations became slightly toxic again and thus unacceptable for injection into humans on a large scale (especially by Americans into Bangladeshis). Ruth Rappaport of Wyeth was therefore going to reduce the somatic antigen content of their preparation by nine-tenths, and to use a new reagent for toxoiding the toxin, namely glutaraldehyde. The Wellcome Laboratories had also experienced reversal of formaldehyde toxoiding, and since this was a phenomenon which they had never experienced with crude toxin, they proposed a for-malinised crude anaculture. A comparison of the protective capacity of such a crude preparation with that highly purified toxoid might be useful. The minutes record that while it was agreed that an anaculture might make a better vaccine, it would not answer the question as to whether antitoxin was protective. The Wellcome Laboratories were also prepared to provide a purified preparation of a different type of toxin antigen, namely, Finkelstein's choleragenoid, which was antigenic but not toxic.

When the Committee met again a few months later (in October 1971), it was reported that Wyeth Laboratories had produced two pilot lots of purified toxin, 1090 and 1100, with the somatic antigen content reduced to 1/10th to 1/100th that of 00101. But even these preparations stimulated production of antibacterial antibodies in rabbits. The answer to the scientific question of the role of antitoxic immunity was going to need drastic purification of the toxin.

With these technical problems, and with the uncertainties about the future of the laboratory in war-torn East Pakistan, research on preventive immunization against cholera was at a low ebb.

By the time the Cholera Committee met again in March 1972, the war was over and the new state of Bangladesh had come into existence. The words "Pakistan-SEATO" had been removed from the title of the Cholera Research Laboratory, and its future for the next six months had been assured by an agreement whereby AID and the International Rescue Committee were to provide $500,000 to the Laboratory to pay local expenses in the training of medical personnel engaged in relief and rehabilitation work as part of the total effort of the International Rescue Committee (see Chapter 11). This arrangement had been largely due to the efforts made by Colin MacLeod in the State Department just before he set off for Dacca on a mission to assess the work of the

Laboratory. On his way, he died suddenly in London on 11 February 1972, at the age of 63. The NIH was now engaged in working out a longer-range future for the Laboratory, and the Director (now Dr. R. Q. Marston) had asked the Cholera Advisory Committee to determine whether there was sound scientific justification for maintaining access to a population in which cholera was endemic. By the end of the meeting, the Committee was able to tell the Director that they believed the NIH did have a valid stake in taking the toxoid work as far as field trials in Bangladesh, or elsewhere. The expected cost of $1,500,000 per year to maintain such a capability "did not bother them" because there were many additional studies that could be made in the field, such as the development of a single method for rehydrating children suffering from cholera or other diarrhoeal diseases, such as those caused by *Escherichia coli*.

Verwey's toxoid subcommittee had come to the conclusion that Wyeth Laboratories' new lot of glutaraldehyde-treated toxoid, lot 1110, should be tried in the field. (There appeared not yet to be any Wellcome toxoid to hand.) Testing of the Wyeth toxoid in American human volunteers should be completed by mid-November, a new field-test–sized lot of toxoid should then be delivered by Wyeth Laboratories by June 1973, and field trials could begin in August 1973, with full field trials in 1974. At least two years would be needed, unless the toxoid was hopeless from the start. The committee was unanimously agreed that these field trials of toxoid should be carried out even though there was no evidence that toxoid conferred longer-lasting protection than whole-cell vaccine, and if the Dacca population were not to be available for such tests, other suitable locations must be sought. The Chairman thought that work up to the point of having a preparation providing prolonged protection could be done in the United States with volunteers, but his committee did not agree, since the results obtained in a cholera-endemic area would be better than those possible in the non-endemic area of the United States.

This was to be the last meeting of the Cholera Advisory Committee. The committee did not meet again in the second half of 1972 because the Cholera Research Laboratory in Dacca had not been able to resume research activities since no agreement had yet been made with the new government of Bangladesh, and since development of the toxoid had not reached a stage that needed discussion by the Committee. Responsibility for the Cholera Research Program, including the Laboratory in Dacca, was internally transferred from Seal's office (as Scientific Director of NIAID) to the Geographic Medicine Branch of NIAID, which had been supporting cholera research under the U.S.-Japan CMSP. Carl Miller was to be the cholera program officer of the Geographic Medicine

Branch, and the Ad Hoc Cholera Toxoid Committee would continue to advise. Accordingly, and in response to an administration directive to reduce the number of committees, the Cholera Advisory Committee was formally abolished on 21 March 1973. The short-term support for the Cholera Research Laboratory that had been agreed with AID and the International Rescue Committee was coming to an end, but the Laboratory was going to continue as an international organization (see Chapter 11).

A "Cholera Toxoid Workshop" met in June 1973 to consider a further batch of toxoid, 11201, prepared by Wyeth Laboratories, the somatic (bacterial) antigen content of which had been reduced to a level that met the Committee's criteria. It had been toxoided with glutaraldehyde to a satisfactory degree of non-toxicity, but needed to be used in higher doses to stimulate as much antitoxin response as the formalinised toxoid. R. O. Thomson of the Wellcome Laboratories reported on a new toxoid preparation, but this had not yet been tested in the United States. It was decided that the Wyeth toxoid 11201[35] was "as good as we are likely to have without extensive further research and that it should serve for the purpose of the initial field trial". The following day, the Ad Hoc Committee on toxoids met to receive a report from George Curlin, who was going to be responsible for the field trials of cholera toxoid in his capacity as epidemiologist to the Laboratory. He had prepared a full protocol for the field testing of cholera toxoid in Bangladesh, and this was agreed. As yet, there were no plans to test the Wellcome toxoid in the field. By this time, Willard F. Verwey had been appointed Director of the CRL, in 1974.

Field Trials of Cholera Toxoid

The field trial of Wyeth toxoid began in Bangladesh in July 1974. It was the biggest field trial ever carried out at Dacca, involving 92,838 people, or 60 percent of the population under surveillance. Two sub-cutaneous injections of 100 µg each were given at 6-week intervals to about 43,000 persons (males 1 to 14 years, females 1 year to adult), and tetanus-diphtheria toxoid was administered as a placebo to an approximately equal number in the same community. The incidence of cholera (El Tor biotype) began to rise in September 1974 to reach a maximum in October. The mortality rate in the field trial area was above the 10-year average, thus providing an excellent opportunity to assess the protective value of toxoid, making it possible to determine protective efficacy down to a level of 18 percent. Curlin presented the results of this field trial to the Ad Hoc Committee in January 1975.

35. Later, another batch, 20101, containing less somatic antigen, was produced.

They were most disappointing. There appeared to be 40 percent protection in the first 6 weeks, but after 9 weeks this protection was gone. Those who received two injections were no better off than those receiving one. The toxoid protected only against Inaba serotype infection, not against Ogawa.

As Curlin told the meeting, "this field trial was a most rigorous test of the protective effect of antitoxic immunity". There was no doubt that, with the particular preparation of toxoid, protection against cholera was achieved but this protection was no more than an intellectual exercise in confirming an expectation that could reasonably have been predicted from animal experiments [e.g., 147]—in practical terms, it was worthless since at best it was only 40 percent effective, and it was transient.[36]

Since toxoid had failed, the Ad Hoc Committee turned, at their meeting in April 1976, to the idea of a combination of whole-cell vaccine and toxoid, and since it was the Wyeth toxoid that had failed, they proposed to use the Wellcome toxoid.[37] And instead of using the vaccine that had been used before, they proposed, for technical reasons, to use a Wellcome vaccine. The idea of being "scientific" seemed to have departed, but not to have been replaced by practical realism. It would have been more scientific, surely, to consider altering only one variable at a time, i.e., to test the unknown combination of a known vaccine with a known toxoid rather than the unknown combination of an unknown toxoid and an unknown vaccine. It might have been more realistic to test a crude, i.e., unaltered, toxoid, with or without whole cells. We are by now well-informed as to the immunogenic efficacy of unaltered whole bacterial cells, but we know very little about the possible efficacy of the unaltered soluble products of these cells. The proposed test of the combination of whole cells and the Wellcome toxoid has, in fact, not been carried out and by the autumn of 1980 it was decided never to carry it out. Many trials have been carried out over 10 years in Dacca, without any striking success, and there may be political objections to further tests on the population under surveillance, especially since we have seen that preventive inoculation, even it if were 100 percent effective, could not reach all the threatened population in time,

36. The account of this field trial of the toxoid has not yet been published in detail, despite the urging of many of those who believed that the reporting of the essentially negative data was of equal importance to reporting of positive data. It was briefly reported by Curlin and others at the 12th Joint Conference of the Cholera Panel of the U.S.-Japan CMSP in Sapporo in 1976 [91].

37. This had been prepared by formalinising (with a slight excess of formalin) a toxin preparation highly purified by a different method from that of Wyeth Laboratories.

and would therefore not be cost-effective in comparison with the high effectiveness of treating patients by intravenous and oral rehydration.

Why was the trial of cholera toxoid such a miserable failure, when antitoxic immunization against diphtheria and tetanus is such a success? Was it because the toxoid was so emasculated by over-purification that it was unable to elicit an effective avid antitoxin? We may never know the answer, but even if unrefined toxin were to elicit highly protective antitoxin, would these antibodies be delivered in the right place, i.e., the gut, and even if they were, would the protection last more than a few months? The goal of the cholera research program was always not only to produce effective immunity to the disease, but long-lasting immunity, comparable with that achieved with other infectious diseases, and particularly the exotoxinoses. Could such lasting immunity to cholera ever be attained by any antigen or combination of antigens?

Cholera differs from most other infectious diseases, particularly tetanus and diphtheria, in two important respects: (1) the incubation period of the disease, and the duration of the disease, are very short: and (2) the infecting organism, and the toxin by means of which the harmful effects are brought about, are confined to the lumen of the gut.

Both these characteristics of the disease were recognized by Colin MacLeod at the outset, when, at the inaugural conference of the laboratory in Dacca in December 1960, he presented a paper on "Some requirements for a field trial of cholera vaccines". He stated:

Because cholera is a superficial infection of the intestinal mucosa and because it has such a short incubation period, it might be anticipated that protection of the bowel from infection would require the protective antibody on the mucosal surface at the time the bacteria are ingested. The short incubation period of 12 to 72 hours and the superficial character of the infectious process make it appear improbable that the secondary immune response, rapid as it is in development, could come into operation soon enough and with sufficient intensity to prevent a second attack. It might be expected for these reasons that immunity following an attack would last only for the period during which antibody in the blood is present at such levels that protective amounts can find their way to the mucosal surface.

The wonder is that these prophetic words were forgotten, even by MacLeod himself, in the years that followed; they apply as much to antitoxic antibodies as to the antibacterial antibodies MacLeod had in mind at the time.

In his presidential address to the American Society of Immunologists in 1952, MacLeod had already presented a theory relating the duration of natural or induced immunity to infectious diseases to the length of the incubation period [266]. The theory was that long-lasting immunity depended not on the maintenance of a protective level of antibody, but on the rise in antibody following the secondary stimulus resulting from the challenge of a new infection. Unless an antigen continues to be present in the body and to stimulate antibody production, as may perhaps be the case with certain viruses, the antibody level must decline. Like all the proteins in the plasma, the antibody protein, i.e., the immune globulin, must have a turnover, and there is no reason why the half-life of an immune globulin should be different from that of any ordinary globulin, or that the level of antibody to one particular antigen should decline any faster or slower than the antibody to any other antigen. Long-lasting immunity must therefore depend on the anamnestic response[38] to secondary antigenic stimulus of infection. Once the body has experienced an antigen and produced antibody to it, the antigen is permanently imprinted on the antibody-producing cells. When these cells encounter the antigen again they respond by making fresh antibody, more rapidly and more copiously than at the first encounter. Animals receiving primary antigenic stimulus, either naturally as a result of infection or artificially by injection, develop antibody which comparatively slowly reaches a low peak, then falls off in the course of time to a vanishing level; but if there is a secondary stimulus, even at such low level, there is a rapid development of a high level of antibody, and with subsequent stimuli even greater levels of antibody are attained even more rapidly [11]. The secondary response develops about three days after the secondary stimulus, i.e., the second contact with the infectious agent; but in cholera this secondary response comes too late. Most infectious diseases have an incubation period of more than three days between the contact with the infectious agent and the development of clinical symptoms; therefore, the development of these symptoms is frustrated by the protective level of antibody already arisen as the result of the secondary stimulus. Cholera has an incubation period of less than 3 days—it is only 12 to 72 hours—and therefore it could be argued that the disease could develop in an immunized subject with a low antibody level, and the epithelial cells of the gut irretrievably poisoned, well before the development of any secondary immunity. In fact, MacLeod made only a passing reference to cholera in putting forward this hypothesis, which he developed mainly with influenza and the common cold in mind, with their incubation periods of 1 to 3 days. He believed that permanent immunity did not occur with these diseases, but in the case of influenza it was not yet fully realized in 1952 that there were several types (and variants of the types) of the

---

38. The "not-forgetting" response.

virus, and that immunity to any given variant was in fact long-lasting, but the body had to encounter all the many types before it became immune to influenza.

MacLeod's hypothesis that a short incubation period frustrates the secondary immune response does not appear to gain much acceptance today (but see Pierce, section 4 of this chapter), and the fact remains that in cholera-endemic regions the (not very striking) natural immunity of adults to the disease does appear to be due to the anamnestic immunological response.

We have already seen that the immunologically inexperienced children of Bangladesh have little or no cholera bacterial antibodies[39] circulating in their blood, and are more prone to get cholera and less easily immunizable than the immunologically more experienced adults who have cholera antibodies in their blood, are less likely to get cholera and more easily immunizable (for a few months). In fact, by far the greatest proportion of adults in Bangladesh do not get cholera, and at least part of the reason for this is that they experience the cholera vibrio every year and so maintain a protective level of antibody. In their case, if they do not die of cholera as the result of infection, the anamnestic response must come into play and produce higher levels of antibody in the serum. These serum levels do not seem to reach great heights, perhaps because the antigens are not presented parenterally but in the lumen of the gut.

But whatever the levels of antibody, whether antibacterial or antitoxic, parenterally in the serum, they may be largely irrelevant to protection against the vibrio in the gut, and the toxin it produced there, beyond the reach of parenteral antibodies. Different types of antibody are produced parenterally and enterally—IgG and IgA, respectively. In the case of the other two toxinoses, diphtheria and tetanus, where antitoxic immunity is effective, there is no particular problem—the antitoxins evoked by parenteral stimulation and circulating in the serum as IgG antibodies act parenterally on toxins produced parenterally. But in cholera the organism multiplies enterally and the toxin acts enterally. While the fact that immunity to cholera, even if not long-lasting, can be attained with parenterally administered antigens suggests that some serum IgG antibodies may leak into the gut and play a part in protection, it is probably the IgA antibodies that are the most effective. These IgA antibodies arise in the lymphatic tissues beneath most mucous surfaces of the body, and are liberated on the mucosal surfaces as secretory IgA. It follows that if IgA antibodies are needed for protection, the

---

39. Curiously enough, children, inexplicably, have higher antitoxin levels than adults [91].

antigenic stimulus should be applied to the mucosal surface from the lumen of the gut, that is, the protective antigens should be introduced orally, as they are in the disease. This subject will be dealt with in section 4 of this chapter.

The efficacy of enteral immunization with Rappaport's highly purified glutaraldehyde toxoid was tested in human volunteers at the Center for Vaccine Development[40] at the University of Maryland School of Medicine in Baltimore by M. M. Levine and his colleagues and compared with that brought about by artificial induction of the disease [249]. Volunteers received primary immunization either by the parenteral injection of 0.2 mg of the toxoid, or introduction of 2 mg of the toxoid directly into the small intestine by means of an intestinal tube. They then all received 2-mg enteral booster doses 4 and 8 weeks later. When these volunteers were challenged by giving them a cholera culture (Inaba serotype) to swallow (after sodium bicarbonate to neutralize the acidity of the stomach), they all developed cholera, not significantly different from that in non-immunized controls. Increasing the dose of toxoid fourfold made no difference. Thus, oral administration of the highly purified glutaraldehyde toxoid was no better at protecting humans in Baltimore, indeed, rather worse, than parenteral administration of the toxoid had been in protecting humans in Dacca. Similar results had been with enterally presented whole-cell vaccine.

However, further tests at the same center showed that volunteers who had been given the disease were subsequently completely immune to challenge with the vibrio. For the first time, people in a non-endemic area—immunological virgins as far as cholera was concerned—had been successfully immunized against cholera. Clearly, the whole living culture contained an immunizing antigen that was not present in a whole-cell vaccine or in the highly purified glutaraldehyde toxoid. What was it? Perhaps a clue is offered by the fact that the Ogawa disease protected against Inaba challenge and *vice versa*, and in all cases of protection no cholera vibrios could be found in the stools of the volunteers. These findings were interpreted as showing that antibacterial immunity protected against cholera and antitoxic immunity did not. Since there was cross-protection between the two serotypes, it was further concluded that a protective antigen common to both serotypes was involved. It

---

40. This facility was set up under the auspices of the NIAID when tests on humans at the Maryland House of Correction were discontinued. The volunteers are college students and other adults living normally in the community, from whom informed consent is obtained. Informedness is determined by means of written examinations after instruction. The volunteers often perform better in these examinations than advanced medical students or doctors.

was considered that it might be the toxin, and that the absence of vibrios in the stools of protected volunteers was due to neutralization of toxin, which is known to favour growth of the organism by provoking the secretion of fluid into the gut. These considerations were thought to be ruled out by finding that samples of intestinal fluid of protected volunteers contained no organisms, whereas those from the controls were heavily colonized. But what was not commented on was the further finding that the early samples were not colonized, and became colonized only late in the incubation period, or during diarrhoea. This would be consistent with the suggestion that the organisms proliferate in the gut of the non-immune only after some time, when the toxin has promoted the flow of fluid into it. Thus, the native toxin (not emasculated by overpurification and treatment with glutaraldehyde) does not seem to have been ruled out as the common protective antigen.

3. Does Mucin Protect Against Cholera After All?

There is another aspect of immunity to cholera that should be considered: that of a possible antitoxic effect of antibacterial immunization. Willard Verwey was always more interested in cellular antigens of the cholera vibrio than in those secreted extracellularly. He believed that antibacterial antibodies would in effect be antitoxic, not by neutralizing the toxin, but by preventing it from being delivered to its site of action. His interest in cholera was first aroused in 1958 when Yashi Watanabe of the Kitasato Institute in Tokyo came to work with him in his laboratory in Galveston. Verwey had been separating and investigating bacterial cellular antigens and Watanabe got him interested in cholera antigens. Their work resulted in the isolation of the Ogawa and Inaba lipopolysaccharide antigens, the latter of which was shown to produce a fair degree of immunity against cholera at the PSCRL. In 1972, at the Tokyo meeting of the cholera panels of the U.S.-Japan CMSP, Verwey put forward a hypothesis of antibacterial immunity. He and his colleague H. R. Williams had shown that when the cholera vibrio was inoculated into an agar gel the colony of cells spread through the gel, but if antibacterial immune serum was incorporated in the agar the colony did not grow through the cell. The mobility—but not the multiplication—of the vibrio had been inhibited. This inhibition of mobility resulted from the fact that although the vibrio continued to grow by cell division in the presence of the antibody, the divided cells would not separate from each other as they normally do, and the cells could not migrate through the agar when they were not separated from each other. He suggested that the same would be true of vibrios growing in gel-like antibody-containing mucus surrounding and covering the internal villi, and thus the vibrios would not be able to reach the epithelial cells and deliver toxin to them; instead, they would run harmlessly down the lumen of the gut [437].

This hypothesis was further supported when the Galveston group showed that when vibrios were inoculated into ligated intestinal loops of rabbits immunized against the vibrios, the vibrios remained in the fluid area of the loops, whereas in non-immunized rabbits the vibrios penetrated through the mucous layer down to the crypts between the villi [388, 461]. Verwey presented his hypothesis in its final form at the 12th conference of the cholera panels of the U.S.-Japan CMSP in Sapporo in 1976, but, sadly, it was garbled because the full text failed to reach the editors. Verwey died in Flagstaff, Arizona, in May 1979 after a protracted and bravely borne illness, before proper justice could be done to his hypothesis. He believed that the pathogenesis of cholera infection took place in 10 stages: (1) Multiplication of the vibrios in the lumen of the gut. (2) Invasion of the mucous layer. (3) Penetration into the intervillous spaces and crypts. (4) Adherence of the vibrios to the mucosa. (5) Production of toxin near the mucosal cell membrane toxin receptors. (6) Dissociation of vibrios and mucus. (7) Beginning of fluid secretion. (8) Removal of vibrios and mucus. (9) Continuation of fluid secretion. (10) Shedding and replacement of mucosal cells. Thus, antibacterial immunity does not function by killing the organisms but by interfering with their mobility, thus preventing them from delivering the toxin close to the toxin receptors on the membranes of the cells in the crypts between the villi, where the main toxin action takes place, as we shall see in Chapter 9. The toxin receptor in these cell membranes had been identified as a ganglioside which has a very strong affinity for the toxin (see Chapter 10), so much so that even if antitoxin were present near the cell membrane the receptor might successfully compete with the antitoxin for the toxin and fix it first, and once fixed the toxin would inevitably do its damage.

Mucus may therefore play a part in protecting the wall of the gut from the cholera vibrio, but immobilization of the vibrio with antibody may be frustrated because the vibrio, as we have seen, produces a mucinase, and if the mucinase liquefies the mucin the vibrio, even with antibody attached to it, may still be able to reach the mucosal surface. Therefore, should the cholera vaccine not after all (but for a different reason) contain, in addition to antibacterial and antitoxic components, a mucinase, as Lowenthal at WRAIR suggested in 1956 [261] when mucinase was still fashionable? Is this another argument against over-purification of the cholera immunizing agent?

4. The Immunology of the Enteron, and Future Hopes[41]

Cholera is a non-invasive infection of the intestinal mucosa, with no penetration of the mucosa by the organism or any of its products, except for the toxin that binds to the membranes of the most superficial layer of cells it encounters, i.e., the brush border cells covering the villi and the smooth cells of the intervening crypts. Therefore, any effective immune mechanism would have to operate at the mucosal surface within the lumen of the intestine, away from those parenteral elements that protect against parenteral microbial infections, i.e., the white cells of blood that phagocytose (envelop) invading organisms, and the complement of blood that plays a part in the immune bactericidal process. The only protective mechanism in the gut would appear to be humoral (i.e., dissolved in extracellular body fluid) antibodies that agglutinate the organisms, immobilize them in the mucus, interfere with their attachment to the mucosal surface, and neutralize the toxin. The antibodies must be in the lumen or at the mucosal surface to be effective, and they arrive there from two sources. One source is serum antibodies arising from systemic antibody-producing sites such as the spleen, or distant lymph nodes. These are mainly IgG antibodies, with perhaps a very small proportion of IgM antibodies. They leak into the gut through the intact mucosal membrane by inefficient passive processes, so that only a very small proportion of them reach the mucosal membrane or the lumen. If the serum concentrations of these IgG antibacterial and antitoxic antibodies are high enough, some may leak into the gut to protect against experimental cholera, but high levels of serum antibodies are not sustained for long. This is probably why parenteral immunization against cholera is possible, but short-lived. The other source of antibodies in the gut is the IgA, or secretory, antibodies that are actively secreted from local production sites, so that the transfer from interstitial fluid to the gut is relatively efficient.

The history of the earlier work on IgA antibodies is briefly as follows: Heremans in Brussels showed that the IgA antibodies (unlike IgG and IgM) are characteristic of the mucosal surface [193]. They are produced at the mucosal surface as dimers (i.e., double molecules) and are actively concentrated by the mucosal epithelial cells. In these cells, the dimer combines with a product of the epithelial cell, namely, the secretory piece, identified by Tomasi in Buffalo [419], and the combination of dimeric IgA and secretory piece is then actively secreted by a mechanism

41. This section is in effect an edited transcript of a tape-recorded discussion with N. F. Pierce of the Johns Hopkins University School of Medicine.

that is efficient both in trapping the IgA and secreting it. Secretory IgA is elaborated by lymphoid tissue that is ultimately incorporated into the mucosal structure, and is located so as readily to encounter antigens present on the mucosal surface. Moreover, IgA is more resistant than IgM to the proteolytic enzymes present in the gut because of its dimeric structure. There is also some evidence that the secretory piece–IgA dimer sticks to the mucosal surface in a way that may prolong its presence at that site. Thus, IgA has several advantages for immunological protection of the mucosal surface. The gut is the best studied mucosal immune system, but it is likely that many of the lessons learned from it will apply also to other mucosal surfaces, such as those of the respiratory and genital tracts and the conjunctiva of the eye.

The lymphoid tissue that elaborates secretory IgA takes the form of patches of clusters of germinal centres—Peyer's patches—that are superficially located on the wall of the intestine. (In the entire small intestine of the rat, there are about 30 Peyer's patches, each about 3 mm in diameter.) These patches are separated from the gut lumen by only a single layer of epithelial cells (M cells) which form a modified epithelium. The M cells have a greater pinocytotic capacity than the brush border cells of the epithelium, i.e., a greater ability to pass antigens across the membrane by actively engulfing small volumes of fluid containing them in minute incuppings or invaginations to form fluid-filled vacuoles which discharge their contents within the cells. Thus, these cell membranes enhance the transfer of antigens from the lumen to the underlying immuno-competent lymphoid tissue of the Peyer's patches. There are analogues of Peyer's patches in the respiratory tract, located primarily at the bifurcation of bronchii, almost as though they are posed where the impingement of antigen would be the greatest; whether they exist on other mucosal surfaces that can mount local immune responses, such as those of genital tracts and the conjunctiva of the eye, has not yet been established. Cebra of the Johns Hopkins University showed that the Peyer's patches appear to be the nursery for cells which ultimately appear as plasma cells that produce IgA antibodies, whereas the cellular products of systemic lymph nodes or spleen produce largely IgG or IgM [84]. A plasma cell is a differentiated lymphoid cell containing a small nucleus suspended in a large volume of cytoplasm (intracellular fluid) which contains the machinery for making antibodies; other lymphoid cells have a large nucleus surrounded by only a small rim of cytoplasm.

In many respects, the mucosal immune system acts independently of the systemic immune system. It is not completely independent since there are important interactions between the two systems, but the mucosal system does appear to be oriented towards the outside world (i.e., the lumenal surface of the small intestine, or enteron, in cholera), where it responds to absorbed antigens and in turn puts the antibody product back onto the mucosal surface of the outside world, rather than into the parenteral circulation.

The background of the cellular traffic in the mucosal immune response stems from the observation by Gowans at the University of Oxford that in rats the cells which appear as IgA-producing plasma cells in the lamina propriae (the layer of connective tissue containing blood and lymph vessels underlying the epithelium of the mucous membrane) arise from precursors in the Peyer's patches [170]. In the lamina propriae between the Peyer's patches there are numerous lymphoid cells, i.e., small lymphocytes and plasma cells. The plasma cells account for about 10 percent of the total lymphoid cell population of the gut, and they produce mostly IgA antibody. Gowans showed that plasma cells appear in the lamina propriae after originating in the Peyer's patches and leaving the Peyer's patches as immature dividing blast cells (i.e., precursors of cells) which then migrate through the intestinal lymphatics into the systemic circulation. They then find their way by an apparently selective homing mechanism back to the lamina propriae of the gut, where they lodge and live out their lifespan of four to five days, producing IgA antibodies which are then secreted to the mucosal surface. These cells are continuously replaced by fresh cells arriving from the circulation.

Thus was set the stage for Nathaniel F. Pierce, director of the cholera research program of the JHCMRT in Calcutta from 1966 to 1968 and now of the Department of Medicine of The Johns Hopkins University School of Medicine, to carry out pioneer studies on the immunology of cholera toxin in the enteron, where the toxin is produced and where it acts. These studies may well revive the flagging hopes of immunizing against the disease. They also add much to the growing knowledge of the immunology of the mucosal surface of the intestine, and of other mucosal surfaces. They arose from work done while Pierce was on sabbatical leave working on rats with J. L. Gowans [353][42] at the Sir William Dunn School of Pathology at the University of Oxford.[43]

Pierce set out to attempt to elicit a mucosal immune response to the

42. Now Secretary of the Medical Research Council of Great Britain.

43. W. E. van H, who worked at the Sir William Dunn School, claims some credit for this fruitful meeting. Pierce had asked him for suggestions where he might spend his sabbatical leave learning a different aspect of immunology from that which he had been practising; van H offered him the choice of chemical immunology with R. R. Porter, Nobel Prizewinner in the department of biochemistry at Oxford, or cellular immunology with Gowans. During his sojourn in Oxford, Pierce was a Visiting Fellow of van H's College, St. Cross College.

cholera vibrio and its products, and to ask how protective that response could be. The Johns Hopkins group's early studies on immunity to cholera had been done on dogs, which proved to be particularly useful for this purpose since C.C.J. Carpenter had first shown that cholera could easily be induced in them by feeding large numbers of vibrios by mouth. Thus, they had an intact adult model allowing immunization by various means and routes, and assessment of the protection thus induced [381, 382]. The Hopkins group had considerable experience with dogs as a model for evaluating parenteral bacterial and toxin vaccines at a time when the role of IgA antibodies was not yet understood, and the major indicator of protection was high values of serum (IgG) antibody.

Pierce's early work on mucosal antigenic stimulus and mucosal antibody response consisted of studies on dogs that had been immunized parenterally with toxoid and thus protected by the serum IgG leaking into the gut. The dogs were then followed for some months until the protection had subsided and the serum antitoxin titres had fallen to near baseline levels. At that point, Pierce attempted to boost the immunity in the dogs by feeding them cholera toxoid by mouth. There was no change in the serum antitoxin level, which remained at a low level that would not ordinarily be protective, but when the dogs were challenged several weeks later by feeding the vibrio they were found to be highly protected [356]. Pierce subsequently showed that they could not protect the dogs if they immunized only by mouth, using the same inactivated toxoid. This failure of toxoid to immunize by mouth is critical, since later it was shown that active toxin by mouth does immunize. It was also shown that dogs immunized and protected by parenteral priming and oral boosting with toxoid did have a detectable mucosal antitoxic response (as determined by biopsy), although there was no change in the serum antitoxin level. This mucosal response was brief; it occurred a few days after the oral booster, with a peak at 5 to 7 days; then there was a rapid decline in IgA antibody-producing cells within the next 2-3 weeks [352, 357]. Nevertheless, when animals immunized by this regimen were challenged up to a year later there was still substantial residual protection. The challenge was fierce—10^{11} vibrios—producing diarrhoea in susceptible animals within 8 to 16 hours, compared with an incubation period sometimes longer than 48 hours in the natural disease in humans. It is not known how the animals were protected— it may have been due to lingering undetectable but still protective antibody levels or to the animals' anamnestic response taking place within a few hours. Whatever the mechanisms, it is important to recognize that prolonged protection was obtained by a particular regimen which, although it included parenteral priming, still produced a vigorous mucosal response.

After Pierce's sojourn at Oxford, he returned to Johns Hopkins to continue the studies on rats he had started in Oxford and to resume his studies on dogs with the view to finding ways optimally to stimulate a local response to a defined antigen of the cholera vibrio, then to assess the nature, magnitude and duration of the protection that such a response might evoke, hoping thus to obtain a better understanding of the workings of the local immune system. As we have already seen, dogs were useful animals for studying protection by immunization; rats were useful for the demonstration of mucosal immune response, the conditions under which it occurs, and the factors controlling it. Pierce dealt entirely with cholera antitoxic immunity because of its advantages as a model in which he could measure the immune response by microscopic examination of specimens obtained from biopsies of intestinal tissue. This was done by first incubating the specimens with pure cholera toxoid which would fix to the cholera antitoxin in them, then "staining" them with pure cholera antitoxin coupled with fluorescin, an easily detectable dye. Thus, the fluorescin dye would mark the toxoid which in its turn had marked the antitoxin in the specimen. By this means, he was able to detect those plasma cells producing cholera antitoxin, and so enumerate antitoxin-producing cells at any site in the gut, and thus directly measure the magnitude of the immune response. He showed in dogs that the amount of antibody secreted into the gut is, as might be expected, directly related to the number of plasma cells producing that antibody in the mucosa, so that a count of fluorescently labelled cells in the lamina propriae is a direct measure of the mucosal antibody response.

One of Pierce's goals was to develop a technique for stimulating a mucosal antitoxic response solely by oral immunization. He confirmed that rats, like dogs, were primed when given a parenteral dose of cholera toxoid, so that when subsequently given the toxoid intestinally (i.e., enterally) there was a vigorous local mucosal immune response, but no priming took place when the first dose of toxoid was given intestinally. He continued to search for ways of stimulating local immune response without parenteral priming, because purely enteral immunization would be closer to what happens in the natural disease, and would take fuller advantage of the design of the mucosal immune system.

Pierce then discovered that cholera toxin—the active whole molecule rather than inactive toxoid—was strikingly effective mucosal antigen, both in priming and boosting. It was markedly different from toxoid, which was ineffective in priming. This raised the question of whether the immunological superiority of toxin was due to either or both of the two properties of toxin that are lost during toxoiding, viz.: (1) The ability avidly to adhere to the cell membrane receptor for the toxin inherent in its choleragenoid component (the B-component), but absent in chemically (glutaraldehyde or formaldehyde) inactivated toxoid. (2) The ability to produce diarrhoea inherent in its A-component.[44] Pierce was able to get an indirect but effective answer to this question by determining how effective choleragenoid was as an immunogen. He found that choleragenoid could evoke enteric priming when given intestinally, but was substantially poorer, both in priming and in boosting, than the whole intact toxin. Therefore, the receptor-binding capacity of intact toxin played a part in its superior immunogeniety, but was not the whole answer—both the binding activity and the choleragenic activity were important in eliciting the priming response, i.e., both the A- and B-components were necessary.

Several workers had shown that cholera toxin, when parenterally administered, was a potent modulator of immunological activity in that it might either enhance or suppress immune response to other antigens administered at approximately the same time, depending on the dosage of the toxin and on when it was given in relation to the other antigen. In general, if given at the same time as the other antigen, response to that antigen was enhanced; if given several days before, response was suppressed. Other data show that other agents which affect the level of adenylate cyclase activity (as does cholera toxin) in lymphoid tissue also modify immune responses, again enhancing or suppressing, again depending on the timing of the two events. Cholera toxin, being both an antigen and an activator of adenylate cyclase at the same time, therefore appears to enhance the immune response to itself. In the sense that the avid receptor binding property and the adenylate-cyclase activating property of cholera toxin both promote its immunogenicity, it seems that in this toxin we have an antigen that is especially suited to provoking an immune response. It is especially suited as a mucosal antigen because the membrane-binding property appears to enhance trapping of the toxin in mucosal lymphoid tissue, so preventing it from slipping past to reach the systemic lymphoid tissue. As an activator of

44. It would be helpful at this stage to anticipate some of the discussion in Chapter 10 on the molecular nature of cholera toxin and its mode of action at the chemical level. The cholera toxin molecule consists of two components, B (for binding) and A (for active). The B-component is Finkelstein's inert choleragenoid, and the A-component is an enzyme that activates another enzyme, adenylate cyclase, in the toxin-susceptible cells of the intestinal epithelium. Avid binding of the B-component to the toxin receptor (ganglioside) in these cells facilitates the passage of the A-component through the membrane to reach the adenylate cyclase and activate it. This activation of adenylate cyclase results in the pouring of fluid and electrolytes into the lumen of the gut, so producing diarrhoea.

adenylate cyclase, it might also be expected to enhance response to other concurrently administered protective antigens, such as bacterial vaccine. However, it should be noted that the administration of cholera toxoid and toxin together gives no greater antitoxin response than that due to toxin alone; that is, cholera toxin does not enhance the immunogenicity of cholera toxoid.

The toxin has certainly proved to be an important tool for studying mucosal immune response because it has been difficult to find other protein antigens that are effective in eliciting a local immune response when applied to a mucosal surface. In the rat, a priming response can be elicited with 1 microgram (a millionth of a gram) of cholera toxin, in contrast to the many milligrams (thousandths of a gram) of other proteins.

Pierce has also used cholera toxin for the study of immunological memory, i.e., the anamnestic response, which is probably important for the prolongation of protection. Since discrete primary and secondary responses to cholera toxin can be shown, it is possible to assess memory. If a rat is given a single enteral priming dose of a few micrograms of toxin (not enough to induce a loose stool), and a boosting dose is given two weeks later, a fully developed local immune response will be developed. A similar response will develop if the booster is delayed eight weeks, but then the dose will have to be four to eight times greater. If the booster is delayed 32 weeks, a maximal response can still be obtained with a dose not much greater than that used at 8 weeks. Immunological memory therefore exists, but there is some other mechanism that suppresses the anamnestic response but which can be overcome by a comparatively moderate increase in the boosting dose of antigen. The memory response is maximal at two weeks and long-lasting; the suppressive response is maximal at eight weeks and is also long-lasting. It now appears this suppressive response arises from parenteral antibodies depressing the enteral response. In this respect, local mucosal immune response to locally applied cholera toxin is different from the parenteral immune response to parenterally applied antigens such as tetanus or diphtheria toxoid, where the longer the interval between priming and boosting, the better the immune response.

The time course of the secondary response to a booster dose of cholera toxin in the rat is rapid enough in usual immunological terms, but slow in relation to the incubation period of the disease. A significant response is not seen in the lamina propriae of previously primed rats until three or four days after boosting. As we have already discussed, this suggests that it is unlikely that an anamnestic response to cholera infection (or reinfection) in humans previously primed (artificially or by natural infection) would appear fast enough to abort the natural disease which appears within an incubation period of one to three days after infection. The secondary response reaches its peak five to seven days after boosting, long after the epithelial cells have been irretrievably poisoned by the toxin. The secondary response may well explain the normal clearance of antigen (i.e., infecting vibrios and their products) during the normal recovery of the disease, which (in the absence of antibiotics) is five to eight days. Thus, the anamnestic response may be a "clean-up" response but not a prophylactic response. But perhaps it could be considered as an adjunct to a therapeutic process. The recovery from cholera is due to the natural shedding of epithelial cells (which takes place whether the cells are poisoned or not) in the normal course of events and their replacement by fresh unpoisoned cells in an environment that has been cleared of the vibrio and its products by the anamnestic clean-up response.

The question we now have to consider is whether the information gained from the studies on the mucosal immune response can be applied to the practical problem of immunizing humans against cholera. The field experiences reported in this chapter show that the parenteral administration of antigens, whether in the form of bacterial vaccines or purified cholera toxoid, is not worthy of further consideration. Parenteral immunization does not produce antibodies of suitable concentration at the mucosal surface. Moreover, Pierce's observations on rats have shown that parenteral administration of antigen, even when used only for priming to be followed by enteral boosting, may actually suppress mucosal response to enterally presented antigens if these are not presented in very high concentrations. Thus, purely parenteral immunization, or parenteral priming followed by enteral boosting, appear to be ruled out, leaving only the possibility of enteral immunization.

The next question, referring only to antitoxic immunization, is what form the toxin antigen should take. We have already discussed the total inefficacy of inactivated toxin in the form of toxoid. The next antigen to consider is choleragenoid, the binding component (B) of cholera toxin. We have already seen that choleragenoid, owing to its avid capacity to bind to the mucosal surface, can induce mucosal immunity (as tested in the rat) when presented enterally both as a primer and a booster. But choleragenoid is not nearly as effective an antigen as the whole toxin, because the adenylate cyclase activating component (A) which stimulates the local immune response is missing [351]. In practise, the comparative deficiency of choleragenoid might perhaps be overcome by using large doses of it.

Let us now consider the practicability of cholera toxin as an enteral antigen. This may appear to be a hazardous undertaking, but we shall see that possibly the immunizing dose need not be large enough to induce diarrhoea. Pierce tested the immunological efficacy of the toxin in dogs. At first, he tried multiple enteral application (by means of tubes inserted into the intestine through the mouth) of doses of pure toxin, or the equivalent amount of crude toxin, that caused diarrhoea. After many such treatments, the dogs ceased to have diarrhoea, and biopsy showed a huge local immune response, at least 10 percent of all the plasma cells of the gut producing IgA antitoxin. The doses of toxin were then reduced in size and frequency. When Pierce administered two small doses (reduced 16-fold) the dogs were no longer protected by the pure toxin, but, significantly, they were protected by an equivalent amount of the crude toxin, which produced virtually no diarrhoea. What was it about the crude toxin that protected the animals? Was it that the toxin was not emasculated as an immunogen by being purified? Or were other antigens involved? This seems to be a most important question, needing an answer. Pierce also tried choleragenoid in the same way, and found poor protection. This may have been due to choleragenoid not being capable of activating adenylate, as already discussed, but it must be borne in mind that the choleragenoid was purified—perhaps crude choleragenoid, like crude toxin, might prove to be a good local immunogen. This question will arise again in the next section of this chapter.

Before proceeding to the next section we should briefly discuss other aspects of Pierce's work possibly affecting diseases other than cholera. The mucosal immune system, from the mouth and nose to the anus, is important because it is the route of entry, apart from breakages of the skin, for most pathogenic microorganisms, and it has to bear the brunt of all exposures of outside antigens. Some of the pathogenic organisms, like typhoid or dysentery bacilli, are capable of breaking through the mucosal epithelium and so exposing themselves to the parenteral immune system, but others, like cholera and whooping cough bacilli, remain on the mucosal surface, and protection against them and their product depends on the secretory IgA antibodies of the mucosal immune response. Recent work in Pierce's laboratory has shown that priming in one mucosal area can also prime another area, but that the secondary response takes place only in the area where the booster is applied. We have already referred to Gowans's demonstration that cells arising in Peyer's patches go through the circulation and then return to the lamina propriae of the mucosa as IgA-producing plasma cells. There is evidence that these cells migrate through the mucosal immune system with much traffic between them, suggesting, for example, that a response to an antigen in the gut may evoke a similar IgA response in the saliva. Pierce has shown that the antibody-producing cells home back selectively to the organ where the booster is applied, regardless of where the primer was applied. It seems that when a Peyer's patch is primed, distant Peyer's patches may also be primed, even if not directly exposed to the antigen. Thus, if the colon is primed, a secondary response may be elicited in the trachea—a truly distant organ—provided the second application of the antigen is in the trachea. Thus, it is conceivable that immunization against whooping cough and other diseases caused by organisms entering by the respiratory tract—mycoplasma, *Haemophilus influenza*, the meningitis organism in children—might be achieved by swallowing the primer and sniffing the booster up the nose. The gut is particularly well suited to priming because it is easily reached and it not only provides the largest of the mucosal surfaces, but its IgA antibody-producing lymphoid tissue is more highly developed (for example, priming the trachea will prime the colon only poorly, but priming the colon will prime the trachea quite effectively). But it must be stressed that a study of the possibility of practical applications of this distant effect of priming has not yet been undertaken.

5. Texas Star

R. A. Finkelstein, bearing in mind that experience of cholera in cholera-endemic areas seemed to confer protection against the disease in adults, had long dreamed of enteral immunization against cholera by means of a single oral dose of an attenuated living culture of the organism, as is now done in immunizing against poliomyelitis. He recognized that the cholera vibrio should be counteracted enterally at the site where it appeared. In a paper received for publication in March 1969, announcing the purification of cholera toxin and the discovery of choleragenoid, Finkelstein [131] already had in mind an attenuated strain of the vibrio that he was later to succeed in producing. His statement has already been quoted in this chapter, but it is worth restating: "If choleragenoid is the precursor of choleragen, it might be possible to isolate a stable mutant, which one might predict would be incapable of causing cholera, and which would potentially provide the ideal immunizing agent—a living attenuated vibrio, capable of multiplication in the gut and stimulation of both antibacterial and antitoxic immunity at the important local level".

Finkelstein's search for a non-toxic mutant of the vibrio did not start with a choleragenoid-producing mutant in mind, but rather with one that produced no toxin antigen at all. In collaboration with his Texas colleague Randall K. Holmes, who was interested in the genetics of bacterial toxin production, he and their colleague M. L. Vasil treated cultures of the cholera vibrio with the mutagenic agent nitrosoguanidine and looked for organisms that no longer produced toxin. Their method was to test whether the active filtrate of the organism produced a precipitate with antiserum against choleragenoid. Failure of precipitation would mean that the organism was producing neither cholera toxin nor choleragenoid. By this means, they were able eventually to isolate a strain M13 that appeared not to produce toxin. In rabbits, the mutant strain was prototrophic, i.e., when introduced into the small intestine it colonized it. When 10^{10} of these organisms were fed to six volunteers each in the Center for Vaccine Development and Control at the University of Maryland, they failed to produce cholera, but they protected the volunteers against subsequent challenge with a virulent vibrio. However, there were problems, the chief of which was that the mutant 13 was unstable, since they were able to isolate from one of the volunteers a cholera vibrio that had fully regained its capacity to produce toxin [135]. This, and the thought that a non-toxinogenic mutant would in any case not produce antitoxic immunity and the further thought that it could not be expected to protect against diarrhoeal disease caused by *E. coli*, which produces a diarrhoeagenic toxin which is immunologically, structurally and in biochemical mode of action practically indistinguishable from cholera toxin (see Chapter 10), caused Finkelstein to abandon the atoxic mutant.

He then returned to the suggestion he had made in 1969 of trying to find a mutant that would produce choleragenoid but not cholera toxin. There was good reason for his not having taken up his own suggestion earlier, before he embarked on the search for a non-toxinogenic mutant. In 1969, it was not yet known that cholera toxin consisted of choleragenoid, the cell membrane-combining B-component that was attached by non-covalent links to the enzymic A-component responsible for the toxin's activity (see Chapter 10). To test for strains producing only B and not A, it was necessary to have separate antisera to each of the two toxin components. The presence of toxin would be indicated by precipitation with both anti-A and anti-B sera, and the presence of choleragenoid by precipitation only with the latter. When these two antisera became available in 1975 Finkelstein had the means of identifying non-toxinogenic choleragenoid-producing (A^-B^+) mutants of the vibrio. During 1976, he and his students screened 30,000 to 40,000 mutants of the classical vibrio 569B strain in vain for one that produced choleragenoid but not the toxin. In 1977, they were joined by Takeshi Honda, on leave from the Research Institute for Microbial Diseases in Osaka. The procedure he used was to screen mutants first for those that did not produce precipitation with anti-A antibody, i.e., did not produce toxin, and then take such mutants and seek those that produced precipitation with anti-B antibody, i.e., produced choleragenoid. Honda screened more than 60,000 mutants of the 569B Inaba serotype of the classical vibrio biotype without success. They then turned their attention to another strain of the vibrio, a hypertoxinogenic streptomycin-resistant 3083 Ogawa serotype of the El Tor biotype that Finkelstein had isolated during his tour of Vietnam. After mutagenesis and screening about 3,000 mutants, they eventually found a mutant that produced as much choleragenoid as the wild (i.e., non-mutated) type of the organism. They named this mutant Texas Star-SR (SR signifying streptomycin-resistant) [207]. It was prototrophic, i.e., it multiplied within the infant rabbit gut, and after 16 serial passages from one rabbit to another, it showed no evidence of reversion to toxicity. Doses of 10^{10} organisms of the mutant were avirulent to infant rabbits, whereas 10^2 of the wild (i.e., normal) type were lethal. Culture filtrates, even when concentrated 100-fold, showed no toxicity by the most sensitive of tests. They grew the mutant on a large scale in fermentors and found no trace of toxin in the culture filtrate, even when they worked up 40 litres of it; on the other hand, they isolated choleragenoid from these filtrates that was identical with the choleragenoid they knew.

When the Texas Star was inoculated in the gut of chinchillas, it caused no cholera in them, and when these same animals were challenged three weeks later with large doses of the wild type they were protected, both against colonization by the vibrio and against outpouring of fluid. The question of whether humans can be protected against cholera, and against *E. coli* diarrhoea, by Texas Star is under test at present in the Center for Vaccine Development and Control in Baltimore. Finkelstein is confident about the outcome of these tests. He points to the immunity generated by colonization with toxin-less (A^-B^-) mutant 13 in human volunteers who were protected only by the cell antigens of the vibrios (but perhaps also by soluble antigens other than toxin or choleragenoid?). With the antitoxic immunity that should be induced by the choleragenoid of Texas Star, the protection should be so much the better, and it might also protect against the related *E. coli* enteropathies which are far more important world-wide as causes of sickness and death than cholera. Moreover, Texas Star, being a mutant of the El Tor vibrio which adheres much better to the wall of the gut than the classical vibrio, should be a better colonizer of the gut than the classical vibrio.

Certainly, immunization by means of a living culture could have many advantages: (1) It might be possible to immunize with a single dose, as with poliomyelitis. (2) The colonizing culture, besides producing bacterial somatic antigen and toxin antigen, produces other antigens, some of which might have protective potential, e.g., mucinase, which might nullify the immobilizing and thus "antitoxic" effect of bacterial somatic antigen suggested by Verwey, and neuraminidase, which might increase the number of toxin receptors in the gut (see Chapter 10).

(3) Antigens are presented in their native state, unemasculated by the manipulations of biochemists and therefore perhaps capable of producing better, if not more, antibodies. (4) The antigens are delivered at a site which is surrounded by the mucosal surfaces capable of producing antibodies which in turn are delivered to that site.

But will colonization by Texas Star induce better protection than the natural disease? In the natural disease, cholera toxin is produced, and it will be recalled that Pierce's studies suggested that the toxin is a better immunogen that Texas Star's choleragenoid, apparently on account of its ability to stimulate adenylate cyclase. On the other hand, Pierce showed that crude toxin was a better immunogen than refined toxin, and his experiments with choleragenoid were necessarily made with refined material (which had to be refined in order to separate it from the toxin); perhaps unrefined choleragenoid, as produced in the gut by Texas Star, may be a better immunogen than Pierce's experience suggests.

And how long will protection last? We have noted already, in the discussion of the earlier vaccine trials at the PSCRL, that experience of the natural disease must protect, at least to some extent, against recurrence of the disease, since adults in cholera-endemic areas are less prone to the disease than infants, and more likely to be protected by parenteral vaccination. On the other hand, there are records in Dacca of people getting cholera two years running. It is difficult to get data on the recurrence of cholera in individuals, because the attack rate, even in a bad epidemic, is only 1 in about 200. The chance of finding someone having had two attacks of cholera is therefore 1 in about 40,000. Nevertheless, W. E. Woodward (son of Theodore Woodward of the original Inner Circle), by conscientious study of the careful records of the Matlab thana surveillance area of the PSCRL in Dacca, identified 14 persons with two documented cholera infections. Of these 14 people, 5 suffered severe enough diarrhoea to be hospitalized and intravenously rehydrated; in 3 of them, the cholera recurred within a year, in the fourth after 2 years and in the fifth after 5 years. All but this one of them (who was 19 years old and had his recurrence after 2 years) were between 3 to 5 years old at the first onset [466]. Woodward states: "It is clear that in endemic cholera areas the risk of infection does decrease with age, as the population gradually acquires specific immunity. We feel it reasonable to conclude, however, that the risk of reinfection is probably only slightly less than the risk of initial infection". George Curlin, who organized the toxoid trials in Matlab thana, has expressed the same opinion (private communication, 1979). On the other hand, studies with volunteers at the Center for Vaccine Development and Control at the University of Maryland showed that artificially induced infection conferred protection lasting two to four years [249]. Whether the degree of immunity arising from 100 percent effective artificial infection is the same as that arising from natural infection has not yet been established.

6. Is Immunological Protection
Against Cholera Feasible or Necessary?

If the short incubation period of cholera does indeed frustrate the anamnestic response, then it would seem that immunity to cholera must depend on the rapidly declining level of antibody present at the time of infection rather than the antibody produced in response to infection. This might suggest that enterally induced immunity to cholera is unlikely to last for more than one or two years. This would be long enough for people in a cholera-endemic area to be immunized well in advance of an epidemic, and so some of the arguments against the cost-effectiveness of preventive immunization would be met. But it would still be necessary to immunize the entire population every one or two years. Annual immunization of visitors to cholera-endemic areas may be feasible, but is it feasible for the whole of the local population? However, perhaps it would not be necessary for the whole of the population, but only for the youngest members of it. According to Pierce (private communication, 1979), epidemiological evidence suggests that cholera immunity in endemic areas is acquired incrementally, eventually producing a substantially immunized adult population. If this acquisition of immunity could be imparted by means of oral vaccine to young children, substantial numbers of them could be saved, and so remain on the road to protective immunity which would be sustained by further natural exposure to infection.

But even if active immunization against cholera were a practical proposition, would it be practised in endemic areas? Consider the case of another toxinosis, tetanus, which is spread as widely about the world as cholera and the other diarrhoeal diseases. Possibly as many babies die of tetanus every year on the Indian subcontinent as of cholera [434]. Yet tetanus is easily, surely and cheaply preventable by parenteral immunization with tetanus toxoid. Moreover, the population by far the most at risk is easily recognized—they are new-born babies dying of umbilical tetanus, which can easily be prevented by immunizing mothers before they are born, even before they are conceived. Yet immunization of pregnant women or post-pubertal girls against tetanus is hardly practised on the Indian subcontinent, even though two or three doses of toxoid within six months will confer immunity to tetanus, probably for life. The irony is that even findings of the Cholera Research Laboratory in Dacca (now the ICDDR/B, see Chapter 11) show that tetanus is a greater menace in Bangladesh than all the diarrhoeal diseases put together, of which cholera is in the minority. A recent (November 1980) issue of *Glimpse*, the ICDDR/B monthly newsletter, reports one of the Centre's own findings that whereas all diarrhoeal diseases in Bangladesh account for "about a third of all deaths" (mainly in children), tetanus accounts for "about 40% of all neonatal deaths". Nor are children immunized against diphtheria, which is also easily preventable. So is it realistic to believe that immunization against cholera, perhaps every year or two, of at least the young children in that subcontinent is likely? And if new-born babies in Africa and South America are also not protected against tetanus and diphtheria, is it likely that effective steps will be taken to protect them against *E. coli* diarrhoea with Texas Star?

There is another and far better way of preventing diarrhoeal diseases— avoidance of infection by not ingesting the faeces of diarrhoea patients. This was achieved in the Western world towards the end of the nineteenth century by separating the water supply from sewage. Such provision in the diarrhoea-endemic countries of the world is for the present only a distant dream, but perhaps the politicians whose duty it is to realize that dream should not be diverted from that duty by taking the easy but useless way out of flying in packages of vaccine, whether useless or not, in times of epidemic crisis.

However, nature has arranged matters so that tetanus, which is hardly curable, is easily preventable; whereas cholera and other diarrhoeal diseases, which are not easily preventable, are easily curable, as we shall see in Chapter 9.

IX

The Simple Cure of Cholera and of Other Infectious Dehydrating Diarrhoeal Diseases

The discovery that sodium transport and glucose transport are coupled in the small intestine, so that glucose accelerates absorption of solute and water, was potentially the most important medical advance this century.

—Editorial in the *Lancet,* 5 August 1978

1. The Normal Physiology of the Small Intestine

By what means does cholera toxin bring about so great an accumulation of an aqueous solution of salts in the alimentary tract that a patient may discharge as many as 30 litres of it a day, or more than twice his body weight, in the course of the disease?[1] To understand the physiology of this morbid process, we must first have some understanding of the normal physiology of fluid movement into and out of the alimentary tract—in through the mouth, back and forth through the mucosal walls of the alimentary tract, and out through the anal orifice. The alimentary tract in humans consists sequentially of: the mouth; the oesophagus; the stomach; the pylorus; the small intestine (or small bowel), comprising the duodenum ("12 finger breadths", 20 cm), the ligament of Treitz, and the jejunum (100 cm), passing without sharp distinction to the ileum (160 cm) [30];[2] the ileocoecal valve; the large intestine (or large bowel), comprising the caecum, the ascending, transverse, descending and sigmoid colons, the rectum and the anal canal, ending in the anal orifice (Figure 9.1).

1. A patient under therapy, that is; he could of course not do so unless he were being continuously rehydrated as fast as he was being dehydrated!
2. Note that the average length of the small intestine in the living human is about 280 cm, contrary to the figure of 500 cm in revered anatomical textbooks such as Gray's.

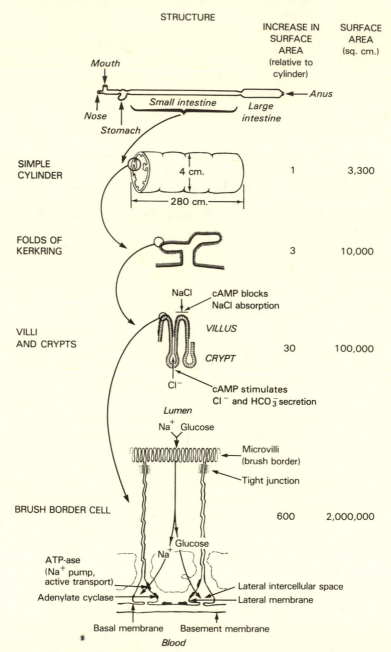

STRUCTURE		INCREASE IN SURFACE AREA (relative to cylinder)	SURFACE AREA (sq. cm.)
SIMPLE CYLINDER		1	3,300
FOLDS OF KERKRING		3	10,000
VILLI AND CRYPTS		30	100,000
BRUSH BORDER CELL		600	2,000,000

FIGURE 9.1. The small intestine and its components. Adapted from figures by Code *Proc. Cholera, Res. Symp., Honolulu 1965,* Washington, D.C.: U.S. GPO, 1965), Wilson (*Intestinal Absorption,* Philadelphia, W. B. Saunders Co.) and Field (*Acute Diarrhoea in Childhood,* Eds. Elliott, Knight, Amsterdam, Oxford, New York, Elsevier-North Holland, 1975).

The stomach is the acidic and peptic digesting vessel, with little movement of salt and water in either direction through its mucosal walls. Its contents are passed to the small intestine, which is slightly alkaline and tryptic, where they are further digested. In the duodenum, the nutrient contents are quickly brought into equilibrium with the blood by the rapid movement of large quantities of water in both directions through the mucosal wall, carrying salt in both directions and nutrients outward only to the blood, and with some net gain of fluid in this section of the gut. This process continues in the jejunum, and as the contents progress further there is progressively less gain of fluid in the gut, so that by the time the ileum is reached water is absorbed from the gut and its contents thus reduced to a small volume. This reduced volume of indigestible material, by now extracted of its nutrients, is then passed on to the colon, where the contents are further dried out by absorption of water and thus prepared and retained for disposal when it is convenient.

In the course of a day, a healthy person will ingest, in one form or another, about 1.5 litres of water and excrete 0.3 litre in the faeces, having disposed of 1.2 litres in the form of urine, sweat and respired water. The stomach and small bowel will receive 7 litres of fluid from various secretions (saliva, gastric juice, bile, pancreatic juice), and a further 8.5 litres will pass from the blood through the mucosal walls into the small bowel. Thus, 17 litres of water enter the small intestine; 16 of them will be absorbed from it [77, 191] and 1 litre will be delivered to the colon, which will in effect absorb 0.7 litre (in the course of which 2.8 litres will pass inwards through the mucosal wall and 3.5 litres will pass out to the blood), leaving 0.3 litre to be excreted in the faeces. Thus, about 16 litres of electrolyte solution move into and out of the small intestine in a day, with no net movement, in a healthy man [77].

The passage of these 16 litres of fluid into and out of the small intestine is the end result of an enormous traffic of fluid continuously back and forth through the cells of the gut epithelium between the lumen of the gut and the blood vessels supplying the walls of the gut. It can be calculated from the available data on the unidirectional flux of sodium ions and water that this amounts to at least 100 litres a day [26, 404]. This volume passes through an enormous surface of cell membranes lining the gut epithelium. If the small intestine were a simple cylinder 280 cm long and 4 cm internal diameter, the surface would be about 3300 cm^2 (Figure 9.1), but the lumenal surface of the small intestine is highly convoluted, first by the folds of Kerkring, the surfaces of which are covered by villi, finger-like processes 0.5 to 1.5 mm long, with the crypts of Lieberkuhn in between. The surfaces of the villi and the crypts are lined with epithelial cells. The lumenal borders of the crypt cells are smooth, and those of the villi are lined in their turn with microvilli about 0.001 mm long. All these folds, villi and microvilli enlarge the lumenal surface of the small intestine by a factor of about 600, bringing it to 2 million cm^2 (Figure 9.1), or say the size of a carpet 20 × 10 m, fit for the Palace of Versailles! In comparison with this enormous surface, the volume of 100 litres of fluid passing back and forth through it becomes small enough to be comprehensible—a twentieth of a millilitre, a mere drop, per cm^2 per day—next to nothing in a minute. It also becomes easy to see that a small unbalancing of the traffic of fluid, favouring movement towards the lumen, could quickly bring about a catastrophic accumulation in the small bowel.

The crypt cells are immature cells which originate and proliferate with a one-day generation time, and rise up the sides of the villi as they mature, and as they do so they acquire microvilli. These mature cells, because of their microvillous lumenal surfaces, are known as "brush border cells". When they reach the tips of the microvilli, they are shed and replaced by other mature cells. The lifetime of an epithelial cell, from crypt to microvillus tip, is about a week. In the course of a day, about 250 g of cells are liberated from the entire gastrointestinal tract [463]. Thus, intestinal epithelial cells are continuously replicating cells, unlike the discontinuously replicating cells of liver, kidney and bone, or the non-replicating cells of nerve and muscle. It is this fact that epithelial cells of the gut are continuously replaced within a week that puts a limit on the duration of cholera. Once a cell has been poisoned by cholera toxin, it malfunctions irretrievably, but when it is replaced, and the toxin is no longer present in the small intestine, the intestinal epithelium can function normally.

It has long been thought that the functions of secretion and absorption of water and electrolytes are divided between the epithelial cells, the immature crypt cells being secretory and the mature villus cells being absorptive [141]. The 20-fold enlargement of the surface of the lumenal membranes of the mature villus cells by the presence of microvilli (Figure 9.1) suggests all the more that these cells should be absorptive. We shall see that the secretory and absorptive functions of crypt and villus cells, respectively, have recently been experimentally confirmed.

Forty years ago, Florey suggested a reason for the constant secretion and absorption of fluid in the small intestine: "It may be necessary for a constant secretion of fluid to take place from the crypts of Lieberkuhn to keep food particles in suspension while they are attacked by pancreatic enzymes, and as the products of digestion are absorbed water and salts go with them. One may envisage a circulation of fluid passing out from the crypts of Lieberkuhn into the lumen and back into the villi" [141].

2. Choleraic Morbid Physiology of the Small Intestine

In the normal person, absorption and secretion are balanced, but in the cholera patient, secretion in the small bowel is increased while absorption is diminished, to the extent that there can be a net secretion of up to 30 litres of fluid a day, the average being about 6 [191]. This morbid phenomenon, as Hendrix of the Johns Hopkins Medical School has pointed out [191], "has been a stimulus to reexamine intestinal secretion, a phenomenon that since the review of Florey et al. has been largely ignored or was believed not to exist".

When cholera toxin is introduced, or produced, in the small intestine, it is rapidly and irreversibly bound to the epithelial cells, but there is a lag period of about 30 minutes before fluid begins to accumulate. The maximum rate of fluid output is reached after 3 to 4 hours, and continues at this rate for 10 to 12 hours and gradually declines over the next 12 hours [355]. The Johns Hopkins group showed in human cholera patients in Calcutta [7], and in experimentally infected dogs in Baltimore [382], that fluid accumulates only in the small intestine, and that the colon continues to absorb isotonic fluid throughout the disease. The JHCMRT group showed that in human cholera patients, fluid accumulation occurred throughout the length of the small intestine with the rate of accumulation per unit length decreasing from the duodenum to the ileum [9], and this was confirmed by their colleagues in Baltimore by direct observations in surgically separated sections of the small intestines of dogs with experimentally induced cholera [54]. This quantitative variation may be a reflection of the increasing absorptive capacity in the same direction in a normal person, which we discussed earlier. But there is also an important qualitative variation in this direction; it appears, both in human cholera patients and in dogs experimentally challenged with cholera vibrios or exotoxin, that the important loss of bicarbonate is more than twice as great in the ileum as it is in the jejunum [177]. Since the flow of water and electrolytes takes place in both directions through the mucosal wall of the intestine—from intestinal lumen to the blood on the serosal side of the mucosal wall, and from the blood to the lumen—it follows that accumulation of fluid in the intestine could be the consequence of three effects: (1) the inhibition of absorption from the gut, (2) stimulation of secretion into the gut, and (3) a combination of reduced absorption and increased secretion. We shall see all three hypotheses have been favoured in their turn and that it seems now that the third is the most likely, with the emphasis perhaps more on secretion than absorption.

After the NAMRU-2 group had carried out their careful determinations of water and electrolyte losses in cholera patients during the epidemic in Bangkok in 1958, they considered the three hypotheses[3] above and came to the conclusion that the first—the inhibition of absorption to varying degrees by the "*V. comma* or its products" would provide "a simple mechanism to explain the origin of the diarrhoea fluid" [456]. Phillips was soon persuaded—and he soon persuaded others—that a product of the cholera vibrio brought about the inhibition of the absorption of sodium by poisoning the "sodium pump"; and in this he was the first, or among the first, to suggest that a product of the cholera vibrio specifically affected the mucosal cells of the gut in such a way as to bring about an accumulation of fluid in the gut. The sodium pump is a structure and/or a mechanism involving the energy-rich substance ATP[4] and an enzyme, the sodium- and potassium-dependent enzyme ATPase, that breaks it down to release energy. The pump is present in the cells of higher animals. In the brush border cells of intestinal epithelium it is located on the lateral and basal membranes (see Figure 9.1). Its function is to "pump" sodium and potassium ions through these membranes from inside the cell into the lateral and basal spaces between and beyond the cells, which are richer in sodium than the cell interiors. From these spaces, the sodium, carrying water with it, finds its way under simple hydrostatic pressure to the basement membrane of the intestinal epithelium where the blood vessels are. Thus, if the action of the sodium pump were inhibited, the absorption of sodium and water from the gut would be reduced.

The movement of sodium through a sheet of cells can be studied electrically in an Ussing chamber.[5] If a sheet of biological tissue (often a piece of frog abdominal skin is used) is mounted in an Ussing chamber in such a way as to form a septum between two halves of the chamber, and each half is filled with a warmed, oxygenated physiological salt solution, and electrodes are placed in each, an electrical potential difference will be seen between one-half of the chamber and the other, i.e., between one side of the sheet of tissue and the other. If this

3. In fact, they still had to consider a fourth hypothesis, namely that there was a transudation of plasma through a desquamated epithelium, since this idea was to await its death knell until the next year (1959) in Bangkok from the demonstration by Gangarosa that the mucosal epithelium in cholera was anatomically intact and by Gordon that large molecules did not leak through it. The NAMRU-2 group had found it "difficult, however, to reconcile the rapid return of bowel function, in patients recovering from cholera, with widespread mucosal damage, hence other diarrhoea-provoking mechanisms should be considered".

4. Adenosine triphosphate—this substance, when broken down by another enzyme in another way, is very important for another reason, as we shall see in Chapter 10.

5. For a clear explanation of the workings and applications of the Ussing chamber, see 122.

potential difference is nullified by passing a short-circuit current (SCC) in the opposite direction, then any subsequent variations in the SCC will be a measure of the active transport of sodium (or chloride) ions across the sheet of tissue.

In October 1959 Comdr. G. S. Huber joined NAMRU-2 in Taipei and familiarized himself with the Ussing short-circuited frog-skin preparation. He and Phillips placed frog abdominal skin in an Ussing chamber and studied the effect of cholera stool, extract of normal stool, cholera culture filtrate and uninoculated cholera culture medium on the SCC needed to nullify the potential difference between the sides of the skin. Cholera stools and culture filtrate produced a rapid[6] and sharp fall in SCC; extract of normal stool and uninoculated culture filtrate had no such effect. They reported their studies of the "unique action of Vibrio cholerae and/or its products" at the inaugural meeting of the Pakistan-SEATO Cholera Research Laboratory in Dacca in December 1960, and Graham Bull, who presided over the section in which the theory of sodium pump poisoning was presented, found this a "convincing explanation" for the large loss of water and electrolytes through an apparently intact mucosa. For the next few years, this was the dominant idea—indeed, the only idea—for the chemistry underlying the morbid physiology of cholera [338]. At the next meeting under the SEATO Cholera Research Program, in Honolulu in January 1965, Phillips reported further that the fluid which gathered in rabbit ileal loops after the introduction of cholera vibrios also appeared to inhibit active transport of sodium in the short-circuited frog skin in the Ussing chamber [345]. By this time, he was less confident of the inhibition of absorption by cholera toxin than he had been at the Dacca meeting. In a further paper with his colleagues Craig Wallace and Quentin Blackwell at the Honolulu meeting, on the absorption of water and electrolytes by cholera patients, it is stated that

> these studies are consistent with the hypothesis that the primary defect in cholera is an inhibition of active Na^+ ion transport from gut lumen to plasma. On the other hand, they are not inconsistent with the alternative hypothesis that the major defect in cholera is an increased filtration of protein-free plasma into the gut lumen with or without inhibition of Na^+ transport. We have previously pointed out that a comparatively brisk mesenteric blood flow is essential for the production of dehydration in cholera.

The idea of filtration under pressure of protein-free plasma from blood

---

6. If they had foreknowledge of what was learned later, this rapid fall would have warned them that this was not an effect of cholera toxin, which requires a lag period of some hours before its effect takes place, as we have seen.

vessels into the gut was later ruled out by Carpenter and by his colleagues who showed that in fact in experimental cholera in dogs the rate of fluid loss was unaffected by a marked decrease in superior mesenteric blood pressure [55]. However, we shall see that there is indeed an increased flow of protein-free electrolyte solution from the plasma into the gut, due not to filtration from the blood, but to secretion of ions into the gut by the epithelial cells.

The notion of a poisoned sodium pump in cholera appeared to receive its death blow at the same Honolulu meeting. A.H.G. Love, a pupil of Bull's at Queen's University, Belfast, then working with Phillips in Taipei, reported on studies of the movement of two different (and therefore distinguishable) radioactive sodium isotopes in opposite directions through the walls of rabbit ileal loops. He showed that in the cholera-infected loop, although there was a net movement of sodium into the loop, the movement out of the loop, as shown by one radioactive sodium isotope, was normal; it was the increased movement into the loop, as shown by the other radioactive isotope, that caused the net accumulation of sodium in the loop [259]. At the same meeting, two other members of NAMRU-2 reported that ammonium salts could have an effect on the frog skin similar to that which Phillips had observed [304]. It seems very likely that Phillips was observing something with his short-circuited frog-skin preparation that had nothing to do with cholera toxin. Yet his efforts were not wasted; these experiments did sharply focus attention on the correct idea that the accumulation of fluid in cholera was due to the action of a product of the cholera vibrio that could be found in cholera culture filtrates and in cholera stools, that affected ion transport in the intestinal epithelial cells, and whose action could be determined by electrical means in the Ussing chamber. We shall see that the Ussing chamber was to be put to good effect when the frog skin was replaced by a more relevant sheet of intestinal mucosal cells. And we shall see that Phillips was perhaps partially correct (though for the wrong reason), because recent work suggests that inhibition of the sodium pump is involved in cholera intoxication accounting for a proportion of fluid accumulation in the gut.

Love's suggestion that the accumulation of fluid in cholera was due to stimulation of secretion of ions and water into the gut rather than inhibition of absorption from it [260] gained further support from experiments on dogs by Iber and others at Johns Hopkins University [212], but we shall see that the fact of the matter probably is that in cholera there is both some reduction of absorption from the lumen of the gut and perhaps a larger stimulation of secretion into the gut, the inhibition of absorption and stimulation of secretion taking place respectively in mature villous and immature crypt cells in the intestinal epithelium. These findings are the outcome of joint efforts by the Johns Hopkins group and Michael Field of Harvard University, in which studies were made of ion movements across sheets of intestinal epithelium mucosa stripped of the muscle layers and fixed between the two cells of an Ussing chamber [122]. In order to discuss this work, it is necessary to anticipate an important discovery that had recently been made by Field (among others), and will be discussed in Chapter 10, namely, that cholera toxin stimulates an enzyme, adenylate cyclase, in intestinal epithelial (and all other) cells, which leads to the formation of a substance called, for convenience, cyclic AMP, or cAMP, by means of which cholera toxin promotes its action on cells. Addition of cAMP to cells has the same effect as cholera toxin. It is more convenient to use. The substance theophylline (which occurs in tea) also has this effect, since it inhibits the enzyme (diphosphoesterase) that breaks down cAMP. Field found that when theophylline was added on the serosal (i.e., opposite the mucosal or lumenal) side of a short-circuited sheet of intestinal epithelium in an Ussing chamber, there was in effect a suppression of sodium and chloride absorption from the lumenal side and a stimulation of chloride secretion into the lumenal side [398]. Thus, whereas in the untreated epithelial sheet sodium ion is absorbed and chloride ion hardly moves, in the theophylline-treated sheet sodium ion hardly moves and chloride ion is secreted, and the abolished movement of the positively charged sodium ion is equal to the opposite movement of the oppositely charged chloride ion. The question now was how these two processes could take place simultaneously. The answer lay in the fact which we have already noted, namely, that absorption takes place in the mature villous cells of the intestinal epithelium, and secretion takes place in the immature cells of the crypts of Leiberkuhn which lie between the villi.

The suggestion that stimulation of secretion and inhibition of absorption by cholera toxin might take place in the immature crypt and mature villus cells, respectively, was made at the Johns Hopkins University by Carpenter and his group in the Department of Medicine on morphological grounds [111], and by Hendrix and his group in the Department of Pathology on physiological grounds [192, 374]. Hendrix and his colleagues showed that when villus cells were selectively damaged by instilling strong salt solution into the intestinal lumen, leaving the crypt cells intact, there was no decrease in cholera toxin-induced secretion. They concluded, therefore, that this induced secretion took place in the undamaged immature crypt cells. Field and his colleagues now tackled the problem in the reverse way—what would be the effect of cholera toxin on a colony of nothing but villus cells? They knew that the intestines of teleost fish did not contain crypts and therefore they experimented on sheets of intestinal epithelial cells from the wild flounder, containing only well-developed brush border cells, mounted in an Ussing chamber. When cAMP or theophylline was added on the serosal side, there was no net secretion of chloride ions, thus confirming that the toxin-induced stimulation of chloride secretion does not take place in mature epithelial cells [122]. This further supported the hypothesis of the anatomical separation of secretory immature cells and absorptive mature cells in the crypts and on the villi, respectively.

There appears to be little doubt that cholera toxin stimulates secretion in crypt cells, but some doubt as to whether it suppresses absorption in villus cells. The experiments of Hendrix cited above suggest that absorption is not suppressed, and Hendrix produces other arguments in support of this suggestion, namely, that in cholera the daily stool output is greater than the volume of fluid absorbed by the gut, and that experiments such as those of Love mentioned above have shown that in cholera-intoxicated rabbit ileal loops sodium movement outwards (i.e., absorption) was normal, whereas inwards (i.e., secretion) it was increased [191]. On the other hand, experiments by Nellans and his colleagues at the University of Pittsburgh [303] seem to suggest that at least some sodium absorption is suppressed by cholera toxin. They showed that at the level of the brush border membrane of the rabbit ileum, about 20 percent of the movement of sodium cations and chloride anions was mediated by an absorption process (from lumen to epithelial cell interior) in which these ions were obligatorily coupled, and that this absorption was inhibited by theophylline, which, as we have seen above, imitates the action of cholera toxin. Theophylline did not inhibit sodium absorption in the absence of chloride, nor chloride absorption in the absence of sodium. In other words, cholera toxin will inhibit some sodium absorption, but only in proportion to the amount of chloride present (Figure 9.1). The Pittsburgh workers postulated that the driving force for this coupled absorption of sodium and chloride was the sodium pump, thereby at least partially rehabilitating Phillips's theory of sodium pump poisoning by cholera toxin. We shall see that Phillips was to show later in another way that sodium absorption was suppressed in cholera patients—when they were given hypotonic or isotonic saline they were unable to absorb electrolytes, just as Hermann had observed in 1830 that cholera patients in Moscow did not absorb the salts of his artificial mineral water.

3. The Glucose Effect

We have seen that the accumulation of isotonic fluid in the gut in cholera is due to the toxin-induced combination of reduced absorption of fluid from the gut and increased secretion of fluid into it. The toxin-poisoned pathway for the absorption is not the only pathway for absorption of fluid. There are other pathways that are not affected by cholera toxin. There is one that comes into play when certain sugars, notably glucose, are present; and there is another that comes into play when certain amino acids, notably glycine, are present. The exploitation of the toxin-resistant glucose-activated pathway[7] has led to a highly simplified method of treating and curing cholera that is applicable to other diarrhoeal diseases as well, and therefore of great relevance to many more countries and many more people than those affected by cholera.

In 1949, R. B. Fisher and D. S. Parsons in the Department of Biochemistry at the University of Oxford reported a series of experiments on the stimulatory effects of glucose on the absorption of fluid by the small intestine. They devised a means of isolating a segment of rat intestine, transferring it to a bath, and bathing it inside and outside with oxygenated fluid in such a way that it survived, isolated from the body, with a viable, properly functioning mucosa [136, 137]. As a first test of the utility of this surviving intestinal preparation, they studied active absorption of the simple sugar glucose (grape sugar, blood sugar, a monosaccharide,[8] the principal source of energy for most organisms) from the lumen of the intestinal segment, and were able to determine what part of the glucose absorption was due to utilization of the glucose by metabolism and what was due to translocation of it through the intestinal wall. A few years later, they studied the absorption of another simple sugar, galactose [138], and showed that this too was absorbed, and that this absorption, like that of glucose, was an "active" process, not simply diffusion. In the course of these experiments, they made the important discovery that during the absorption of glucose, water was absorbed along with it, but not during the absorption of galactose. P. F. Curran of the Biophysical Laboratory of Harvard University showed in 1960 that glucose also promoted the active transport of sodium and chloride ions through the mucosal wall from the lumen to the serosa, and that it was this process that carried the water through [92]. Schultz and Zalusky of the U.S. Air Force School of Aerospace Medicine showed that this effect was not, as had been previously thought, due to the

---

7. The glycine-activated pathway has not been much exploited (see below), for the simple reason that glucose is cheaper and easier to obtain.

8. Glucose and fructose (fruit sugar) are the monosaccharide moieties of the disaccharide sucrose, the common sugar derived from sugar cane or beet; glucose and galactose are the monosaccharide moieties of the disaccharide lactose, or milk sugar; the disaccharides are cleaved into their constituent monosaccharides by disaccharidase enzymes.

nutritive properties of glucose as it metabolized, but to transport of a ternary complex of a glucose molecule, a sodium ion and a water molecule [389].

What is important to our present considerations is the fact that this glucose-coupled mechanism of absorption of sodium and water remains intact in cholera-intoxicated intestinal epithelial cells. This was in effect first reported at the Honolulu conference in 1965 by A.H.G. Love, who had been carrying out experiments in Phillips's NAMRU-2 in Taipei. He showed that in ligated ileal loops in normal rabbits, as little as 10 mM glucose increased net movement of sodium and water out of the gut, without affecting the movement of sodium into the gut. Sodium and water accumulated in infected ileal loops in the absence of glucose, due to greatly enhanced inward movement and unchanged outward movement; but when glucose was present in the infected loops, the absorption of sodium and water was so much enhanced as to overcome the effect of cholera toxin and promote net absorption. Similar results were found with cholera patients. Thus, it seemed that glucose still promoted the absorption of sodium and water in the gut, even when it was poisoned by cholera toxin [259]. Two years later, at the meeting of the Cholera Panel of the U.S.–Japan Cooperative Medical Science Program in Palo Alto, there were half a dozen reports from the Johns Hopkins groups in Baltimore and Calcutta, and from the CRL, on experiments in animals and experiences with human cholera patients amply confirming the conclusion that in cholera the glucose-stimulated pathway for the absorption of electrolytes and water was unaffected.

But these reports at the Honolulu and Palo Alto conferences did not arise directly from Fisher and Parsons's observations at Oxford, nor from Curran's at Harvard. They arose from experiments carried out by R. A. Phillips on human cholera patients in the Philippines with orally administered glucose-containing electrolyte solutions.

4. Early Attempts at Oral Rehydration

Although the regime of isotonic intravenous rehydration has proved itself in the saving of countless lives since it was put on a sound basis by Phillips and his successors, it has in fact got limitations which make it hardly feasible in large-scale epidemics over wide and remote areas of underdeveloped countries. A single patient may need as many as 60 or more one-litre bottles of fluid (see Figure 9.2). The cost of this fluid is high, and the transport of so much bulk can be a severe problem, especially in a country such as Bangladesh where it can be transported only in country boats, which take three days to cover the score of miles from Narayanganj to Matlab Bazaar. The water the salts

FIGURE 9.2. Recovered cholera patient at Pakistan-SEATO Cholera Research Laboratory surrounded by 96 litre bottles for intravenous infusion fluid that had been needed for his treatment.

are dissolved in has to be distilled in order to rid it of fever-producing substances (pyrogens), and the solutions in the bottles have to be sterilized. If sodium bicarbonate is used, it needs special handling. The administration of the fluids needs special skills—finding the appropriate blood vessel (which is often collapsed) and inserting the needle, maintaining the correct flow of fluid, and monitoring the patient. All require, if not fully qualified physicians, at least large numbers of medical aides with adequate training and experience. The NAMRU-3, PSCRL and JHCMRT teams in Thailand, the Philippines, South Vietnam, East Pakistan (Bangladesh) and India dealt expeditiously and efficiently, with a mortality rate of generally less than 1 percent, with all those who came under their care; but those who came under their care were only a small proportion of all those who had cholera.

If the rehydration fluid could be administered by mouth rather than by vein, many of the problems of rehydration would be avoided. The fluid would not have to be sterile because one of the functions of the intestinal tract is to cope with the germs that are constantly ingested by the mouth; there would be no need for the sterile needles and tubes used in the intravenous administration of fluid, and the patients' relatives could administer the fluid by mouth.

As early as 1959 in Bangkok, Phillips was already thinking of oral rehydration. His ultimate dream was that all cholera patients should be rehydrated by mouth, preferably by means of pills dissolved in glasses of water, but he was concerned about how to get, and keep, the fluid down, because, as Sir Leonard Rogers and many others had already observed, attempts to give cholera patients water containing salt and mild alkali by mouth are likely to be thwarted by nausea and vomiting. He believed that he could circumvent this problem by taking the middle ground—rehydrating the patients intravenously at first to correct analkalaemia and regulate fluid balance, thus restoring them to a condition where they no longer vomited, then carrying on with oral rehydration.

There was also the question of whether the gut of a cholera patient, which was rejecting or expelling fluid and electrolyte, was capable of absorbing them when presented to it via the mouth. Phillips, in his physiological way, intended to start by making careful quantitative studies of water and electrolyte movement across the wall of the small intestine in normal subjects and cholera patients in Bangkok, but was unable to make much progress because there were only a few mild cases of cholera in Bangkok in 1960, and the disease came to an end in Thailand by the end of July. But in September 1961, the seventh cholera pandemic broke out with an eruption of an epidemic in the Philippines 25 years after the previous outbreak—this was the first serious El Tor epidemic.

Phillips immediately encouraged his friend Dr. Azurin (at that time director of quarantine in Manila) to cause the Philippine authorities to invite NAMRU-2 (through the Department of State in Washington) to send a team to the San Lazaro Hospital in Manila to help control the disease. Within a few days, the NAMRU-2 team, with Lt. Comdr. Craig Wallace in charge, arrived at the San Lazaro Hospital and by 7 October 1961 set up a treatment centre. Intravenous rehydration of patients was immediately instituted on the lines developed by NAMRU-2 and the death rate lowered from 14 percent to 3.4 percent [450]. As a result of this work, a division of NAMRU-2 was established in the Philippines, and when the cholera returned in the summer of 1962, Phillips was able to take up his experiments on the movement of orally ingested water and electrolyte across the wall of the gut. In July and August of that year, he carried out experiments on 12 cholera patients in the San Lazaro Hospital. They were first brought into fluid, electrolyte and acid-base balance by intravenous rehydration, then given water alone, and hypo-, iso- and hypertonic solutions containing sodium, potassium, chloride and bicarbonate ions. To Phillips's surprise, cholera patients were able to drink two glasses of water an hour without vomiting, and he was encouraged to press on with his observations. Patients given hypotonic solutions were able to absorb water and some potassium and bicarbonate ions, but not sodium or chloride ions; those receiving isotonic solutions absorbed potassium and bicarbonate, but not water or sodium or chloride; those receiving hypertonic solutions containing nearly twice as much sodium chloride as the isotonic absorbed potassium and bicarbonate, but not water and only very little sodium or chloride.[9] Thus, it was evident that electrolyte solutions administered orally could replace the losses of potassium and bicarbonate, and of water if dilute enough, but not sodium or chloride, even when these ions were presented in high concentrations. This inability to absorb sodium and chloride ions was manifest only in patients with cholera; convalescent patients, like normal subjects, were quite capable of absorbing these ions.[10]

At this stage, Phillips had the thought of replacing some of the sodium with a non-electrolyte. He tried several compounds, including alcohol and some sugars, including glucose. Orally administered glucose-electrolyte solutions had, in fact, been used before in the treatment of dehydrated patients. Thus, Darrow and his colleagues at Yale University had administered electrolyte solutions containing glucose with apparent success in the treatment of 250 dehydrated infants in New Haven and Texas [93]; and Chatterjee had claimed successful treatment of 33 mild cases of cholera in Calcutta by means of oral administration of a drug to reduce vomiting, a plant extract to control diarrhoea, and a solution containing 68 mMoles of sodium chloride and 139 mMoles of glucose per litre [68]. Neither of these workers gave any reason for using glucose—perhaps they had its nutritive properties in mind; nor did Phillips give his reason for trying glucose, but as an experienced physiologist he must at least have known—for example—of the paper published in 1960 in the *Journal of General Physiology* by P. F. Curran of the Harvard Medical School on the coupling of sodium transport and glucose transport in the small intestine [92]. Craig Wallace avers that he did, but Sir Graham Bull (see below) believes that he did not. He stated (privately, 1980),

9. These experiments are detailed in NAMRU-2 reports of the time.

10. In the late 1950s, it was quite common practice in the United States orally to rehydrate babies dehydrated by diarrhoea with various hypotonic solutions made up from commercially available powders containing sodium, potassium, chloride and citrate ions (but apparently not glucose), and there were many reports of hypernatraemia in these infants as a result of the occasional use of hypertonic solutions. Apparently, these diarrhoeas were different from cholera diarrhoeas in that the sodium ion appeared to be absorbed.

Unless Bob [Phillips] was being very devious with me I am convinced that his use of glucose in the study on the key patient was purely to make the solution isomolar. You will recall that he had been studying the effects of giving oral fluids of different electrolyte composition and molalities. Some were hypertonic, some hypotonic and others isotonic solutions, but in all of these the only solutes were electrolytes. He needed to test the effect of an isotonic solution with less electrolyte, and glucose was a handy solute. If he was aware of the Fisher et al. studies he certainly did not mention them to me when we sat in his office working out the balances. There is no doubt in my mind that the discoveries of the effects of glucose on electrolyte absorption were independent. I have certainly said so repeatedly in lectures. Quote me if you like.

Phillips studied the effect of glucose in 2 of his 12 cholera patients in Manila in 1962. One, number 18474, male, received orally on 12 July a solution that was isotonic, with an equiosmolar amount of glucose substituted for some of the sodium. Whereas an isotonic solution of the composition of cholera stools would contain a total of about 310 milliosmoles per litre in the form of sodium 145, potassium 10, chloride 110, and bicarbonate 45 milliosmoles per litre (see lines 8 and 9, Table 1.2), this solution contained 310 milliosmoles per litre as sodium 95, potassium 10, chloride 60, bicarbonate 45 and glucose 100. This patient, although drinking an isotonic solution, absorbed both sodium and water. The second patient, number 20646, male, received orally a solution that was isotonic with respect to the salts, but in addition to that glucose was added in increasing concentrations from 50 to 500 mMoles per litre, i.e., the patient was drinking hypertonic solutions. The higher the concentration of glucose this patient drank, the more sodium and water he absorbed. Wallace comments (private communication, 1980): "The first time we used glucose the effect was dramatic—the patient stopped having diarrhoea while receiving it because the glucose was allowing him to absorb fluid he would otherwise have shed—only to have it recur during the control period. It was a phenomenon we could repeat. The entire team realised that Bob had found the key to his dream".

Thus it seemed Phillips had found a means of rehydrating cholera patients by mouth—the glucose-linked mechanism of transporting water and sodium was apparently not inactivated in cholera, so that if glucose was incorporated in a solution of salts and drunk by a patient, he would absorb water and be rehydrated, and at the same time he would absorb sodium, potassium, chloride and bicarbonate and thus be remineralized and realkalinized.[11] Phillips returned to Taipei, where he had been joined on 29 August 1962 by Dr. Graham Bull,[12] then of the British Post-graduate Medical School of London, whom he had invited for some months. They went through the large amount of data that Phillips had just accumulated in Manila, calculating the water balance of the patients who had received these various salt and glucose-salt solutions by mouth. Bull confirmed the findings on cholera patients in experimental animals. He introduced cholera organisms, and toxic culture filtrates, into ligated rabbit intestinal loops by De's method (p. 60), followed by solutions of various concentrations of salt with and without glucose and found essentially the same results as had been found with human patients.

Phillips already had tests under way in the Philippines to determine whether cholera patients could be treated with an oral regime of hypertonic sodium bicarbonate, potassium chloride and glucose, in conjunction with an intravenous regime of isotonic saline. The limited objective of the oral regime was to test whether analkalaemia (acidosis) and potassium loss could be corrected in this way, possibly with some saving of intravenous saline. On 4 August 1962, three patients were treated with this "oral electrolyte cocktail", as it was called, with encouraging results. An advance NAMRU-2 party had returned to Manila in September 1962 with Wallace again as physician in charge. He was instructed to treat 30 patients orally with the "cocktail" (after preliminary rehydration and correction of analkalaemia by intravenous infusion of the usual fluid). Phillips and Bull arrived in Manila a week later on 21 September, and found that there had been 5 deaths among the 30 orally treated patients. Bull immediately made a round of the ward and found that some of the patients whose kidney function was impaired were, in his opinion, "in effect drowning in their own intracellular fluid", which had collected in the extracellular spaces in the lungs, causing pulmonary oedema, followed, in some cases, by death from

11. According to Wallace and to Watten (who had by then left NAMRU-2 to take up an appointment in the United States), Phillips called a press conference before he left Manila to announce that the oral cure for cholera was at hand. At that time, cholera was, states Wallace, a politically explosive matter in the Philippines.

12. Now Sir Graham Bull. When Phillips was working on blood plasma and plasma substitutes in NAMRU-3 in Cairo in 1951, he invited Bull to join him there because he was interested in Bull's technique for measuring very low blood flow through the kidney. He had also caused Bull to be invited to the inaugural meeting of the Pakistan-SEATO Cholera Research Laboratory in Dacca in December 1960. Bull subsequently became a Director of the Medical Research Council's Clinical Research Centre in London and a consultant to the Technical Committee of the Dacca laboratory.

heart failure. Bull then realized, apparently for the first time, that the fluid they were being given orally was not isotonic, but hypertonic, because instead of the glucose replacing some of the electrolytes it was in addition to them. Phillips, in his determination to ensure that the patients would absorb electrolytes, had added glucose to an already isotonic salt solution of salts. Consequently, the glucose had "pumped" the (in effect) overload of sodium of the hypertonic oral fluid from the lumen of the gut into the extracellular spaces of the tissue beyond the wall of the gut; and this excess of sodium—this hypernatraemia—had drawn out water from inside the cells. Wallace comments: "After the fact this probably is true, but it was not that black and white at the time. Also, the adults with hypernatremia did not appear as one would expect—and not as children presented. Further, those patients that did well did very well indeed". In any event, as soon as it was realized that the patients were suffering from hypernatraemia, water was added to the oral fluids and there were no more deaths.

This unfortunate but understandable incident was most distressing to Wallace, who had been in charge of the oral rehydration of these patients. Had they been treated under circumstances where there would have been the normal laboratory backing, it would have been noticed immediately that there was excess sodium in their blood (i.e., they were hypernatraemic), but Wallace had no such backing and therefore no idea what was happening to his patients, and what he should do about them. He states (personal communication, 1980):

Bob was adamant that this must be a simple study—"the 12 year old could do it"! He was even reluctant to let me take a couple of corpsmen with me—and only by chance did we have an EKG [electrocardiogram]. We could do specific gravities and HCO_3—he specifically did not want serum electrolytes [i.e., including sodium]. We argued a great deal about this. He was, as I said, adamant, and was pushed to make it look simple. Incidentally, he had another block, about bacteriology. I wanted cultures on all patients—his remark was that "cholera is a clinical disease"—and Bob was not a clinician. If he'd allowed such studies the use of antibiotics in cholera and the other non-vibrio causes of such diarrhea, with all the spin-offs, would have come to light sooner. This is as I see it—yet, if he'd been swayed from his goal the oral breakthrough might have been a lot longer in coming.

It is clear that Phillips, too, was for several years affected by this incident, although on the surface he remained as laconic and debonair as ever. It was not the deaths that affected him—as a professional, he knew that every time some new advance in the treatment of disease was made it must entail risks. It would show poor understanding to judge this incident harshly, and a lack of gratitude, because the taking of these risks in this case has led, as the quotation at the head of this chapter has it, to crowning of "the most important medical advance this century".[13] What affected Phillips, even when honours were later being heaped on him, was that this incident seemed to him to be a blow to his tidy dream of oral rehydration as a cure for cholera. He did not like things to go wrong. He was so affected that when oral rehydration became a proven reality he was the only one not to realize it. Just as Joseph Priestley is said to have been "the father of modern chemistry [that is, oxygen] who refused to acknowledge his daughter", so Phillips refused to acknowledge the daughter he had fathered. Priestley one can understand because oxygen put an end to his theory of phlogiston as the principal element of matter, but why Phillips refused to acknowledge oral rehydration is a mystery, unless it is that he simply did not like, could not endure, things going wrong. David Nalin (see below), having discussed the matter with Wallace and with Kendrick Hare, believes that the "permanent scar on Bob's mind" was due to Phillips's feeling that if oral rehydration had not been successful in the competent and sophisticated hands of NAMRU-2, it could not work in any hands, and would be disastrous out in the field. However, we shall see that some years later, when oral rehydration had successfully been applied to the actual large-scale cure of cholera in 1968, under his nose, he came around to admitting its efficacy.

Six months after the incident in Manila, at a meeting at the Brookhaven National Laboratory in March 1963 to celebrate the 80th birthday of his old chief at the Rockefeller Institute, D. D. van Slyke, Phillips gave a paper in which he mentioned the physiological experiments he had done in the previous July and August in Manila on the absorption of water and salts from orally administered fluids in cholera patients. He stated: "We have further evidence which suggests that incorporation of glucose in an oral treatment regimen in the average case might completely eliminate the requirement for intravenous fluids". But he added: "I would like to urge caution on this particular point. Such a regimen can only be validated by careful balance studies of the type reported here. The literature on cholera abounds with treatment regimens which have been enthusiastically urged by their proponents in whose hands there has been great success. When the same regimen was tried by others, it appears to be useless" [339]. Nearly two years later, at the second meeting of the Cholera Research Program, in Honolulu in January 1965, he gave a more detailed account of his work in Manila in 1962, but

13. Or, as George Curlin has it, to what "has got to be the most tremendous success story in medicine from basic science to the field".

there was no mention of glucose, and—in the presence of all those cholera experts, who would surely have been interested—no suggestion of oral therapy for cholera [345].[14] Why not? Was he, with the passage of time, too much troubled by the incident in Manila? Another year later, when he gave the Bruce Memorial Lecture to the American College of Physicians in April 1966, he did at least mention oral rehydration with glucose solution in passing, stating that solutions containing 100 mM glucose were effective in mild cases of cholera, but to be effective in more severe cases the glucose concentration had to be raised to 400 mM and this caused severe vomiting and therefore could not be used for therapy [340]. The next year, in November 1967, the year of his triumph, when he received the Albert Lasker Clinical Science Award, Phillips abandoned all hope of oral rehydration. In connection with the vomiting induced by strong glucose solutions, he stated, "Thus the hope for a simple method of treating cholera by this procedure did not materialise" [341].

5. Consolidation of Oral Rehydration

Phillips, it seems, was being governed at that time by whatever it was that upset him in Manila in September 1962 rather than by his usually hard head, for even before he expressed this defeatist conclusion, the possibility of oral rehydration had already been taken up again simultaneously in Dacca and Calcutta, by the PSCRL and the JHCMRT, respectively.

At the PSCRL in Dacca, the question was taken up by Norbert Hirschhorn, who had come to the laboratory in December 1964 from the Office of International Research, NIH, which, as a newly qualified physician, he had joined as part of his military assignment. During the cholera epidemic in the winter of 1966–67 (which was the biggest the PSCRL has so far experienced), he suggested to Phillips (who was by now Director of the PSCRL) that he should be allowed to try oral therapy again because he was concerned that they might run out of intravenous fluids. Hirschhorn relates that Phillips closed the door and told him he would tell him something he was not to tell anybody else. He unlocked a safe and brought out the notes of the fatal trial in the Philippines. He left Hirschhorn to look at the data, with instructions to lock them in the safe again. Hirschhorn did so, then suggested that

---

14. Wallace, who was by then at the JHCMRT in Calcutta, states that there was a great deal of talk about it (unrecorded) at the meeting, and that he and Phillips discussed doing further experiments in Calcutta. Eventually, such experiments were carried out by Wallace's successor in Calcutta, N. F. Pierce.

if an isotonic glucose-electrolyte solution rather than a hypertonic solution were used there should be no risk of hypernatraemia. Phillips replied that the only way to do this was to give an intravenous infusion simultaneously with an oral fluid and "sleep with the patients." This is exactly what Hirschhorn and his colleagues did. They administered the usual electrolyte solution parenterally and an isotonic glucose-electrolyte solution enterally by means of a nasogastric tube (i.e., a tube inserted into the stomach through the nose) to the worst cases, and they set up a cot in the room and stayed with the patients in trepidation, fearing that their confidence might turn out to have been misplaced. But it was not. The patients survived and got well, with far less intravenous fluid than they would otherwise have needed. This initial success apparently encouraged Phillips for the first time, and prompted further studies in collaboration with him, together with the newly arrived physicians D. B. Sachar, J. O. Taylor and J. L. Kinzie, confirming and extending the observations he had made in Manila in the summer of 1962. They showed that in the normal intestine some sugars, e.g., glucose and galactose, which were actively transported through the intestinal epithelium, carried sodium and water with them; sugars that were not transported, e.g., fructose and maltose, did not carry sodium and water with them. They showed further that this effect of glucose was not changed in acute cholera patients; that is, in the cholera patients, there was no impairment of the active transport of sodium across the wall of the gut that was stimulated by actively transported sugars.

These findings were reported for the first time at the second meeting of the Cholera Panel of the U.S.-Japan Cooperative Medical Sciences Program that was held in Palo Alto, California, on 26 to 28 July 1967, and "The implications of this study in delineating the pathophysiology of cholera and in providing a possibly dramatic form of therapy" were discussed [198, 380, 416].

At this same meeting in Palo Alto, members of the Johns Hopkins University School of Medicine, and of the JHCMRT in Calcutta, announced essentially similar experiences and conclusions. In the autumn of 1962, the then Director of the cholera program of the JHCMRT, C.C.J. Carpenter, and his colleague R. B. Sack had paid a visit to the NAMRU-2 group in Manila, where oral therapy of cholera had just been tried. Despite the unfortunate outcome of that trial, Wallace still believed that oral rehydration would be feasible if the correct glucose-electrolyte solutions were used. This was the first Carpenter and Sack had heard of the possibility of oral rehydration. Carpenter was inclined to be sceptical—according to Wallace, very sceptical—about it, and thought it might be worth trying some time. This time did not come until 1966, when Nathaniel F. Pierce arrived in Calcutta to take over the directorship of the cholera program of JHCMRT from Wallace, who had taken over from Carpenter in May 1964. Under Wallace's stimulus, Pierce began testing oral glucose-electrolyte solution. Like Phillips, Wallace was concerned that patients receiving oral fluids should have the same round-the-clock coverage by doctors that patients receiving intravenous fluids required. By the spring of 1967, the Johns Hopkins group under Pierce and J. G. Banwell in Calcutta were getting essentially the same results as the PSCRL group under Hirschhorn and Phillips in Dacca. At the meeting of the U.S.-Japan Cooperative Medical Science Program in Palo Alto in July 1967, Carpenter (who had returned to Johns Hopkins University Medical School) reported on his experiments on dogs in the small intestines of which crude Craig cholera toxin (supplied by NIH) had been introduced. Four hours after this toxin challenge, there was an excretion of isotonic fluid into the gut, twice as much in the jejunum as in the ileum. Perfusion of the gut of unchallenged dogs with electrolyte solutions showed that when glucose was added, absorption of water and salts was increased, and in toxin-challenged dogs the glucose greatly reduced the fluid output into the gut. Once again, it was clear that the glucose-stimulated pathway for the absorption of water electrolytes was unaffected by cholera toxin [8, 15, 47, 348]. Similar results were observed in dogs and rabbits by Hendrix's group at Johns Hopkins, who concluded that active secretion of fluid and electrolyte, rather than failure of absorption, was the functional lesion produced in the gut by cholera toxin. The Johns Hopkins group in Calcutta reported essentially the same observations in human cholera patients, and concluded that in cholera water and sodium moved in both directions, out of the gut and into it, but the flow into the gut was greater than the flow out [8, 9, 15, 47, 59, 348]. They had also studied the effect of glucose on the absorption of water and sodium from the gut of cholera patients, and concluded that glucose enhanced absorption of water and salt without altering the mechanism of cholera stool formation; and that it could be of value in the replacement of fluid and electrolyte losses in cholera patients.

The proceedings of the meeting of the Cholera Panel of the U.S.-Japan Cooperative Medical Sciences Program in Palo Alto in 1967 were brief and fairly informal, and not widely circulated. Both the Dacca and the Calcutta groups eventually published their conclusions on the possibilities of oral rehydration of cholera patients in well-known medical journals nearly simultaneously the following year—the Calcutta group in the May 1968 issue of the *Indian Journal of Medical Research* [347] and the September issue of *Gastroenterology* [349]; the Dacca group in the July issue of the *New England Journal of Medicine* [199]. The Dacca group concluded that "where intravenous fluids are scarce in cholera-affected areas, oral electrolyte solutions containing glucose can supplement parenteral fluids in the treatment of cholera"; the Calcutta group came to the same conclusion, but pointed out that "this report does *not* constitute a recommendation for their general use. . . . Adequate intravenous fluid replacement remains the most important element in the successful management of cholera". Both groups continued their studies on the possibilities of oral rehydration of cholera patients in parallel. We will return first to the Dacca group.

Between July 1967, when, at the meeting in Palo Alto, Phillips joined his colleagues in alluding to oral glucose solutions as "providing a possibly dramatic form of therapy", and November of that year, when he received the Albert Lasker award in New York, he underwent a further change of heart, as we have already seen, and stated that "the hope for a simple method of treating cholera by the procedure did not materialise". After the preliminary experiments on reducing intravenous fluid input in cholera patients by means of oral rehydration with glucose-electrolyte solution, Hirschhorn and Sachar returned to the United States in May 1967, and their places in the clinical research section were taken by David Nalin and Richard Cash. Nalin had learned about the possibilities of oral rehydration when he heard a paper on the subject by Hirschhorn at a meeting in San Francisco shortly before he went to Dacca, and he was eager to take over these studies.

There was no cholera in Dacca that year, and after a few months Nalin and Cash were authorized by Phillips and Hare to proceed to Chittagong, where there was a substantial outbreak. Nalin states that a rather simple protocol had been devised to test the practicability of oral rehydration, and he was assigned to oversee the project, which prior to his arrival had been in the hands of some Bengali physicians because, in Nalin's view, such practical matters were of little interest to the academically inclined scientific staff of the PSCRL. The Chittagong trials appeared to show that oral therapy was "a horrible practical failure", but on analysing the data, Nalin concluded that the reason why they had failed was that the protocol made no provision for linking the patients' intake of oral solutions with their actual losses of fluid. Consequently, some patients were getting too much fluid and others too little, so there was massive over- and underrehydration, and therapeutic failure. Nalin devised a new protocol which he and Cash were able to test on a small number of patients during a small wave of cholera in Dacca in the spring of 1968. These tests confirmed that oral rehydration reduced the need for intravenous fluid, and a paper was sent to the *Lancet*. It was nearly withdrawn, because Phillips was travelling abroad at the time, and when he returned and found that in his absence Nalin and Cash had carried out experiments on oral rehydration after its apparent failure during the Chittagong outbreak, he was displeased. His fears about the possible dangers of this procedure were re-awakened and he was inclined to demand that Nalin withdraw his paper to the *Lancet*. However, Hare "managed to control Bob's pique" and to persuade him that oral therapy could be safely carried out under hospital conditions.

The next step was to carry out a practical field trial. But Phillips still had reservations, for Nalin states that he received a cable from Seal's office, relayed through Hare, telling him to "cease and desist as public health officer from studies of oral therapy". Nalin believed that Seal had been advised that oral therapy might be dangerous, and that his informant had been Phillips.[15] At this point, after a discussion among Mosley (Head of the Epidemiology Division), Hare, Nalin and Cash, Langmuir of CDC was consulted. He agreed to send a number of CDC officers to assist in field studies on oral rehydration under Mosley's epidemiological wing. In this way, Nalin and Cash were able to design the study and supervise the CDC officers without carrying out the study with their own hands, and so avoid being accused of violating the cabled order. Two pairs in succession of CDC officers came to Dacca to carry out field trials in Matlab thana during the cholera epidemic of 1969 (when there was a large number of cases and a shortage of intravenous fluids). The trials were a success. In carefully controlled hospital studies, intravenous fluid requirements were reduced by 80 percent, and in milder cases without shock the need for intravenous fluid was eliminated altogether. It was a *fait accompli*, and Nalin and Cash were now in a strong enough position to present their data to Phillips, who was impressed, and once again converted to the idea of oral rehydration, which he thereafter supported, if he did not enthusiastically advocate it. Indeed, Phillips, Nalin, Cash and others collaborated on a paper on oral maintenance for cholera in adults that was published in the *Lancet* in August 1968 [297]. A number (29) of acute cholera patients were first rehydrated with isotonic intravenous fluid to restore their blood volume and correct their acid-base balance: 10 of them were maintained on the intravenous fluid, 10 received by nasogastric tube a fluid that was slightly hypotonic with respect to electrolytes (254 mMoles/l), supplemented with 111 mMoles glucose/l; the remaining 9 drank the same fluid. They found that, compared with patients receiving only intravenous fluids, patients receiving fluids in the gut by one route or the other needed 80 percent less intravenous fluids to be cured. This greatly reduced requirement for intravenous fluids would

15. Seal cannot recollect such a cable, doubts that he would have used their wording, and no record of it could be found in the files.

make the therapy of acute cholera much more widely available, and mild cases without shock could be treated by oral therapy alone. But they went on to state: "We would emphasise that the continued need for intravenous therapy, and for careful records of intake and output dictate that specially trained staff must supervise the management of cholera patients who are on oral maintenance therapy".

Nalin and Cash continued their investigations on oral therapy for some years. With the staff at Matlab Bazaar, consisting of three physicians, six nurses, three ward-boys and two female attendants, they carried out a trial of oral therapy on a group of 135 cholera patients and confirmed that once the patients were rehydrated intravenously to bring them into fluid, electrolyte and acid-base balance, they could be maintained with a glucose-electrolyte fluid taken by mouth. The ingredients, sodium chloride, sodium bicarbonate, potassium citrate and glucose were obtained at local markets. They were weighted out and put in plastic bags in such quantity that when dissolved in 15 litres of drinking water from a pump well they would give a solution that was slightly hypotonic with respect to salt, and containing 110 mMoles glucose per litre. The use of this fluid enabled them to use 70 percent less intravenous fluid, and the oral treatment regimen became routine at the field hospital at Matlab Bazaar. It could be used without intravenous fluid for mild cases, and it even seemed possible "that if patients with severe cholera were treated from the time of onset, they might be maintained on oral therapy alone". The PSCRL group stated:

> In most areas of the world affected by cholera intravenous fluids are not widely available, and in epidemic conditions stocks are rapidly depleted. Oral maintenance therapy extends the use of limited supplies to far greater numbers of patients. Furthermore, all the necessary ingredients are locally available, can be stored in sealed packets after weighing, and diluted with local water before use. Medical and paramedical personnel were easily trained in the preparation and use of oral solutions [61].

They showed that the absorption of amino acids by the gut, particularly glycine, also stimulated the absorption of sodium and water, and that the effects of glycine and glucose were additive, that is, they were following different pathways through the wall of the gut, neither of them affected in cholera. However, the glycine effect was never applied on a large scale, presumably because glycine is not so easily available in developing countries as glucose [299].

They developed an oral glucose-electrolyte solution, containing a little less sodium and appreciably more potassium than the one previously used for adults, that was suitable for the oral maintenance therapy of cholera patients in all age groups and could be used without previous intravenous rehydration for milder cases that were not in shock [296, 298].

In the meantime, and independently, the group at the JHCMRT in Calcutta were making further observations that were essentially the same as those of the PSCRL in Dacca. In a study of 20 adult males with severe El Tor cholera during May to July 1968, they demonstrated that, after a six-hour period of intravenous rehydration, adequate water and electrolyte balance could be maintained by infusion through a nasogastric tube of a glucose-electrolyte solution. However, at this stage they felt that further studies were needed, and they were not yet ready to recommend the use of orally administered solutions for the routine treatment of cholera [350]. In a further report on this investigation, they stressed that it was unlikely that oral fluids would eliminate the need for intravenous fluids because no other means of fluid replacement would be satisfactory at the time of initial treatment when very rapid fluid replacement is necessary to correct the life-threatening reduction in blood volume and the analkalaemia due to loss of bicarbonate in the stool. In discussing the practical advantages of oral rehydration in areas where cholera is prevalent, they warned: "It should be stressed, however, that this regimen would require at least equally close supervision of the patient as the established method of treatment that depends entirely on intravenous fluids. Regardless of the route of fluid replacement, it is essential that fluid losses be replaced accurately if mortality is to be prevented". They also developed an oral solution that was suitable for the rehydration of children and infants who were most at risk in cholera epidemics and in whom there were technical difficulties in replacing water and salt intravenously [269]. And they made an important recommendation that the efficacy of oral rehydration should be evaluated in persons suffering acute dehydrating diarrhoea that was *not* due to cholera. This was a disorder that often occurs during cholera epidemics and is usually impossible to differentiate from pure cholera on clinical grounds; see Chapter 6 [359]. As we shall see below, non-cholera diarrhoea is not confined to areas where cholera occurs—it is world-wide.

A crucial field trial of oral glucose-electrolyte solution that established its inestimable value in the treatment of cholera beyond any doubt was forced by circumstance on the JHCMRT in the summer of 1971, when its members had to deal with an outbreak of disease among refugees from the war in East Pakistan that led to its independence as the People's Republic of Bangladesh. (See Chapter 11.) The account by Dilip Mahalanabis and his colleagues (three other Indians and one

American) of how they coped with this desperate situation is worth considering in some detail [268].

By the end of May 1971, over 6 million people had fled from the Civil War in East Pakistan and sought refuge in India. In the monsoon months of June and July, cholera broke out in the crowded refugee camps among people who were already weak from starvation, exposure and exhaustion. The death toll was enormous, with a case fatality rate of 30 percent from cholera and cholera-like diarrhoeal disease. At the peak of the epidemic, the JHCMRT sent 2 teams to set up a treatment centre in a subdivisional hospital consisting of 2 cottages with 16 beds at Bongaon, near the border with East Pakistan. When they arrived there on 24 June 1971, there were 350,000 refugees in the immediate vicinity, and 6,000 more pouring in every day. The huge amounts of intravenous fluids, and the transport and the trained personnel, that would be needed to deal with such large numbers effectively simply did not exist; the small amount of intravenous fluids kept at JHCMRT for research purposes was soon exhausted, and supplies from other agencies were limited, and were in any case in a multiplicity of formulations, generally without lactate or bicarbonate. Oral fluids were therefore the only recourse, and the one used contained 3.5 g table salt, 2.5 g baking soda and 22 g glucose per litre (i.e., sodium 90, chloride 60, bicarbonate 30, glucose 122 mMoles/l). Potassium would have been desirable, but it was not obtainable locally. Packets of these ingredients were made up in the library of the JHCMRT in Calcutta. The three simple components were weighed by separate technicians and poured into small polythene bags in a rudimentary assembly line; a fourth technician inserted a label with instructions and sealed the bags with a hot iron. Packets were made up for dissolving in 4 or 16 litres of clean drinking water in drums, and the solutions were dispensed into the patients' cups. Altogether, this "salt factory" turned out enough packets for 50,000 litres of solution and all the materials were obtained locally at a total cost of 750 U.S. dollars.

At the height of the cholera epidemic at the end of June, admissions of patients at the Bongaon Centre reached a peak of 200 a day. The cottages were soon overloaded and patients were placed on the floor, until there was no more floor space; then a large tent containing a hundred canvas cots was set up beside the cottages, often with two adults, or four children, huddled on the same cot.

Patients in shock were treated intravenously at first to counteract fluid deficiency and analkalaemia, and needed less than 3 litres of intravenous fluid when oral supplementation was provided. With these reduced requirements, the meagre daily supplies of intravenous fluids just sufficed.[16] Patients with mild to moderate dehydration, without shock, were given oral glucose-salt solution as soon as they could take it by mouth, within 1 to 4 hours of admission. Adults needed from 10 to 12 litres of solution for recovery. Children who appeared to need potassium were given it often in the form of green coconut water (70 mEq K^+/l). All the patients received tetracycline by mouth. Paramedical workers and relatives were encouraged to give the patients oral solution freely,[17] which they took avidly as long as they were dehydrated; when they were rehydrated, they preferred plain water. It was sometimes difficult to convince paramedical workers, and even physicians, of the massive volumes of fluid needed.

Altogether, 3,700 cholera patients were treated during the 8 weeks from 24 June to 30 August 1971, with an overall case fatality rate of 3.6 percent. In the tent which served as a demonstration ward exclusively under the control of the JHCMRT staff, the case-fatality rate among the 1,200 patients treated was 1.0 percent.

Mahalanabis and his colleagues drew a number of lessons from their experiences: (1) Prepackaging of the glucose-salt mixture and taking it to the field in dry form eliminates error in mixing ingredients on the spot and greatly reduces the cost of transport. Measuring the dry ingredients by volume in teaspoons would simplify matters further.[18] (2) With instructions provided in unmistakably simple terms, intelligent people in camps and villages could be brought to recognize cholera and cholera-like diarrhoea and start oral treatment early. (3) Oral fluid therapy must be started *early* in the illness and *massive* amounts must be given in the initial stage of rehydration. Since overhydration by oral fluids does not occur, the correct amount to give is the amount the patient can take by mouth. (4) Vomiting in the initial stages of rehydration, probably associated with reduced blood volume and/or continuing analkalaemia,[19] can be a serious problem in oral therapy, and is best met by rapid administration of appropriate fluid by any appropriate

---

16. Paramedical workers with no experience of cholera therapy learned how to start intravenous drips after two days of training, but were not experienced enough to judge the required rate and amount of infusion.

17. Some families thought intravenous therapy was more impressive and would try to cajole the staff into using some of their scarce supply, even though the patients were doing well on oral solution alone. Since "saline" was widely known to be a cure for cholera, the oral solution was called "drinking saline", which made it more acceptable.

18. Thus the ingredients for 4 litres of oral solution, in level teaspoons, would be: table salt 4, baking soda 3, commercial glucose (as used in soft drinks), 20.

19. Wallace is satisfied that vomiting can easily be avoided by correcting analkalaemia with oral or intravenous alkali (private communication).

route, including the vein, mouth and the nasogastric tube. The importance of this point could not be overemphasized.

The inescapability of the need for intravenous rehydration in some cases where vomiting cannot otherwise be reduced is also stressed by Nalin and Myron Levine and their colleagues [300] at the Center for Vaccine Development at the University of Maryland School of Medicine in Baltimore.[20] Levine points out that by the time a cholera patient comes for treatment in Dacca or Calcutta he has already been ill for six to eight hours, and what has happened to the patient during that time can at best only be surmised from his history. With the coming of oral therapy, it was assumed, starting with the first stool, that if every volume of stool lost was replaced by an equal volume of fluid given orally, the need for intravenous fluid could be eliminated. If packets of glucose and salts could be got into every home, there need never be another death from cholera. But studies with volunteers in the Center for Vaccine Development suggest that this is not going to be so. In this centre, the natural history of cholera was studied in volunteers from the very beginning of attacks of cholera induced by swallowing large doses of cholera organisms, after neutralization of stomach acidity with sodium bicarbonate. It was observed that in severe cholera there first occurs a six- to eight-hour period of nausea and vomiting which, contrary to previous beliefs, is not due to hypovolaemia and analkalaemia, but to a mechanism which at present is not clear. It is thought to be due to the toxin interfering with the neurological control of the movement of the stomach and causing severe reverse peristalsis. (Shades of Robert Koch! Is this, after all, systemic action of the toxin?) During this six- to eight-hour period of nausea and vomiting, the patient is purging rapidly, at a rate of 800 ml stool per hour, but because of the vomiting he is unable to retain oral glucose-electrolyte solution, even if given warm by means of a nasogastric tube. After six to eight hours, this period of nausea and inability to swallow passes, even though the patient is purging as strongly as ever, and he suddenly becomes able to drink the oral solutions. From this stage on, oral therapy is effective. With most patients coming to treatment centres in endemic areas, this period is over before they are seen by the physician. They arrive with a history of vomiting just when the "toxic phase" is over, and they are rehydrated intravenously or orally. It was this that

---

20. The Center for Vaccine Development is, in fact, a centre for vaccine development. The reason why studies on oral rehydration are carried out there is that the center must be capable of treating cholera patients who volunteer to have the disease induced in them in experiments on cholera vaccines, just as Benenson had to have a cholera ward in a laboratory that was responsible for testing cholera vaccines.

led to the suggestion that restoration of blood volume and correction of analkalaemia by intravenous rehydration caused the nausea and vomiting to go away. But the experiments in Baltimore showed that this was not so. The early part of the natural history of cholera is the period of nausea and vomiting, during which life is in danger unless intravenous therapy is available. When this period is over, the intravenous therapy can be stopped and replaced by oral therapy. Not all patients go through this dangerous period—only those who have a rapidly progressing disease are going to have severe cholera, and this can soon be predicted from the rate of change in the consistency of the stools, and in the increase in their volume. Within a few stools, a judgement can be made as to whether a patient is going to need intravenous treatment. Nalin and Levine concluded that no matter how much progress is made with oral therapy, there will always be a need for treatment centres where a minority of patients can be rehydrated intravenously. They point out that even in Dacca only 5 percent of all outpatients seeking treatment have severe dehydration, and that many more in the villages have diarrhoea and never seek treatment. Consequently, a system of village-level oral maintenance would have to spend a large proportion of its available resources every year in order to reach a very small proportion (about 3 per 1,000) of cases with potentially severe cholera. In Bangladesh, with 80 million people at risk, a system of home therapy would be far more costly, and far less effective, than a system with an adequate number of rural treatment centres where adequate oral therapy could be applied to the most severe cases of diarrhoea, with limited supplies of intravenous fluids for initial rehydration when this is really necessary. Nalin and Levine believe that the logical step is to do further research on the pathophysiology of the early vomiting with a view to finding a means to control it. Then the residual need for intravenous therapy would be eliminated.

It could perhaps be argued that Nalin and Levine take too pessimistic a view when they compare their experiences with the artificially induced disease in artificial surroundings with the natural disease in its natural circumstances. The case rate of the natural disease is very low. In Bangladesh, only 1 out of every 2,000 people exposed to the disease actually gets it; in the Center for Vaccine Development, where the volunteers are first given bicarbonate of soda to neutralize the acidity of the stomach, which acts as a natural barrier to invasion of the gut by the cholera vibrio, and are then given a far greater dose of vibrios than is likely to be encountered naturally, nearly 100 percent of those challenged get the disease. The artificially induced disease is therefore probably far fiercer than the natural disease. Is the "toxic" phase of vomiting perhaps an artifact? Bhide and Modak of the Haffkine Institute showed in 1969 that the stomach is just as capable of reacting to cholera toxin as the small bowel [28]. In nature, the stomach is not exposed to the toxin, but in the artificially alkalinized volunteers in Maryland, the heavy dose of vibrios may multiply and produce toxin in the stomach, and perhaps the resultant accumulation of fluid in it may be the cause of vomiting. How many children and infants suffering from the natural disease actually do go through the dangerous "toxic" phase? They are brought for treatment in a parlous state after six to twelve hours, but would they have got into the parlous state if they had been given oral fluids from the first moment of danger? Moreover, Nalin and Levine, with their volunteers in a well-equipped ward in Baltimore, could not and dared not fail to be far more cautious than circumstances would ever permit under the natural conditions prevailing in a developing country. They could not take the slightest risk; but in a developing country, risks may have to be taken because there are no alternatives to fall back on. And so far we have been considering only one diarrhoeal disease, cholera. In fact, as we shall now see, there are many other diarrhoeal diseases, all over the world, that can be treated by oral rehydration and none of these is as fierce as cholera. While some intravenous rehydration may be essential in cholera-endemic areas, it may not be quite so necessary in other diarrhoea-endemic areas.

6. The Other Diarrhoeal Diseases, World-wide

The seventh cholera pandemic spread cholera farther around the world than it used to be, although the ratio of cases to inapparent infection with the more pervasive El Tor biotype of the vibrio is only about a tenth of that of the classical biotype. The incidence of cholera is still higher in the Ganges delta than elsewhere, and still a very serious cause of deaths, especially in infants. But even in this area, cholera is numerically not the most important of the diarrhoeal diseases. Non-cholera diarrhoea, due mainly to rotaviruses, *Escherichia coli* and dysentery bacilli, far outnumbers cholera diarrhoea. In the Philippines, 95 percent of diarrhoeal disease is not cholera. In other parts of the world, the rest of Asia, Africa and Latin America, non-cholera diarrhoea is responsible for more infant deaths than any other disease in developing countries. Five hundred million episodes of diarrhoea occur in infants every year, killing 5 to 18 million of them [376]. Diarrhoeal disease is not confined to the developing countries. In Europe and North America, it is sixth among the causes of death among children between the ages of 1 and 4 years [376].

These different enteropathies produce diarrhoea in different ways, of which those of cholera and enterotoxic *E. coli* diarrhoea are understood, yet patients can all be treated by oral rehydration. The first demonstration of this was by Nalin and Cash in Dacca. They showed that non-cholera diarrhoeal disease could also be treated by oral glucose-electrolyte therapy in exactly the same way as genuine cholera cases [295]. This realization that other diarrhoeas than cholera could be treated by oral therapy with glucose-electrolyte solutions was tremendously important. It extended the use of the glucose-electrolyte solution from Bangladesh and India to all parts of the world where children suffer from diarrhoea. Hirschhorn and Cash treated Apache children in the Whiteriver Indian Hospital in the Fort Apache Reservation in Arizona by oral rehydration. They were suffering from diarrhoea caused by *Shigella flexneri, Sh. sonnei, E. coli, Salmonella typhimurum* (and possibly by viruses), and, after partial intravenous rehydration, drank the glucose-electrolyte solution avidly to the point of normal hydration, so that the investigators were encouraged to hope that "semi-skilled personnel and family members could be allowed to treat a large proportion of children with diarrhoea in adverse settings" [196]. Children hospitalized with diarrhoea who were strong enough to drink could take enough hypotonic glucose-electrolyte solution for volume replacement and maintenance, and correction of acidosis. This *ad libitum* oral therapy proved to be "effective, comfortable and inexpensive", and the solution was easily made up with standard U.S. measuring spoons; thus, half a level teaspoon each of common salt and bicarbonate of soda, a quarter of a teaspoon of potassium chloride and two tablespoons of glucose, stored in capped plastic vials and dissolved in one litre of water when needed (at a cost of 2.5 U.S. cents), would provide the appropriate solution, which proved to be "most beneficial in areas of the world where infantile diarrhoea is an endemic, debilitating, and often fatal disease" [200, 201].

The most important of the debilitating effects of chronic diarrhoea in children (which Rohde and Northrop class as fluid-electrolyte malnutrition) [376] is the chronic undernourishment (or protein-energy malnutrition) which results from the forced fasting that the diarrhoea imposes, together with anorexia and malabsorption of the reduced nutrients that they are able to ingest [275]. Hirschhorn (whose devotion to the treatment of infantile diarrhoea remains undiminished since he pioneered oral rehydration in Dacca in 1966) has shown that this malnutrition can be reversed with oral therapy, so that the children regain their appetites and flourish, and their mothers are pleased to feed them [197]. Chronic diarrhoea has also recently been implicated in the aetiology of the disease of the eye, xerophthalmia, in India, due to vitamin A deficiency resulting from malabsorption of the vitamin [302].

The principles of oral rehydration are now well understood. The real problem now is the practical, logistical and sociological problem of "taking the science where the diarrhoea is" [376], of how to make the ingredients even cheaper, how to measure them out, what containers to put them into, how to get them to the people that need them, how to transfer responsibility for the therapeutic process from the physician to paramedical staff, and even to the patient's mother.

As to reducing the cost of the ingredients—the only one whose cost can be reduced is that of the sugar. Glucose (as used to sweeten soft drinks) is fairly expensive compared with the ordinary household cane or beet sugar, sucrose (which is a disaccharide—a compound of glucose and fructose), and in many parts of the world glucose is unobtainable. Sucrose as such does not promote the absorption of sodium in the gut, but the gut contains disaccharidase, which breaks sucrose down into glucose and fructose, and Nalin has shown there is no objection to using sucrose since it does in effect promote salt and water absorption in patients suffering diarrhoea from cholera and rotavirus infection very nearly as well as glucose [292, 301, 383]. Thus, all the ingredients for oral therapy can be obtained in market places all over the world.[21]

As to packaging of the ingredients of oral solutions, all kinds of packets and sachets have been made up,[22] and various kinds of measuring spoons for the solids and measuring vessels for the water have been devised [109, 293]. The "appropriate technology" of providing for world-wide oral rehydration is "now a well-established and rapidly growing health resource" [103].

As to the question of delivering the oral therapy to the patient, probably the best way to deal with it is to couple the range of severity of the disease with a range of management. Where the disease is mild enough, it could probably be dealt with by mothers giving the fluid to their sick infants by mouth. The distribution of the ingredients of the fluid is more a matter of good local sense than medical expertise. In Indonesia, for example, oral glucose-electrolyte is distributed throughout the country by a vast network of 70,000 village retailers, together with contraceptives and traditional herbal mixtures. A system like this would probably suffice for a situation when the diarrhoea is not severe. When it is more severe, provision would have to be made for a number of treatment centres where paramedicals could regulate oral therapy under

21. In Bangladesh, for example, crude local salt (*lobon*) and sugar (molasses, *gur*) are used.

22. Thus UNICEF, for example, has made a million packages of Oralyte (3.5 g sodium chloride, 2.5 g sodium bicarbonate, 1.5 g potassium chloride, 20 g glucose—to be dissolved in 1 litre of water), and has stated that it will assist any nation to develop local production facilities [376].

simple instructions, using the pulse and the rate of respiration as guides to the degree of dehydration, and thirst and the number of stools to determine the rate of therapy—after thirst is assuaged, a glass of fluid is taken for each stool [376]; but occasionally intravenous therapy will be necessary and then there will have to be a physician at hand, with the necessary sterile fluid and the equipment for administering it.

The implications of preventing deaths in infants may go beyond the saving of millions of lives every year—there are those who believe that the saving of infants will result in a lowering of the birth rate. Thus, for example, Rohde states that two-thirds of all completed families (i.e., with mothers older than 45 years) in rural Indian villages have had two or more children die, and that women who had lost children when their families were small subsequently showed a higher birth rate—as if they "overshot" the number of desired children when the fate of their children was uncertain [375]. Similar views had previously been expressed by Greenough [176]. It is perhaps this consideration, and the link between diarrhoeal disease and malnutrition, that have led to a reorientation of the objectives of the Cholera Research Laboratory in Dacca. We shall see in Chapter 11 that now, with its name changed to the International Centre for Diarrhoeal Disease Research, Bangladesh, it has broadened its scope: The new centre will "undertake research, training and information dissemination on diarrhoeal diseases and directly related subjects of nutrition and population with special relevance to developing countries" [160].

X

The Biochemistry of Cholera

1. Introduction

Investigations into the immunology of cholera have not yet led to a means of preventing the disease as simple, effective and long-lasting as those that have been so successful with the two other exotoxinoses, diphtheria and tetanus. However, they have brought us much closer to an understanding of the immunobiology of the enteron, which in its turn may still lead to a means of immunizing against the disease, and perhaps against other infectious diseases affecting other mucosal surfaces besides that of the small intestine. Investigations into the physiology of cholera have led to a very simple and effective means of curing not only this disease, but the other infectious diarrhoeal diseases that cause incalculable discomfort, misery, malnutrition and death world-wide. Investigations into the biochemistry of cholera have not yet yielded any knowledge that can practically be applied to the prevention or cure of the disease, but they did lead, during the 1970s, to such an explosion in knowledge of the biochemistry (now, alas, called "molecular biology") of the disease that it is today perhaps better understood than that of any other infectious disease. And it promises to have implications that go beyond the disease itself, and perhaps other diseases, towards an understanding of the cells that make up the organs and tissues of the body, the way they react to the action of hormones and drugs, and the way they interact with each other. Those who were fortunate enough to be concerned in these stirring developments cannot fail to have been moved by the experience, as were those who, in the late 1950s and the 1960s, were the pioneers in the understanding of the nature of cholera and the means of treating it. Perhaps not quite as much moved, for as the field expanded into areas less and less concerned with the disease itself, and passed into hands that had never dealt with the manifestations of the disease, even in experimental animals, let alone suffering humanity, it became more like everyday modern experimental biological science, more competitive and so less humane, less inspiring, less agreeable, less comradely.

Since the developments in the 1970s came from so many directions, it may be helpful to try and summarize them first before giving a more detailed account of them. The period is marked by several milestones in the form of discoveries or developments that themselves generated additional bursts of related research. These milestones were as follows.

1968. The elevation of the understanding of the mode of action of cholera toxin to the realms of biochemistry began with the realization that adenosine-3'5'-cyclic monophosphate (cAMP) could bring about alterations in the transport of ions across intestinal membranes which were very similar to those brought about by cholera toxin. cAMP is the product of the action of the enzyme adenylate cyclase on the substrate adenosine triphosphate (ATP); it is the universal "second messenger" that mediates the effect of many hormones that act by stimulating adenylate cyclase in susceptible cells. This led to the discovery that cholera toxin brought about its effects by activating the adenylate cyclase in intestinal epithelial cells. It was a finding of the utmost importance, for not only did it at last provide a relatively easy way of studying the action of cholera toxin on suspensions of cells *in vitro* rather than in ligated ileal loops or the shaven skin of animals, but, in the wider and more fundamental field of biochemistry, it presented cholera toxin as a tool for the study of the mechanism of action of that universally important but hitherto very unapproachable enzyme, adenylate cyclase. Another important discovery was that the toxin activated adenylate cyclase in all animal cells, not just the epithelial cells of the small intestine.

1970. The next milestone was the preparation of highly purified cholera toxin ("choleragen"), and its distribution to many workers all over the world. Without this, the greater proportion of the work to be discussed in this chapter could not have been done.

1971–1973. Next came the demonstration of the existence of a receptor for cholera toxin, and its identification as a ganglioside—a particular ganglioside, galactosyl-N-acetylgalactosaminyl-(N-acetylneuraminyl)-galactosylglucosyl-ceramide, to give it its full name,[1] or GM_1 to give it its most used name, or GGnSLC, to give it its most sensible name. This ganglioside avidly binds to cholera toxin and its inert component, choleragenoid (see below); it was to play its part in determining the molecular structure of cholera toxin, and in defining the means by which the toxin gains access to the interior of the susceptible cell. This and

---

1. Which nevertheless, by the austere standards of the International Union of Pure and Applied Chemistry, is still a rather trivial name.

other gangliosides appear to be important components of cell membranes and were to be implicated, or suggested, as cell membrane receptors for other bacterial toxins, for hormones and for other active substances, such as viruses and interferon.

1970–1976. During this period, the molecular structure of cholera toxin, or at least our present conception of it, was worked out. In 1969, an inert protein (choleragenoid) of lower molecular weight than the toxin had been found in cholera culture filtrates; it was antigenically related to the toxin, and like it, capable of binding to cells, and, as shown in 1971, to ganglioside. It was shown that choleragenoid, binding to intestinal epithelial cells, blocked the action of subsequently applied toxin. Thus it appeared that choleragenoid was part of the cholera toxin molecule, and was responsible for the binding of the toxin to the ganglioside receptor in the membranes of the susceptible epithelial cells. If choleragenoid was to be an inactive binding component of the toxin, then there was the implication that there had to be another component that was active and capable for activating adenylate cyclase. The idea of a bipartite toxin consisting of a binding (B) part and an active (A) part was readily acceptable at the time, since it had recently been shown that diphtheria toxin had such a constitution. The converging work of several groups soon confirmed that cholera toxin, with a molecular weight of 84,000, was constituted of a choleragenoid B component with a molecular weight of 58,000 (itself consisting of five subunits of molecular weight 11,600) and an active A-component of a molecular weight about 28,000, which in turn consisted of an A_1 subunit which was active only when it was introduced into the cell (see below), and an A_2 subunit which formed the link with the B-component.

1974–1975. The next milestone was the development of a system of "broken cells" which cholera toxin (or its active component) could enter directly, without having to pass through the cell membrane, and so activate the adenylate cyclase system. This led to a much clearer understanding of the action of the toxin. Previously, research had been hampered by the fact that there was a lag of at least 30 minutes between the application of the toxin to the cell surface and the beginning of its effect. The cell membrane had always stood in the way and the toxin had first to combine with the receptor and thus be passed through the membrane before it could reach its target (the adenylate cyclase system on the inner surface of the membrane). This prevented a detailed study of the kinetics of the activation process, and of any requirements it might have. Once activation of adenylate cyclase by toxin takes place, the toxic effect persists for days, long after excess toxin has been removed. (This delayed and persistent action of the toxin is in contrast with that of hormones that activate adenylate cyclase. They act instantly, but only as long as they are present, and the action ceases as soon as the hormone is washed off.) In pigeon red-blood cells (erythrocytes) the adenylate cyclase response to toxin took place after the usual delay, but when the cell membrane was perforated, or lysed, the activation of adenylate took place immediately with no lag, and furthermore the A_1 subunit of the toxin, which hitherto had not been found to have any more than a slight action on intact cells, had the same immediate effect, thus opening the way to a further understanding of the molecular basis of the action of the toxin. Not surprisingly, the idea arose that the A_1 subunit of cholera toxin (like the A subunit of diphtheria toxin) was an enzyme, in this case an enzyme that activated adenylate cyclase.

1975. At this stage, the very important fact was discovered that the activation of adenylate cyclase by cholera toxin or its A_1 subunit required the presence of the compound nicotinamide adenine dinucleotide (NAD), in which adenine diphosphate ribose, ADP-ribose, is coupled to nicotinamide. It had been found that the toxin would not activate adenylate cyclase in suspensions of lysed pigeon red cells unless these lysed cells were suspended in the fluid (the cytosol) that had been contained in their interiors, and the major part of the reason for this was that the cytosol contained NAD. Here again we have a similarity with diphtheria toxin, the active component of which also requires NAD for its action, which is to catalyze the cleavage of adenine diphosphate ribose (ADP-ribose) from NAD and its transfer to another enzyme, in this case the Elongation Factor (EF2), which is involved in protein synthesis. In the course of this reaction, nicotinamide is liberated. It had been shown that in the case of cholera toxin, the ADP-ribose is transferred to an arginine-containing receptor, and this transfer of ADP-ribose may be relevant to the next milestone.

1976–1978. It now became clear that research on the biochemistry of the action of cholera toxin has much wider implications than were first thought possible. It provides an insight into the mechanism of action of adenylate cyclase and the regulation of its activity, and this is a matter of fundamental scientific interest, reaching beyond the simple matter of turning the bowels to water. An important example of this is the way in which the activation of adenylate cyclase by the toxin seems to parallel the regulation of the enzyme under normal physiological circumstances by a substance closely related to the substrate of the enzyme ATP. This is guanosine triphosphate, GTP, which differs only slightly from ATP. The enzyme adenylate cyclase, in addition to having a subunit which carries out the specific catalytic activity of the enzyme, has a regulatory subunit which determines the degree of activity. It is now known that in the normal action of the enzyme, GTP, by binding with the regulatory subunit, causes an activation of the catalytic subunit, and this activation is "turned off" as soon as the GTP is hydrolysed by the enzyme GTP-ase. If artificial, nonhydrolysable analogues are used, the activation of adenylate cyclase persists. Such persistent activation of adenylate cyclase is one of the most striking features of the action of cholera toxin. Thus, it seems that cholera toxin may act by causing in the regulatory subunit of adenylate cyclase an irreversible change rather than the transient on-off changes that occur during the normal regulation of enzymic activity. This is where the cholera toxin-catalysed transfer of ADP-ribose may come in. Recent evidence suggests that this irreversible change in the regulatory subunit of adenylate cyclase may be due to the transfer by the toxin of ADP-ribose to the GTP-ase associated with the regulatory subunit, thus inhibiting it, and thereby preventing the hydrolysis of the GTP, thus blocking the normal "turn-off" of the activation process.

We will now discuss these developments in the chemistry of cholera, as they were seen at the end of 1980, in more detail.

2. The Release of the Second Messenger

In 1971, Earl W. Sutherland, Professor of Physiology at Vanderbilt University, Nashville, was very justly awarded the Nobel Prize for Medicine or Physiology for his work on the second messenger. The second messenger is the ubiquitous molecule adenosine-3′ 5′-cyclic monophosphate (cAMP) that is generated from the substance adenosine triphosphate (ATP) by the enzyme adenylate cyclase which is activated in response to any one of a number of first messengers, the hormones [412]. Indeed, cAMP can simulate so many effects of so many hormones and other active agents in so many tissues and organisms (including plants and slime moulds) that at first it was hard to believe that this one molecule could be so universally active. But this area of research continued to expand so vigorously and fruitfully that there can now be no question about the great importance of cAMP.[2] In a secondary way, the concentration of cAMP in tissues is also regulated by the enzyme phosphodiesterase, which breaks it down, and this mechanism in turn can be controlled by drugs such as theophylline that inhibit the phosphodiesterase and thus allow the buildup of cAMP concentrations.

---

2. Sutherland's discovery came at a time when students were apt to be concerned about whether academic research had any practical applications to the betterment of man's material lot. When asked by a student whether the information he had gained would have any practical application, he replied, "There is one kind of information that I am reasonably sure cannot be applied. And that is information that we do not have" [412].

In 1968, in the comparatively early days of cAMP, Michael Field of the Harvard Medical School (who at the time was not concerned with the cholera problem) showed that the effects of the antidiuretic hormone vasopressin in stimulating the transport of ions across a sheet of rabbit ileal epithelial cells in an Ussing chamber could be imitated by theophylline or by solutions of cAMP itself. When vasopressin was added to the serosal side of the ileal sheet (i.e., the "blood" side, opposite the lumenal side), there was an increase in short-circuit current across the tissue, signifying the passage of ions. The similar increase in SCC brought about by cAMP or theophylline was considerably reduced when chloride or bicarbonate ions were excluded from the solution in the chamber bathing the tissue. It therefore appeared that the SCC elicited by these agents was the result of the active secretion of chloride and bicarbonate ions by the rabbit ileum [125].

Shortly after this, in the spring of 1968, W. B. Greenough, at that time at Johns Hopkins University Medical School, was invited by his former Dacca colleague N. Hirschhorn to come to Boston to give a seminar on cholera in human patients and experimental dogs. Field was one of "all of five people" (Greenough's words) who came to the seminar. It immediately became apparent that Field and Greenough had certain experiments to do together, and within two weeks Field was down in Baltimore with his Ussing chambers to make a start on them. Three or four weeks later, Greenough went to work in Field's laboratory in Boston, where they were better equipped to measure cAMP and adenylate cyclase. They found that when cholera toxin (in the form of a dialysed culture filtrate) was added to the mucosal side of isolated rabbit ileum, these was an active secretion of chloride ions (and a flow of water) from the serosal to the mucosal side, and a consequent increase in SCC similar to that caused by cAMP and theophylline [124]. Similar observations were made with sheets of human intestinal mucosa, in this case also with prostaglandin El, another agent which causes elevations in cAMP levels [1, 123]. In all these experiments, the only difference that was observed between the action of cholera toxin and that of the cAMP-elevating agents was that the latter all acted immediately, whereas the effects of cholera toxin were not apparent until after a lag of at least half an hour. At that time, this lag in the action of cholera toxin was not yet understood, and was for some time to provide a barrier to the detailed understanding of the mechanisms of action of the toxin. As early as 1970, it was realized by Schafer (formerly of the JHCMRT in Calcutta) and his colleagues at the University of Minnesota that the delay might be due to the inefficient or slow entry of the toxin to its site of action within the cell [386]. A similar conclusion was reached by Field [120] when considering some interesting but rather neglected observations in Greenough's laboratory, where it had been found that cholera toxin could cause break-down of glycogen (see below) in disrupted blood platelets without the lag that was characteristic of unbroken cells [468]. We shall see that it was not until 1975 that a comparable system was found for the study of the direct action of cholera toxin on a cell by breaking down the barrier to entry of the toxin. Meanwhile, however, the existence of the lag in the action of the toxin on intact cells had a beneficial influence, since it directed many investigations to the question of how toxin became bound to cells, with the result that more is now known about the cell receptor for cholera toxin than for any other toxin.

In spite of the time-lag difference between the actions of cholera toxin and hormones and drugs, etc., it was becoming clear that cholera toxin was calling the second messenger into action in intestinal mucosal cells. This was directly confirmed by Schafer, who found elevated levels of cAMP in mucosal cells of dogs treated with cholera toxin [386]; and by Chen, Rhode and Sharp at the Cholera Research Laboratory in Dacca, who found elevated levels of cAMP in mucosal cells taken by means of the Crosby capsule from human cholera patients—levels which dropped to normal in convalescence [72, 73].[3]

The elevated levels of cAMP in toxin-treated cells could be due either to the activation of the adenylate cyclase in the gut epithelial cells, or to inhibition of the phosphodiesterase that normally breaks down cAMP in the cell. Sharp and Hynie at the Massachusetts General Hospital in Boston, and Field and his colleagues, showed that it was the former, the activation of adenylate cyclase, that brought about the accumulation of cAMP [223, 396], and that this was not due to the synthesis of new adenylate cyclase in the cells, but activation of the enzyme already present.

At about this time, a discovery was made that had no direct connection with cholera but was important from the point of view of biochemistry; it was that cholera toxin acted not only on epithelial cells of the small intestine, but virtually on all animal cells; the action of the toxin was always to activate adenylate cyclase, but the cAMP that resulted promoted different reactions according to the cell that the toxin was acting on. The first of these activities of cholera toxin that had nothing to do with cholera were shown by Martha Vaughan at the National Heart, Lung,

---

3. In 1963–64 in Dacca, Greenough and Gordon used to discuss what caused the huge outpouring of fluid in cholera, and Gordon began to think of a hormonal mechanism, possibly a pancreatic hormone. To the extent that cholera toxin mimics a hormone by bringing about its effects by raising the level of cAMP in the susceptible tissue, these thoughts were prophetic.

and Blood Institute (NHLBI) in Bethesda, in collaboration with the two seasoned cholera researchers W. B. Greenough and N. F. Pierce of the Johns Hopkins University. Greenough happened to be doing some research on fatty acid metabolism in the then National Heart, Lung, and Blood Institute at NIH in 1967, where he met Vaughan, who had been interested in the hormone-activated break-down of fats (lipolysis) in fat cells since 1960, and had shown that it was mediated by cAMP. This idea did not gain ready acceptance at that time because the only systems in which cAMP was known to play a part were those that had been studied by Sutherland, involving glycogen break-down in liver and the adrenal gland. A role for cAMP in another process in another tissue was more than many people were willing to accept— cAMP could not be taken seriously if it promoted so many different events. But by the time Greenough came to the Heart Institute in 1967, the idea of cAMP as a mediator in hormone-stimulated lypolysis was accepted and Vaughan was focusing attention on fat cell adenylate cyclase. She and Greenough incubated fat cells with cholera toxin, and after a lag phase of one to two hours observed that lipolysis took place [436]. Greenough was later to use this toxin-stimulated lipolysis in fat cells as a means for assaying cholera toxin *in vitro* that was much used at the Cholera Research Laboratory in Dacca. Since the work with fat cells, several other effects of cholera toxin were observed that depended on elevated cAMP levels, including increased glycogen break-down in liver [175, 468], induction of steroidogenesis in cultured adrenal cells [105], inhibition of DNA synthesis in human fibroblasts [202], inhibition of macromolecular synthesis in mouse spleen cells [411] and induction of pineal enzyme in culture [281]. The interesting point about these observations is that cholera toxin, unlike the hormones, has not been found to show any tissue specificity. It seems to be capable of acting on widely differing cells which all react in their own characteristic way, depending on the nature of the cAMP-dependent reaction that takes place in them. This universal action of the toxin suggested that the receptor for the toxin on the outer surface of membranes was common to nearly all cells, and this has proved to be the case.

3. The Provision of Pure Cholera Toxin

Most of the work discussed up to now was done with impure— indeed, highly impure—cholera toxin, in the form of cholera culture filtrates prepared as they were needed (by those who knew at least how to culture the cholera vibrio), or in the form of the freeze-dried Wyeth-001 crude culture filtrate prepared under contract for the Cholera Advisory Committee and distributed on demand to anybody with reasonable credentials who applied for it. But now that studies on the action of cholera toxin had entered the realms of "molecular biology" it was necessary to have pure cholera toxin—a preparation that could confidently be said to consist of the toxin and nothing but the toxin, uncontaminated by any other active material, or by any inhibitory material. We have seen in Chapter 8 how R. A. Finkelstein prepared such a purified toxin, and how he so generously distributed it to those who needed it (and sometimes to those who did not really need it). The great progress that was made in the understanding of the molecular structure of the toxin, and in the biochemistry of its action, would not have been possible without this wide-spread distribution of the toxin, later done by NIH, who contracted for it, and still later by industry that sprang up to meet the demand. Few of those who received the pure toxin from Finkelstein, and used it to good effect, would have been capable of growing the cholera cultures on the necessary scale, and then of going on to extract the toxin from the culture filtrates and purify it to as complete a degree of purity as it is possible to determine. Some might have been able to handle the cultures, others the purification (and the assays of toxin entailed), but few could have handled both. The purification and supply of cholera toxin were important enough. What was also important, and essential in the development of our understanding of the structure of the cholera toxin molecule, was the recognition and isolation, and supply, of choleragenoid, the inert component (B) of cholera toxin that recognizes the toxin receptor on the cell membrane and binds to it, and in so doing facilitates the passage of the active (A) component through the membrane and its access to the adenylate cyclase system.[4]

4. The Toxin Receptor

The discovery and identification of the cholera toxin receptor on the membranes of susceptible cells owes its origin to Paul Ehrlich's dictum *Corpora non agunt nisi fixata* (things will not act unless fixed), and the subsequent discovery by Wassermann and Takaki in 1898 of the fixation of tetanus toxin by nervous tissue, not long after the discovery of the toxin. Ehrlich's side chain theory contained some ideas about the nature and action of toxins that have recently been confirmed, as we shall see

4. Since he started keeping records, Finkelstein provided pure cholera toxin and choleragenoid, free, to more than 400 individuals in most scientific countries on every continent, including Iron Curtain countries. In addition, he provided large quantities of these materials under various contracts.

in this chapter, and some ideas about the generation and nature of antibodies that have not stood the test of time. He held that toxins (and other active substances) contained an active component—the "toxophore"—and a component—the "haptophore"—that fixed the toxin to a receptor in the protoplasm and thus enabled the toxophore to express its activity. This appears to be true of some toxins today. His "side chains" were less fortunate. He held that the protoplasm of the body contained highly complex organic molecules consisting of a stable central group to which were attached less stable side chains. These side chains were the receptors that bound to the haptophore of toxins. When the side chains bound toxins, they split off from the large complex molecules of the protoplasm and became soluble antibodies circulating in the blood; in the meantime, the protoplasm generated more side chains [110]. Wassermann, in Koch's Institut für Infectionskrankheiten in Berlin, pursued both these notions of toxin fixation and antitoxic side chains when he concluded that tetanus toxin, which produced such pronounced neurological manifestations, must be fixed by nervous tissue, and that the receptor was the antitoxin waiting to be separated from the parent molecule. He believed he would have a means of artificial immunization if he could lay his hands on the receptor [451].[5] He and Takaki showed that if spinal cord or brain tissue were emulsified with saline and mixed with a few lethal doses of tetanus toxin and injected into mice, the mice would survive. The material producing this effect was not water-soluble, since if the emulsion of nervous tissue were filtered the residue had the antitoxic property but not the filtrate. They concluded that the toxin was fixed by the nervous tissue injected along with it and was therefore unable to be fixed to the nerve cells of the injected animals. Tissue from other organs such as liver, kidney, spleen, bone marrow, had no such effect. Brain tissue was better at fixing the toxin than spinal cord tissue, which they considered surprising since tetanus toxin was thought—quite correctly—to act on the spinal cord [452].

The phenomenon of the fixation of tetanus toxin by susceptible tissue attracted a great deal of attention, since at that time it was believed that the harmful effects of all pathogenic bacteria were due to toxins (see Chapter 2).[6] Several investigators sought to identify the material

5. Curiously enough, Wassermann referred to the receptor side chains more than once as "toxophores". Presumably he meant "toxophil", the adjective which Ehrlich devised to denote the toxin-binding property of the side chains.

6. Wassermann suggested that the similar searches for toxin-fixing materials should be made in the susceptible tissues of other toxins, but did not suggest what toxins, which is not surprising, because tetanus toxin was the only toxin known at the time that pointed so markedly at its susceptible tissue. We shall see such an opportunity was not to be presented again until more than 70 years later, with cholera toxin.

in nervous tissue that was responsible for the fixation, and the one who came nearest the truth—but not near enough—was the great Karl Landsteiner, then working in the Pathological-Anatomical Institute in Vienna.[7] He removed the acetone- and ether-soluble material from brain, then extracted the residue with hot ethyl alcohol. On cooling the solution, a white precipitate, known in those days as "protagon", settled out, and Landsteiner found that this material had a greater tetanus toxin-fixing capacity than any of the other brain fractions he tested [242]. Protagon is not a single substance, but a mixture, and Wassermann's former collaborator, Takaki (now moved to the Institute of Physiological Chemistry in Strasbourg), believed that its main components, water-insoluble cerebrosides, were responsible for the binding of tetanus toxin, but he was puzzled by the fact that there was far more cerebroside in white matter than in grey, yet grey matter was far better at binding tetanus toxin than white [415]. The problem was then forgotten until 50 years later, when it was taken up again by van Heyningen at the University of Oxford. He confirmed that the tetanus toxin-binding material could be found in the protagon fraction of brain, but it was not the water-insoluble cerebroside in it; it was water-soluble ganglioside that formed an insoluble complex with it [429]. Grey matter was much richer in ganglioside than is white. It had been discovered in 1935 to 1942 by Ernst Klenk of the University of Cologne in the brains of infants dead of Tay-Sachs disease [230]. At the time, all that was known about ganglioside was that it occurred in grey matter, and that it was amphiphilic, that is, soluble both in organic fat solvents, such as chloroform, and in water, because one end of the molecule was fatty, consisting of long-chain stearic acid and sphingosine, and the other end was sugary, consisting of several glucose and galactose residues and N-acetyl galactosamine and, notably, N-acetylneuraminic (or sialic) acid. It was not known how these various residues were put together, nor was it realized that there were several gangliosides, differing in the number of sialic acid residues they contained and where they were attached. By 1961, the structures of the four most abundant gangliosides had been determined by Richard Kuhn [238]. These structures (see two of them in Figure 10.1) are conveniently conveyed in McCluer's notation as GGnSLC, SGGnSLC, GGnSSLC, and SGGnSSLC, where G=galactosyl, Gn=N-acetylgalactosaminyl, S=sialosyl, L=lactosyl (i.e., galactosyl-glucosyl) and C=ceramide (i.e., stearylsphingosine) [264]. The only sialyl residue that is not split from the ganglioside molecule by the enzyme sialidase (or neuraminidase, produced by the cholera

7. He joined the Rockefeller Institute in New York in 1922, and won the Nobel Prize for Physiology or Medicine in 1930.

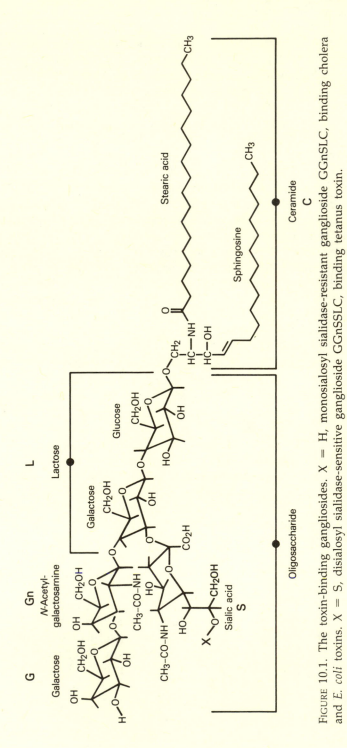

FIGURE 10.1. The toxin-binding gangliosides. X = H, monosialosyl sialidase-resistant ganglioside GGnSLC, binding cholera and *E. coli* toxins. X = S, disialosyl sialidase-sensitive ganglioside GGnSSLC, binding tetanus toxin.

vibrio) is the one directly attached to the galactosyl moiety of the lactose component. Van Heyningen showed that the ganglioside that fixed tetanus toxin best was the sialidase-labile GGnSSLC [431]. This seemed at the time to be a useful step forward in the study of the mode of action of tetanus toxin at the molecular level, and it may well turn out to have been so, but as yet little further progress has been made.

In 1970, van Heyningen set out to find the cholera toxin receptor in the same way as Wassermann and Takaki had set out 72 years previously with tetanus toxin. Scrapings of epithelial cells from rabbit small intestine, and suspensions of tissues from the liver, kidney, spleen and lungs, were suspended in solutions of crude cholera toxin (NIH's Wyeth-001), stood for some time, then spun down and the supernatants tested for toxicity in the rabbit skin by Craig's method. The small intestine scrapings readily fixed the toxin, but the other tissues appeared to have little or no such capacity. Thus there appeared to be a cholera toxin receptor in the intestinal scrapings. What was it? Before proceeding with the fractionation of the chemical components of intestinal scrapings, a suspension of brain tissue was tested at the suggestion, and indeed insistence, of van Heyningen's technician. It seemed hardly worth testing brain tissue—obviously it could not be regarded as a susceptible tissue for cholera toxin, and in any case it had been shown that of all the large number of toxins tested in 1959, only tetanus toxin was fixed by brain tissue or by protagon. (Cholera toxin was not tested at that time for the good reason that its discovery was not announced until later that year; see Chapter 2.) But astonishingly, brain tissue fixed cholera toxin far better even than intestinal scrapings. Could the cholera toxin receptor possibly also be a ganglioside? The cholera toxin fixing capacity was found in the water-soluble (i.e., the ganglioside-containing) fraction of the total lipids of the intestinal scrapings, and not in any other component, and when mixed brain gangliosides were tested they were found to have an amazing capacity to bind, and to deactivate, cholera toxin. Van Heyningen then proceeded to Baltimore, where, in collaboration with the experienced cholera workers Greenough, Pierce and Carpenter, it was shown that mixed gangliosides inactivated cholera toxin also in the rabbit intestinal loop test and the fat cell test (see above), as well as in the rabbit skin. The paper describing the finding was delayed, having been rejected by *Nature*, and appeared in the *Journal of Infectious Diseases* in October 1971 [433]. By this time, the identity of the particular cholera toxin-binding gangliosides had been established by King and van Heyningen in Oxford.[8] It was not the

8. And announced by van Heyningen at a seminar at Johns Hopkins University, where P. Cuatrecasas, working with ganglioside prepared by van Heyningen and supplied to him by Greenough, was subsequently able to confirm this finding.

sialidase-labile tetanus toxin-binding ganglioside GGnSSLC, but a ganglioside differing from it by one sialic acid residue, viz., the sialidase-stable GGnSLC, galactosyl-N-acetylgalactosaminyl-(N-acetylneuraminyl)-galactosylglucosyl-ceramide, generally known as GM_1. King and van Heyningen resolved mixed brain gangliosides into their main component species and tested their effect on the toxicity of cholera toxin in the rabbit skin, and on its ability to activate adenylate cyclase. Some anomalous results were initially obtained in the adenylate cyclase tests where more concentrated toxin was used. Sialidase-labile gangliosides, such as SGGnSLC (GDla), seemed also to deactivate the toxin, but this was shown to be due to their being converted to GGnSLC by the sialidase present in crude and partially purified preparations of the toxin. When Finkelstein's pure toxin was used, this anomaly was not observed [224]. The specific and avid binding of (a molecule of) cholera toxin by four or five molecules of GGnSLC was subsequently confirmed at Johns Hopkins University by Cuatrecasas [89], and at Gothenburg University by Holmgren and Svennerholm [206].[9]

There seemed to be some possibility of practical applications of this discovery to the prevention of cholera. Thus it had been the hope, for example of Nalin and Cash at the Cholera Research Laboratory in Dacca, to find a way of absorbing or deactivating the toxin, as a possible means of treating the disease [294]. If ever there were a substance capable of blocking the action of the toxin, it was surely ganglioside, which could block nearly 20 times its weight of toxin. It had already been shown in the rabbit ileal loop that ganglioside was effective only if added together with or before the toxin—if added only five minutes after the toxin, it was ineffective. Therefore, ganglioside could not undo any harm the toxin had already done, but at least it might prevent any further harm by further-produced toxin, or perhaps it could be used as a short-term prophylactic to be taken by people in imminent danger of getting cholera. There would be no need to isolate the ganglioside, since an emulsion of brain was effective, 1 gram of guinea pig brain tissue being capable of blocking the equivalent of 26 litres of a potent laboratory culture of the cholera vibrio, probably at least 20 times as much toxin as any patient is ever exposed to. Van Heyningen had visions of Bengali mothers giving their families a spoonful each of goat brain gruel three or four times a day during the cholera season as a day-to-day prophylactic, but these hopes are unlikely to be fulfilled. Richard Cash gave such a brain gruel to a small number of volunteers at the Maryland House of Correction before challenge with live vibrios and found that they were, if anything, slightly worse off than volunteers

9. Svennerholm was one of the early workers on the separation and chemistry of gangliosides, and thus had samples of the various species readily available on his shelves.

who did not receive the gruel (private communication, 1975). Joseph Staerk had a similar experience with experimental dogs at the Behring Institute in Marburg (private communication, 1976). Another prophylactic possibility could be based on the observation that sialidase converts gangliosides that do not bind the toxin into the sialidase-stable cholera toxin binding ganglioside GGnSLC. It is interesting that the cholera vibrio is perhaps the best-known source of sialidase (or neuraminidase, as it is often called). Could this sialidase play a part in the natural history of the disease by making more receptors available for the toxin? If so, should any active immunizing agent against the disease contain an anti-neuraminidase element? Incubation of intestinal scrapings with sialidase leads to a considerable increase in their ability to bind the toxin [224], which is due not only to conversion of sialidase-labile ganglioside to cholera toxin-binding ganglioside, but also, apparently, to the unmasking of otherwise unapproachable ganglioside binding sites possibly by breaking down glycoproteins [153]. Pretreatment of dog intestine with sialidase makes it produce more fluid in response to cholera toxin [407]; treatment of adrenal cells with sialidase increases their responsiveness to cholera toxin [189]; pretreatment of pigeon red cells with sialidase increases the activation of the adenylate cyclase in them by cholera toxin (King, private communication, 1974). But there may be an opposite side to the coin: Not all the toxin that is bound by cells is necessarily functionally bound [226], and if the toxin were impotently to be bound in this way by an excess of receptors, the neuraminidase would have the effect of diminishing rather than increasing the toxic effects of the disease.

If the binding of cholera toxin by ganglioside has no practical application at present to the prevention or cure of the disease, it has proved to be of great importance in elucidating the structure of the toxin, and the way it acts on susceptible cells. The fact that ganglioside bound cholera toxin and blocked its action on otherwise susceptible tissue suggested that ganglioside was the toxin receptor in the cell membrane. This idea was supported in many ways. Thus, Cuatrecasas made the interesting observation that if rat fat cells were suspended in a solution of ganglioside the ganglioside became functionally incorporated in the cell membrane, for if the ganglioside were GGnSLC the cell acquired an increased capacity to bind cholera toxin and an increased lipolytic response to the toxin [89]. Similarly Gill and King found that pigeon red cells would absorb ganglioside, with increased stimulation of adenylate cyclase by cholera toxin [157, 226]. The fact that the response of cells to cholera toxin can be increased by the incorporation of exogenous ganglioside suggests that the response of the normal cell is limited by the number of available functional toxin receptors, but

not all incorporated and toxin-binding ganglioside is necessarily functional. King incorporated radioactive GGnSLC into pigeon red cells and
measured toxin binding and response of adenylate cyclase to it, and
found a discrepancy between the amount of additional toxin bound
and the degree of enhancement of adenylate cyclase activation. Thus
there was only a doubling of biological response to a tenfold increase
in toxin-binding, which indicated that a substantial proportion of the
exogenous ganglioside was incorporated in the cell membrane in such
a way that it could still bind toxin, but the bound toxin was unable
to fulfill its function of activating adenylate cyclase [225]. This suggested
that the functional cholera toxin receptor was not simply GGnSLC, but
GGnSLC in a particular surrounding. Previous evidence had already
suggested that even for toxin-binding, without considerations of enhanced
action, ganglioside as incorporated in the cell membrane was more
efficient than free ganglioside [225].

The number of cholera toxin molecules that bind to cells varies a
great deal. The pigeon red cell binds less than 100 toxin molecules
[226], whereas human fibroblasts [23] and bovine intestinal epithelial
cells [203] bind as many as a million toxin molecules, perhaps not all
functionally. The amount of toxin bound is roughly proportional to the
GGnSLC content of the cell [23, 203], and cells which do not contain
this ganglioside do not bind cholera toxin, nor do they respond to it.
This point about ganglioside-free cells was made by Cuatrecasas's group
by extensively subculturing transformed cell lines from mouse embryo
kidney and so causing them to lose ganglioside from their membranes.
Cells subcultured less than 60 times and containing some detectable
GGnSLC bound some toxin, which activated cellular adenylate cyclase;
cells subcultured more than 200 times, and containing some detectable
ganglioside but no detectable GGnSLC, bound considerably less toxin,
but what was bound stimulated adenylate cyclase in proportion; a
different subculture cell line contained very little ganglioside of any
kind and bound hardly any toxin, but on treatment with sialidase became
more sensitive to toxin, presumably because whichever ganglioside it
contained was converted to GGnSLC [203]. The Cuatrecasas group went
so far as to state, probably with justice, that the ability of a cell to
react to cholera toxin was a more reliable indication of the presence of
GGnSLC in its membrane than chemical methods, which have a lower
limit of about a million molecules per cell; if an animal cell does not
respond to cholera toxin, it does not contain GGnSLC. There remains,
of course, the possibility that a cell with no endogenous ganglioside
might absorb exogenous gangliosides that may be present in its culture
medium; indeed, another cell line, lacking the machinery for making
GGnSLC, responds poorly or not at all to cholera toxin, but the response

is markedly increased after treating the cells with GGnSLC but not with any other ganglioside [289]. All this evidence supports the suggestion that the ganglioside GGnSLC is the receptor, or the principal component of the receptor, for cholera toxin in the cell membrane.

We know what component of the cell membrane is the receptor for cholera toxin; we also know what part of the cholera toxin binds to the receptor. It is choleragenoid, the inert protein discovered by Finkelstein that is immunologically nearly, but not quite, identical with cholera toxin, and of a smaller molecular weight (59,000 compared with 84,000). Finkelstein's discovery and purification of choleragenoid is nearly as important as his work on cholera toxin.

In the early work on the binding of cholera toxin by ganglioside, van Heyningen, wishing to study whether choleragenoid was also bound, and having no means of measuring its activity since it had none, intended to study interaction of pure cholera toxin and pure choleragenoid with ganglioside in the analytical ultracentrifuge, as he had done 10 years previously with tetanus toxin [435]. In order to do this, concentrated solutions of the toxin and choleragenoid (2 mg in 0.2 ml) were mixed with concentrated solutions of ganglioside (1 mg in 0.2 ml), but as soon as this was done, dense precipitates fell out in both mixtures, thus showing that both cholera toxin and choleragenoid were bound by ganglioside [433].[10] The binding of choleragenoid was subsequently confirmed by Cuatrecasas with radioactive choleragenoid [90]. N. F. Pierce carried out the next important experiment with choleragenoid. Finkelstein had recently shown by immunohistological techniques that choleragenoid, as well as cholera toxin, was bound to the membranes of intestinal epithelial cells [329], and Pierce showed that if choleragenoid were placed in an ileal loop in the dog, and followed an hour later by cholera toxin, there was no fluid accumulation. The choleragenoid had blocked the cholera toxin, molecule for molecule, and, since it was known to bind to ganglioside, it presumably pre-empted the toxin receptors in the epithelial cell membranes [346]. King and van Heyningen then showed that if choleragenoid were allowed to react with ganglioside GGnSLC, then it would no longer block the action of cholera toxin, because, being already bound to the ganglioside it could no longer bind to the cell receptor [225]. Pierce's experiment was most important because it was the first indication that cholera toxin had a binding component that was not an active component. Since choleragenoid was smaller than cholera toxin, the active component must be in the difference

---

10. This abrupt precipitation caused anguish to Finkelstein, who had generously provided amounts (2000 µg) of his precious products which, especially in those days, were considered very large.

between the two. This prepared the ground for the idea that cholera toxin, like diphtheria toxin, was a bipartite toxin, consisting of a cell receptor binding part and an active part.

The ganglioside GGnSLC may be the receptor, or the principal component of the receptor, in the cell membrane for cholera toxin, but cholera toxin is a foreign invader. What part does ganglioside play in the normal functioning of the cell? Paul Ehrlich put this question of the normal function of receptors 80 years ago in his Croonian Lecture to the Royal Society of London:

> That these are in function specially designed to seize on toxines cannot be for one moment entertained. It would not be reasonable to suppose that there were present in the organism many hundreds of atomic groupings destined to unite with toxines, when the latter appeared, but in function really playing no part in the processes of normal life, and only arbitrarily brought into relation with them by the will of the investigator. . . . One may therefore rightly assume that these toxophile protoplasmic groups in reality serve normal functions in the animal organism, and that they only incidentally and by pure chance possess the capacity to anchor themselves to this or that toxine [110].

It has been suggested that gangliosides may form part of the cell membrane system that normally transmits information from outside the cell to its interior [139]. In this connection, it is interesting that several hormones (which also appear to consist of binding and active components) appear to be bound by ganglioside in cell membranes [246]. For example, thyroid plasma membranes bind both the thyroid stimulating hormone, thyrotropin, and tetanus toxin, and, like tetanus toxin, thyrotropin is bound by the ganglioside GGnSSLC [245]. There has also been speculation on a possible role for ganglioside in the regulation of cell growth, since the membranes of malignantly transformed cancer cells (whose prime characteristic is their lack of proper regulation of cell division) have altered glycolipid patterns, glycolipids being compounds including, but not restricted to, gangliosides [87]. Exogenous glycolipids have also to have an inhibitory effect on the growth of some normal cells [222].

5. The Molecular Structure of Cholera Toxin

The elucidation of the structure of cholera toxin began in 1969 with Finkelstein's purification of cholera toxin (with a molecular weight of 84,000) and his demonstration and purification of the closely related inert protein choleragenoid (with a molecular weight of 59,000), and with his further demonstration that choleragenoid was a derivative of the toxin rather than a precursor of it, or an independently synthesized protein. He showed that when a solution of toxin was shaken, it broke down to choleragenoid (and noticed that both the toxin and its inert derivative could be dissociated by heating at a low pH into subunits of molecular weight approximately 15,000 [134]). He then treated cholera toxin mildly with the anionic detergent sodium dodecyl sulphate (SDS), which dissociates proteins into their constituent peptides, and found that the toxin was resolved into two species—one with a molecular weight of 56,000 and the other with a molecular weight of 28,000. Choleragenoid was unaffected by this treatment with SDS [130], and appeared to be the component with the molecular weight of 56,000 [258]. Finkelstein and his colleagues suggested, as we have already seen, that the choleragenoid component of cholera toxin was responsible for binding the toxin to the membrane of the susceptible cell [329], and had concluded that a different, "toxophore"[11] group of the toxin molecule was responsible for the toxic activity. It was natural to look to the other, smaller, component with a molecular weight of 28,000 for the toxic activity. When this component was treated with a sulphydryl reducing agent, its molecular weight further decreased to 23,000, suggesting that a peptide of molecular weight of 5,000 had been split from it.

To return to the choleragenoid component of the toxin—Finkelstein's group showed that if cholera toxin or choleragenoid were boiled with SDS (rather than treated gently, see above), the choleragenoid component of molecular weight 56,000 was broken down into subunits of molecular weight about 10,000, whereas the other component, of molecular weight 23,000, was unaffected.

These findings were soon essentially confirmed by other workers. Thus Lonnroth and Holmgren in Gothenburg also found two types of subunit on treatment of cholera toxin with SDS—Finkelstein's component with molecular weight of 28,000, which they called H (for heavy), and his component with a molecular weight of about 8,000 which they called L (for light)—and they suggested that the toxin consisted of one H subunit and seven L subunits. Neither of these subunits was toxic, but recombination of L with H in various proportions did restore some

---

11. Paul Ehrlich's word for the hypothetical active part of a toxin. He turned out to have been right (at least in the case of cholera, diphtheria and some other toxins) to suggest such an active component of a toxin, and to suggest further that the toxin had to be bound by a different component, a "haptophore", to the receptor. Finkelstein, having borrowed Ehrlich's toxophore, missed the opportunity of calling his choleragenoid the haptophore.

toxicity [257]. Dissociation of toxin into subunits (with urea) and re-combination with some return of toxicity were also achieved by Fin-kelstein [128].

S. van Heyningen, then at the University of Oxford, dissociated cholera toxin in a different way. He bound the toxin to a suspension of ganglioside made water-insoluble by complexing with cerebroside, washed the complex free of excess toxin, then eluted it with urea solution. The choleragenoid portion of the toxin remained fixed to the ganglioside complex and the urea solution contained a substance with a molecular weight of about 28,000. This material had some slight toxicity when tested in the rabbit skin, suggesting it might be the active component of the toxin [423]. The clear demonstration of the activity of this component had to await the discovery of a "broken cell" preparation, discussed in the following section.

Thus it seemed in 1974 that cholera toxin consisted of two types of component which were normally associated by non-covalent forces that could be broken down by fairly mild treatment with reagents such as urea, detergents, dilute acids. These components were the possibly toxic one (now known as A, for active) with a molecular weight of about 28,000 (diminished to 23,000 on reduction with sulphydryl reagents), and the inert ganglioside-binding one (now known as B, for binding) with a molecular weight of about 56,000 (broken down into subunits of molecular weight 8,000 to 15,000 on more severe treatment with SDS, urea, detergents). The exact number of subunits in the B-component was the subject of debate for some time, but was finally settled by the determination of the full amino acid sequence of this subunit, which allowed precise calculation of its molecular weight. There appear to be 103 amino acids and one intra-chain disulphide bond, giving calculated molecular weights of 11,590 [240], 11,600 [291] and 11,637 [241], which is consistent with the choleragenoid component having five subunits, i.e., molecular weights of 57,950, 58,000 and 58,185, respectively. The arrangement of the toxin molecule with one A-component and one B-component consisting of five subunits has led to a proposal by Gill that the five B subunits take up the conformation of a ring, with the A-component at the core [155]. This has been supported to some extent by Ohtomo's electron micrographs of the toxin, which show two main conformations: a ring with a central core, or a conical structure, likened to a Japanese tea whisk. Choleragenoid appears as a ring with no central core [312]. It has already been mentioned that the A-component, molecular weight 28,000 can be dissociated by sulphydryl reduction to two peptides, A_1 with a molecular weight of 23,000, and A_2 with a molecular weight of 5,000. The A_1 component is the active component, with the ability to activate adenylate cyclase (see next section), and the A_2 component is thought to be the connecting piece holding A_1 within the B subunit assembly [155].

The idea of a bipartite toxin molecule, with distinct active and receptor-binding components, would probably not have flourished nearly so quickly if the ground had not already been prepared for it by A. M. Pappenheimer and D. M. Gill shortly before in a splendid culmination of Pappenheimer's 36 years of work on the structure and mode of action of diphtheria toxin [79, 325]. They had shown that diphtheria toxin consists of two peptide chains, A (for enzymically active) and B (for binding), linked together by easily cleavable peptide and sulphydryl bonds. The B part is responsible for the binding of the toxin to the receptor (as yet not identified) on the membrane of the susceptible cell, and thus facilitates the entry of the A part into the cytoplasm of the cell, where it catalyses a reaction which leads to a blocking of protein synthesis in the cell. This reaction catalyzed by the active enzymic component of diphtheria toxin is highly relevant to cholera toxin, since it is very similar to a reaction that appears to be promoted by the A_1 subunit of cholera toxin. The diphtheria toxin-catalyzed reaction is: NAD + EF-2 = ADPR-EF-2 + nicotinamide + H^+. NAD is nicotinamide adenine dinucleotide (see Figure 10.3), which consists of nicotinamide joined to adenine diphosphate ribose (ADPR or ADP-ribose); it is cleaved by the diphtheria toxin enzyme into free nicotinamide and ADPR, which is at the same time coupled to the protein-synthesising enzyme Elongation Factor-2, thus inactivating it. This enzyme-catalyzed transfer of ADP-ribose from nicotinamide to another substance is called ADP-ribosylation. It is an expression we will use again. Now it seems there are other bipartite toxins and active substances: the exotoxin of *Pseudomonas aeruginosa* has since been shown to be very similar to diphtheria toxin, and it blocks protein synthesis in the same way, by ADP-ribosylating EF-2. Tetanus toxin has been shown to consist of two separable components, "light" and "heavy", which are separately inactive, but active when joined together again; the heavy component is bound by the ganglioside GGnSSLC [see 425, 427]. The enterotoxin of *E. coli* is apparently constituted in exactly the same bipartite fashion as cholera toxin, and promotes the same reaction within all animal cells containing the ganglioside GGnSLC in their membranes (see below).

This bipartite structure is not confined to bacterial toxins. The plant poisons abrin and ricin are similarly constituted, and it is possible to form hybrids of abrin A-ricin B and ricin A-abrin B. The cell membrane receptor for the B components is not known, but it has been shown that the A-component is an enzyme that blocks protein synthesis in a manner that has not yet been defined [314]. The glycoprotein hormones (i.e., thyroid-stimulating, luteinising, and follicle-stimulating hormones and human chorionic gonadotropin), and even the virus-induced antiviral agent, interferon, are apparently also composed of active (alpha) components, thought (in the case of the hormones) like cholera toxin to stimulate adenylate cyclase, and binding (beta) components, thought to bind to ganglioside receptors in susceptible cell membranes [236]. But perhaps it is too early to form a serious judgment of the validity of these suggestions. However, the fact remains that active proteins like bacterial toxins and hormones act on components located within cells, and to gain access to these components they must pass through the cell membranes. They cannot, like small-molecular drugs, simply drift through the membranes; therefore, they have to have another means of getting through. The bipartite mechanism, by which one, inert part binds to the membrane and facilitates the passage of the other, active part through it, certainly seems to operate in the case of the bacterial toxins and the plant poisons we have discussed. The toxins act on intact cells only after a lag period, and then their action persists long after the toxin has been washed off the cells; in contrast, the hormones activate adenylate cyclase instantly as long as the hormone remains bound to the cell, and their action ceases as soon as they are washed from the cell.

6. The Development of the Perforated Cell

Research into the detailed mechanism by which cholera toxin activates adenylate cyclase was hampered for some years by the fact that the bipartite toxin needed time to work its way, or the active component's way, through the barrier of the cell membrane; and then, as long as the cell was intact, it was difficult to find out what was happening inside it. In Greenough's laboratory at Johns Hopkins University, Zieve had shown that when mechanically disrupted blood platelets were treated with cholera toxin they responded immediately, without the characteristic 30-minute lag, but the significance of this report went largely unnoticed [468]. Five years later, the problem of getting at the cell interior was overcome in a different way when D. M. Gill came on sabbatical leave in 1975 from Harvard to spend a term working with Carolyn King in W. van Heyningen's laboratory in Oxford. In that short period, much was achieved. Gill and King soon found that the pigeon red-blood cell provided a handy means of studying the action of the toxin [157]. Pigeon red cells are convenient to use since they are easy to obtain and quick to prepare as a homogenous preparation of washed cells since they centrifuge down readily because of their heavy nuclei.[12] Like all other animal cells, they respond to cholera toxin with increased levels of cAMP, after the usual lag of 30 minutes. But Gill and King circumvented this lag by perforating the cell membrane, and thus giving the toxin direct access to the cell interior. The perforation of the cell membrane was neatly accomplished by treating the cells with another toxin, the theta toxin, or haemolysin, of *Clostridium welchii* [402], which produces holes of 50–70 nanometres diameter in the membrane, ample for the passage of exotoxins and other macromolecules. When such perforated pigeon red cells were treated with cholera toxin, the adenylate cyclase was stimulated immediately, and if higher concentrations of toxin were used it was possible to activate the adenylate cyclase to much greater levels than in intact cells, which suggested that the response of intact cells was limited (e.g., by the number of toxin molecules that could be accommodated on the cell surface ganglioside receptors).

It was obvious from these results that if the lag between the binding of the toxin and the activation of adenylate cyclase could be abolished by the simple expedient of punching holes through the membrane, then the lag was due to some time-consuming event within the cell membrane, an event that had nothing to do with the activation of adenylate cyclase. Gill and King concluded that the lag phase represented the time during which the toxin—or its active component—became buried within the cell membrane and then travelled across it to reach the inner side of the membrane, and probably to penetrate the intracellular space itself. During this period, the toxin was "eclipsed" as far as extracellular antitoxin was concerned. For the first couple of moments of the lag phase, the toxin was still partially accessible to extracellular antitoxin, but if antitoxin was added to intact cells more than 2 minutes after the toxin it was powerless to prevent the development of adenylate cyclase activation 20 minutes later (a well-known observation by many workers with different types of cells). On the other hand, if toxin-treated pigeon red-blood cells were perforated in the presence of antitoxin at some time after the lag—when adenylate cyclase activity had started to rise— the process of activation was stopped as soon as the antitoxin came in contact with the internal contents of the cell; but antitoxin could not reverse such activation as had already occurred. Nor was it possible to

---

12. This highly successful "ornithological gimmickry", as it was called by J. P. Craig, was due to the fact that Gill wanted to use turkey red-blood cells, as had been used by Michael Field for certain studies with cholera toxin. The chief of the animal house at the Sir William Dunn School of Pathology told Gill that there were no turkeys, but plenty of aged pigeons, surviving from the days when Lord Florey had used them for studies on atherosclerosis.

reverse activation by thorough washing of the red cell membrane, or by dissolving the toxin-activated adenylate cyclase with help of a detergent [16]. This permanent and irreversible activation of adenylate cyclase that occurs after treatment with cholera toxin is a unique and important feature, with far-reaching implications for the mechanism of action of adenylate cyclase, as we shall see.

These observations with the pigeon red-blood cell suggested that the activation of adenylate cyclase was brought about by an antitoxin-sensitive portion of the toxin which actually reached the inside of the cell. By this time, it needed no great stretch of the imagination to suppose that it was the A-component of the toxin that was involved in the process, especially since it had already been shown in Finkelstein's laboratory that the inert B-component (choleragenoid) of the toxin remained on the outside of the cell during intoxication, saturating the ganglioside receptors and so preventing any further toxin from having any further effect (but remaining free to combine with external antitoxin, which reacts with both the A- and B-components of the toxin [329]). Once the perforated cell became available, it was a relatively simple matter to confirm the supposition that the power to activate adenylate cyclase resided in the A-component. S. van Heyningen and King used the preparation of the A-component obtained by eluting it with urea solution from a suspension of toxin absorbed on ganglioside-cerebroside, leaving the B-component still absorbed. It may be recalled that the preparation showed slight toxic activity in the rabbit skin [423]. It was added to intact and to perforated pigeon red-blood cells and the activation of adenylate cyclase determined. In the intact cell preparation, it produced a very slight rise in adenylate cyclase activity, following the usual lag. This small degree of activity was not blocked by ganglioside, as is the activity of whole toxin on intact cells; it was assumed that the A-component could penetrate the membrane without assistance, but only very inefficiently. In perforated cells, the preparation of A-component acted with immediate and dramatic rise in adenylate cyclase activity, which could be blocked by antitoxin, but not by ganglioside. Gill and King prepared the A-component in another way, by dissociating the toxin with SDS and separating the A- and B-components electrophoretically, and found the same results with intact and perforated cells.

These observations pointed clearly to the concept of the toxin-receptor combination's being concerned only with the toxin's gaining access to the interior of the cell, and therefore being replaceable by a hole in the cell membrane. This concept was further supported by the finding that the toxin receptor in the cell membrane, ganglioside which combines only with the B-component, had no effect on the activity of the whole toxin or of the A-component in perforated cells: It did not block their activity in such cells, and it did not enhance their activity when intact cells had exogenous ganglioside incorporated in their membranes prior to being perforated. Moreover, when choleragenoid was added to intact cells before perforation, it did not block the activity of subsequently added cholera toxin.

S. van Heyningen and King suggested, since the A-component has a slight action on whole cells, that the function of the binding of cholera toxin to the cell receptor might simply be to bring about an increased concentration of toxin close to the membrane surface, and so increase the chance of entry (by relatively non-specific means) of the A-component [428]. Gill has suggested a rather less passive role for the B-component, namely, that once the B-component has combined with the ganglioside molecules they actually extend some distance into the membrane, thereby providing some kind of channel for the A-component to pass down [155]. These concepts imply that the A-component is detached from the B-component, which it leaves behind on the membrane surface while it finds its way separately into the interior of the cell. This may well be so in the natural course of events but it may not necessarily be so, in the laboratory at any rate. S. van Heyningen attached the A- and B-components to each other by means of covalent linkage (instead of the natural non-covalent linkage) and found that this complex was still fully capable of activating adenylate cyclase in the intact pigeon red-blood cell after an initial lag. He suggested that either enough of the A-component extended into the cell interior to activate the adenylate cyclase, or a still active portion of it was split off by intracellular proteases [426]. It has in fact been claimed that active fragments can be split off from the A_1 subunit by proteolytic action [277].

7. The Function of NAD

An essential prerequisite for the action of cholera toxin on the perforated cell has so far only been touched on; it is the presence of an adequate concentration of nicotinamide adenine dinucleotide, NAD. When Gill first started working with perforated red blood cells he found that cholera toxin or its A-component acted on them only poorly unless they were suspended in their cytosol, that is, the juice from their interiors. Evidently, there was something in the cytosol that was necessary for the activation of adenylate cyclase by the toxin. He found that addition of NAD to perforated cells separated from the cytosol to some extent improved their response to the toxin, and, conversely, treatment of the perforated cells with a NAD-destroying enzyme, glycohydrolase, to remove residual free and bound NAD completely abolished the responsiveness of the cells to the toxin [157]. This very important discovery was due to two fortunate circumstances: the first that Gill had come to Oxford fresh from investigations at Harvard University on the part played by NAD in the action of diphtheria toxin; the second that the only birds available at the time in the Sir William Dunn School of Pathology were Lord Florey's gerontic pigeons, because it so happens that the pigeon red-blood cell does not possess an NAD glycohydrolase. Most other cells contain such an enzyme bound to their membranes, which is activated on lysis and immediately breaks down endogenous or added NAD. Had the perforated pigeon red cell been endowed with such an enzyme, cholera toxin would not have had any effect on it. Gill's findings with avian red-blood cells were soon confirmed with various other broken cell preparations, such as rat liver membranes [273] and sarcoma cell membranes [140, 459], and even with solubilized adenylate cyclase from rat liver [424], in which cholera toxin and its A-component were able to activate the enzyme as long as NAD was present.

Note that on p. 273 it is stated that Gill originally found that NAD "to some extent" replaced cytosol. This was because NAD was not the only component of cytosol necessary for the activation of adenylate cyclase by cholera toxin. Reduced glutathione and adenosine triphosphate, and an unidentified macromolecular factor, were apparently also needed for complete action of the toxin. The importance of glutathione lies in its reductive capacity, which enables it to promote the separation of the A_1 and A_2 subunits of the A-component by reducing the disulphide bond joining them (i.e., A_1-S-S-A_2 + H_2 = A_1SH + A_2SH). Thus the requirement for glutathione is abolished if purified A_1 is used rather than A in the activation of adenylate cyclase in perforated pigeon red-blood cells, and Gill found that the delay of about one minute normally observed in the action of the toxin in perforated red cells was abolished if the toxin were preincubated with an excess of reduced glutathione, which suggests that the delay was probably due to slower reduction of the A_1-A_2 disulphide bond by the small concentration of endogenous glutathione in the cytosol. He also found that even greater activity could be induced by pretreatment of the toxin with a mild detergent such as SDS, as well as with glutathione [156]. These results suggest that the active species A_1 needs to be completely dissociated from B and from A_2 before it can act, and that therefore the holotoxin AD, as synthesized by the cholera vibrio, should not act without being dissociated into $B + A_2 + A_1$ by passing through the cell membrane-receptor system, but this concept is challenged by S. van Heyningen's demonstration that when the A + B components are covalently cross-linked (and therefore not separable by the membrane-receptor system), the resultant preparation is still fully active not only on perforated red cells, but also, even more surprisingly, on intact cells (see above). This finding will be discussed again below.

The apparent importance of ATP in the toxin-stimulated activation of adenylate cyclase[13] in pigeon red-cell membranes was first discussed by Gill in 1976 [156], and observed also by others working with the adenylate cyclase of purified liver membranes [273]. The precise role of the ATP has yet to be defined. The specificity as to the purine base component (see Figure 10.3) seems not to be critical, since other nucleoside triphosphates are also effective. Indeed, we may have here anticipated the discussion in the next section by reporting that the possibility has been suggested that the ATP is substituting for another nucleotide, guanosine triphosphate, in the activation process.

The function of the unidentified, apparently protein, "cytosol factor" [156], and perhaps even its necessity for the action of the toxin, is still obscure, but in connection with the preceding sentence it may be worth considering observations not directly connected with cholera toxin. It was found that a cytosolic fraction from rat liver enhanced the basal and hormone (glucagon)-activated adenylate cyclase of liver membranes. The effect of this fraction could be mimicked to some extent by GTP, and could be produced by enzymes that broke down GTP, and by trypsin, which breaks down protein. It was suggested that the cytosolic factor was a soluble complex of GTP and a protein which affects the responsiveness of adenylate cyclase under normal conditions in the cell [174].

It might now be useful to consider in more detail the two main theories of the action of cholera toxin at the molecular level which were current in the period 1975–76.

The enzymic theory of Gill [156, 157] proposed that the active subunit of cholera toxin, having passed through the membrane and into the cell interior, acts enzymically to promote some reaction which requires the co-factors NAD, ATP and cytosol factor. There were several points in favour of this theory. Under favourable conditions (perforated red cells, plenty of NAD and cytosol, SDS to separate A from B, glutathione to split the -S-S-bond between A_1 and A_2) the amount of A_1 needed to produce a measurable effect on adenylate cyclase seemed to be as little as one molecule per cell—indicating a catalytic reaction. Under these optimal conditions, the rate of activation was directly proportional to the concentration of A_1, and in perforated cells the activation process was smoothly dependent on temperature and took place, albeit slowly, even at 0° C. This is in contrast with the activation in whole cells,

---

13. Obviously, ATP is needed for the action of adenylate cyclase, since it acts on it to convert it to cAMP, but we are now concerned with the activation of the enzyme by the toxin, which is a separate event preceding the action.

which involves the membrane phase and is therefore dependent on the state of mobility of the membrane lipids, with the consequence that below a certain critical transition temperature, though the toxin may bind to the cell, it cannot intoxicate it.

Another group, that of Flores and Sharp at Harvard University, having also found that the action of cholera toxin on broken liver cells needed NAD and cytosol factor, also proposed that the toxin acted enzymically, possibly by ADP-ribosylating the adenylate cyclase (and activating it), as diphtheria toxin ADP-ribosylates the protein-building enzyme known as Elongation Factor-2 (and inactivates it) [140]. However, there was no direct evidence in support of this enzyme theory. The problem with the enzymic theory until recently was that the reaction supposed to be catalyzed enzymically by A_1 could not be identified. Gill, having played such an important part in the demonstration that diphtheria toxin catalyzed the cleavage of NAD into ADP-ribose and nicotinamide, naturally could not fail to have entertained, from the time he first observed the necessity for NAD for the action of cholera toxin, the notion that cholera toxin acted on NAD, and that this action should liberate nicotinamide and ADP-ribose, and that the ADP-ribose should combine with something. The question was, what? But he cautiously did not publish this notion in the beginning because attempts made in 1975 to show that cholera toxin induced the formation of ADP-ribose, or nicotinamide, were not successful. Gill showed that ADP-ribose added as such did not support the activation of adenylate cyclase, which indicated that if ADP-ribose were involved it must be via a direct transfer reaction to some cellular component. We shall see that it was not until very recently, in 1978, that such a reaction was detected in association with the activation of adenylate cyclase.

In the meantime, the absence of a firm demonstration of a reaction enzymically catalyzed by cholera toxin encouraged the other main theory for its action. This was the mobile receptor theory of Cuatrecasas's school [23]. These workers proposed that cholera toxin acted not enzymically but stoichiometrically, like certain hormones, by interacting first with the ganglioside receptor, then directly with the adenylate cyclase in the cell membrane. As it seemed unlikely that every ganglioside molecule was directly in contact with an adenylate cyclase molecule, it became necessary to postulate that the toxin-receptor complex moved within the plane of the membrane (during the lag period) until it came in conjunction with an adenylate cyclase molecule. A conformational change in the enzyme was then brought about by contact with the toxin-receptor complex, which resulted in an irreversible activation of the adenylate cyclase. This mobile receptor theory grew out of the finding that activation of adenylate cyclase by cholera toxin in fat cells occurred only after a lag phase, whether the cells were intact or broken [385]. In addition, the presence of toxin in the cytoplasm of toxin-treated cells could not be demonstrated and the dependence of the activation on the presence of NAD could not be confirmed [21] (this may have been due to incomplete removal of endogenous NAD). It was concluded therefore that the intracellular component of the cell was not important for activation, that the toxin—or any active subunit—did not penetrate right through the membrane, and that activation of adenylate cyclase was purely a membrane-mediated event, involving the movement of the toxin-receptor complex to the adenylate cyclase. There was some evidence that such a movement of ganglioside could occur. In cholera toxin-treated lymphocytes, gangliosides were shown to move within the plane of the membrane and form aggregates, or "caps"; and exogenous and GGnSLC ganglioside incorporated artificially in the cell membrane also underwent redistribution in the membrane after reacting with cholera toxin. However, the same phenomenon could be induced with the inert choleragenoid, without effect on adenylate cyclase, so it follows that the redistribution of a toxin-receptor complex within the membrane could not be responsible *per se* for the activation of adenylate cyclase [366]. Cuatrecasas also observed movement of ganglioside within the cell membrane in lymph node cells under the influence of cholera toxin by labelling the toxin with fluorescein, thus making it visible under the microscope, and found this movement had a time course comparable with the typical lag in activation of adenylate cyclase [85]. Cuatrecasas' mobile receptor theory seemed to gain support from S. van Heyningen's artificially coupled complex of the A- and B-components of the toxin which still had nearly undiminished activity on whole or perforated red blood cells. This was awkward for the theory of enzymic activity of the A_1 subunit, which needed to be separated from A_2 and B before it could act, but as we have seen, there were suggestions for getting round this awkwardness, viz., intracellular proteases might split off a still catalytically active part of the A_1 component, or the ganglioside-B-A_2-A_1 complex might project far enough through the membrane for the A_1 component to reach the adenylate cyclase on the inner side of the membrane.

This mention of adenylate cyclase on the inner side of the cell membrane brings us to another point, this time awkward for the mobile hormone receptor theory of the action of cholera toxin, which demands that that is where the adenylate cyclase should be; at least, it is awkward in the case of real cholera. It is true that adenylate cyclase resides on the inner side of the red blood cell membrane, and perhaps of most cell membranes, but in the intestinal epithelial cells the situation seems to be different. In these cells, the adenylate cyclase is not to be found on the inner side of the membranes which bind the toxin, but in the basal and lateral membranes of the cell (where the other ATP-splitting enzyme, the Na-K-dependent ATP-ase, is also situated, see Figure 9.1) [326]. In these cells, the active component of the toxin, having penetrated to the cytosol, could easily diffuse to the other side of the cell where the adenylate cyclase is situated.

The mobile receptor theory of the action of cholera toxin was formulated when it was believed, perhaps correctly, that the activity of hormones lay in the act of their binding to susceptible cells, and when it was discovered that cholera toxin was bound by ganglioside on the outer membrane of cells. In the first flush of that discovery, and in the absence of any other ideas, there was a tendency to assume that the binding of toxin by ganglioside was a central part of the process of the activation of adenylate cyclase. Now that we know that ganglioside, important as it is for the action of the toxin on the intact cell, is irrelevant to the action of the toxin in cells whose interiors can be reached in other ways, we can turn again, perhaps with some relief, to the enzymic theory of action of the toxin.

8. The Present Position

In the years after the role of NAD in the action of cholera toxin was firmly established, many workers were persuaded of the enzymic action of the toxin, and they sought to define more precisely the putative reaction that the A_1 subunit might catalyze. At the same time, research on adenylate cyclase itself was proceeding, and there were numerous reports in which the action of cholera toxin threw some light on the mechanism of action and the regulation of activity[14] of this important generator of the second messenger in the normal unintoxicated cell. One early such observation was that of Field in 1974 [121], subsequently confirmed by Cuatrecasas [21], that adenylate cyclase which had been activated by cholera toxin appeared to become more responsive to the action of such hormones as adrenaline and glucagon. Field suggested that cholera toxin either modified the cell membrane in such a way that the hormone receptors were more closely coupled to the catalytic component of adenylate cyclase, or that the toxin directly modified the catalytic component of the enzyme, making it more sensitive to the action of hormones. The former possibility, involving the membrane, seemed less likely since it had been found that when the activated

14. It should be noted that enzymes (all? most? some?) have, in addition to an active component which carries out the catalytic function, a regulatory component, which, through being affected by other agents, determines the degree of catalytic activity.

adenylate cyclase from toxin-treated liver membranes was solubilized it still retained some sensitivity to hormones, which is not the case with the non-activated enzyme after solubilization [16, 248]. In 1975, the other group at the Harvard Medical School, Flores and Sharp, pointed out several similarities between the effects on adenylate cyclase of cholera toxin and of Gpp(NH)p, a non-hydrolysable analogue[15] of guanosine triphosphate. Both these agents enhance the sensitivity of adenylate cyclase to hormones; both cause the activation of adenylate cyclase in such a way that the activation persists through washing and solubilization; both interfere with the activation of adenylate cyclase by fluoride (which is thought to convert adenylate cyclase to an un-regulated form in which the total potential activity is expressed).

Flores and Sharp found that the actions of cholera toxin and Gpp(NH)p were mutually exclusive—pretreatment of rat liver membranes with cholera toxin prevented subsequent activation by Gpp(NH)p. The toxin and the guanyl compounds seemed to have as their common target the regulatory component of adenylate cyclase [140]. This regulatory component was shown to be that part of the enzyme to which the guanyl compounds bind, thereby removing some kind of restraint on the enzyme's activity [333]. Flores and Sharp further suggested that one way by which the active component of cholera toxin might affect the regulatory component of adenylate cyclase could be for the toxin to catalyze the transfer of a break-down product of NAD to the regulatory component—the way diphtheria toxin transfers the ADP-ribose break-down product of NAD to the enzyme Elongation Factor-2 (which is a protein that also reacts with guanyl compounds). To use the jargon, they suggested that cholera toxin ADP-ribosylates the regulatory component of adenylate cyclase.

Thus, in 1975–76, it seemed that cholera toxin might act on the regulatory component of adenylate cyclase in some way that resembled the action of guanyl nucleotides in their regulation of the normal enzyme. The nature of the actual reaction catalyzed by cholera toxin remained undetermined, but 1976 saw the beginnings of an under-standing of it when Moss and Vaughan at the National Heart, Lung and Blood Institute showed that very high concentrations of toxin or its A subunit could bring about the hydrolysis of NAD to nicotinamide and ADP-ribose [289]. This was a simple splitting of NAD into its ADPR and nicotinamide components (i.e., NAD glycohydrolase activity), not involving, as in the case of diphtheria toxin, the simultaneous transfer of one of the split products to some acceptor compound (i.e.,

---

15. The number of intimidating shorthand names for reagents is increasing—the non-hydrolysable (i.e., non-break-downable) analogue of GTP is guanylylimidodiphosphate, or Gpp(NH)p, when an NH group takes the place of an oxygen atom (see Figure 10.3).

transferase activity). The need for such high concentrations of toxin suggested that this hydrolase activity was not the main activity of the toxin. Indeed, it turned out not to be an activity of the toxin at all, but of a contaminating enzyme, for S. van Heyningen showed two years later that when cholera toxin was purified sufficiently it lost this NAD glycohydrolase activity without loss of its ability to activate adenylate cyclase [414]. However, by this time Moss and Vaughan had demonstrated NAD transferase activity by cholera toxin, when they found that in the toxin-induced break-down of NAD nicotinamide was liberated and ADP-ribose was transferred to the amino acid arginine (and not to any other amino acids). Moss and Vaughan made the suggestion that the target for ADP-ribosylation by cholera toxin might be an arginine residue on a protein, such as adenylate cyclase itself or some related component of the adenylate cyclase system [290].

Thus, the problem of the activation of adenylate cyclase was now being approached on two fronts. On one front, several groups of workers were chiefly concerned with the effects of cholera toxin and GTP on the regulatory component of adenylate cyclase, and on the mechanism by which hormonal effects were enhanced; on the other front, several groups were attempting to identify the target for the toxin-catalyzed ADP-ribosylation which could result in the activation of adenylate cyclase. These two lines of research came together in a single solution, namely, that cholera toxin ADP-ribosylates, and thus modifies, the protein that controls the regulatory component of adenylate cyclase. This protein is closely associated with, and may indeed be, the regulatory component. Before discussing this work in detail, we should consider the way in which GTP is now thought to regulate the activity of the regulatory component of the adenylate cyclase.

Various schemes have been put forward to account for the enhancing effect of hormones on GTP-dependent activation of adenylate cyclase. On the one hand it has been proposed that hormones act by promoting the dissociation of the inhibitory GDP from the regulatory site of the enzyme, leaving it free to combine with fresh GTP. In other words, hormones regenerate the basal enzyme [31]. On the other hand, it has been suggested that hormones act by increasing the rate of change from an initially inactive "transition" form of the enzyme-GTP complex to a highly active form [387].

Neither of these schemes is entirely satisfactory in view of the finding that turkey red-blood cell membranes possess a GTP-splitting enzyme— a GTP-ase—which is activated by hormones, and is itself closely associated with the GTP-binding regulatory component of adenylate cyclase [63]. It is proposed that the enzyme-GTP complex is the active form of the enzyme which normally breaks down immediately due to the hydrolysis of the GTP by the GTP-ase associated with the regulatory component. The active enzyme-Gpp(NH)p remains irreversibly activated because Gpp(NH)p is insensitive to the GTP-ase. In the absence of hormones, GTP alone does not cause overall activation of the enzyme; in the presence of hormones, the rate of formation of the enzyme-GTP complex is increased, as also is its rate of degradation by GTP-ase. Thus, the adenylate cyclase is in a permanent state of oscillation in which the relative rates of formation and break-down of the enzyme-GTP complex determine the overall level of activity. It is on the degradation of the enzyme-GTP complex by the GTP-ase associated with the regulatory component that the effects of the action of cholera toxin are now thought to be exerted.

It has already been pointed out that the actions of cholera toxin and the non-hydrolysable analogue of GTP (i.e., Gpp(NH)p) are very similar. They both bring about persistent activation of adenylate cyclase, an activation which is greatly enhanced by hormones. The effects of these two agents are mutually exclusive, which indicates that they have a common target. Since it has already been established that the persistence of the effect of Gpp(NH)p is due to its resistance to hydrolysis by the regulatory GTP-ase, it seemed reasonable to suggest that cholera toxin might also prevent the action of GTP-ase in "turning off" the activation of adenylate cyclase. This was indeed shown to be the case when it was shown that cholera toxin inhibits the hormone-sensitive GTP-ase activity of the regulatory component of the adenylate cyclase of turkey red-blood cells [64]. Thus, in the presence of cholera toxin and GTP, the activated form of the enzyme-GTP complex gradually accumulates since it is no longer continuously degraded by the GTP-ase. In the presence of hormones as well, the rate of formation of enzyme-GTP is greatly enhanced, and with the turn-off mechanism inhibited, very high levels of adenylate cyclase activity develop. These findings have been confirmed with mammalian cells [217, 251]. A further important finding was that the action of the toxin in inhibiting the GTP-ase was dependent on the presence of NAD [64]; this brings us back to a consideration of the reaction that is actually catalyzed by the A_1 component of cholera toxin.

Following the findings of Moss and Vaughan on the NAD-ase action of cholera toxin, many attempts were made to determine whether cholera toxin catalyzed the ADP-ribosylation of an identifiable membrane component. Some of these attempts were abortive, since it was found that very high concentrations of toxin ADP-ribosylated the toxin itself— the A-component, but not the B—and it did not seem possible that this bizarre phenomenon could be relevant to the natural action of the toxin. Some of the initial problems were due to the numerous nucleotide-

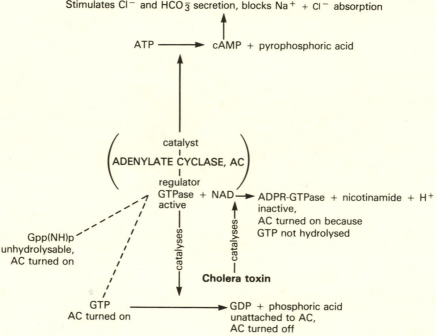

- - - - - signifies attachment

FIGURE 10.2. A view held in 1980 of the possible mode of action of the A_1 enzymic component of cholera toxin. The structures of the various compounds are shown in Figure 10.3. The catalytic activity of the enzyme adenylate cyclase that gives rise to elevated levels of cAMP is under the control of a regulatory component that is itself, or is closely associated with, a GTP-ase. As long as this regulator is combined with GTP, or its unhydrolysable analogue Gpp(NH)p, the adenylate cyclase is "turned on"; cholera toxin inactivates the GTP-ase by ADP-ribosylating it by the cleavage of NAD, thus preventing the hydrolysis of GTP to GDP (guanosine diphosphate), thus keeping the adenylate cyclase permanently turned on. This view is by no means proven, and is, like most ideas, almost certainly wrong, at least in detail; but it may be a rough indication of the truth of the matter.

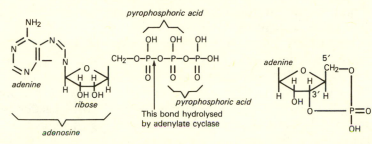

ATP, adenosine triphosphate (a nucleotide)   **cAMP, adenosine-3′5′-cyclic monophosphate**

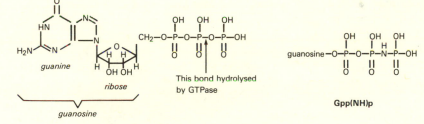

GTP, guanosine triphosphate (a nucleotide)

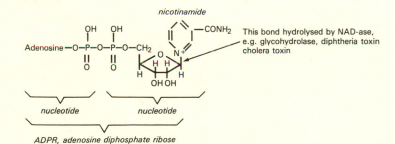

NAD, nicotinamide adenine dinucleotide

FIGURE 10.3. The structures of the main components in Figure 10.2. The names of the constituent parts of the molecules are given in italics.

binding proteins in the cell membrane, not all of which had any relevance to the action of adenylate cyclase. Pfeuffer showed that there were four major GTP-binding proteins, of molecular weights 80K, 52K, 42K and 23K, in the pigeon red-cell membrane. Solubilized adenylate cyclase which was still responsive to GTP contained only 42K and 23K proteins, and of these it seemed that the 42K component constituted the GTP regulatory component of adenylate cyclase [217]. Gill and Meren found that the 42K membrane component was ADP-ribosylated by cholera toxin in the presence of NAD, and conversely, ADP-ribose was removed from the 42K component when it was incubated with toxin and nicotinamide [158]. In other words, as with diptheria toxin and the ADP-ribosylation of Elongation Factor-2, the reaction was reversible; thus NAD + 42K = ADP-ribose-42K + nicotinamide + H^+. Thus, it seems that the 42K membrane component could be the primary relevant target for the cholera toxin-catalyzed reversible ADP-ribosylation which is associated with the activation of adenylate cyclase.[16] This conclusion was further supported by some neat cross-reconstitution experiments by Cassel and Pfeuffer, who mixed purified toxin-stimulated regulatory component of adenylate cyclase with purified non-activated catalytic component of the enzyme and thus activated the enzyme [62].

Taken as a whole, these results, and several we have not discussed, now afford a reasonably plausible explanation of the action of cholera toxin at the molecular level, which we may summarize thus: The regulatory (42K) component of adenylate cyclase binds GTP and in so doing activates the catalytic component; it is identical with, or embraces, a GTP-ase which under normal circumstances hydrolyses the bound GTP, thereby turning off the activation of the catalytic component. Subunit A_1 of cholera toxin is an enzyme that hydrolyses NAD and in the same act transfers the ADP-ribose component of this substrate to the GTP-ase, thereby inhibiting its activity, thus blocking the turn-off mechanism. Therefore, in the presence of NAD, GTP and cholera toxin adenylate cyclase activity becomes elevated, and remains so. Figure 10.2 and Figure 10.3 summarize, and no doubt oversimplify, the situation.

Thus, we think we now may know how cholera toxin activates adenylate cyclase, thus raising the level of cAMP in the cells of the small intestinal epithelium, but we still do not know how this raised level of cAMP causes a failure of absorption of sodium and chloride ions by the villus cells, and a secretion of chloride and bicarbonate ions by the crypt cells.

16. It seems that the turkey red-blood cell has a NAD-requiring enzyme with ADP-ribosylating activity, and the ability to activate adenylate cyclase. Thus, a vertebrate cell possesses an enzyme very similar in its action to the A_1 component of cholera toxin. If this is the case, it would seem likely that there would be some mechanism for "turning off" the activator enzyme.

XI

The International Centre for Diarrhoeal Disease Research, Bangladesh (ICDDR/B)

1. The Departure of R. A. Phillips

All the American expatriates at the PSCRL in Dacca except the young Public Health Service officers were on two-year contracts. Phillips's contract as Director expired on 31 December 1970. It was decided by the NIH Director, and by him, not to seek renewal. The reason for this decision stemmed from Phillips's loss of capacity to provide leadership to the younger officers. There were several complaints against him: He travelled excessively and so was absent from Dacca for much of the time (six months in 1968). He spent lavishly on travel for himself and for consultants at a time when the laboratory was short of funds for research. This was a source of bitterness for some, since all the staff were restricted to economy class travel while Phillips and consultants travelled first class. Many of these expensive consultants were of little value to most of the staff and indeed were not often seen by the younger officers. He accepted research contracts without consulting the staff that would be responsible for the work. He had opposed the field studies of oral rehydration. Some of the epidemiologists resented his lack of interest in epidemiology, maintaining "he could hardly spell the word". Phillips may not have had much personal interest in epidemiology, but it cannot be said that he opposed it or held it down. It was Phillips who initiated the discussions with Langmuir that led to the assignment of Epidemiological Intelligence Service officers from CDC to PSCRL, who encouraged the further development of the surveillance facility in Matlab thana and the strong program of vaccine evaluation, and so allowed the epidemiology division to become the biggest arm of the PSCRL. Finally, Phillips's capacity to deal with the day-to-day running of the laboratory had become impaired, due no doubt to sleepless nights exacerbated by hard off-duty drinking. He was not available to the staff in the mornings, and there were long delays in his reviewing of the manuscripts of scientific papers they submitted to him.

The atmosphere in Dacca at that time, of expatriates in an Eastern land, at times ill at ease with each other, perhaps making more of a drama of a situation than was justified, could have been drawn from one of Somerset Maugham's short stories. Some of the younger officers (e.g., Nalin and Cash, despite previous disagreements, and Curlin) were sympathetic to Phillips, but there were some young Turks, led by K. J. Bart and W. H. Mosley (whose missionary background and straight-laced outlook could hardly have been sympathetic to Phillips's life-style), who expressed their feelings to the Old Guard—Seal, MacLeod, Langmuir—during a protracted meeting in the Dacca Intercontinental Hotel. The upshot in Washington was, with Phillips's agreement, that his contract would not be renewed. He returned to Taipei, where his home and his family still were, and where for the rest of his years he carried out research in the Kohlberg Laboratory of the Chinese Veterans' Hospital, supported by research grants from the U.S. Navy Office of Naval Research and from private foundations. His interest in the intestinal tract was still strong and he studied the absorption of amino acids among healthy and malnourished Taiwanese people. He tried to develop the possibly excellent idea of lavaging the gut of kidney-diseased people with large volumes of saline, so using the gut as a sort of built-in dialysing machine. In his last months he tried by means of several telephone calls from Taipei to Oxford and California to get this idea patented. His health declined but certainly not his spirit. In the end he was evacuated to the U. S. Air Force Hospital at Clark Air Force Base in the Philippines, and there after a few days he died, on 20 September 1976, at the age of 70 years. His interest in physiology had remained with him until the day before he died, when he described to Filipino medical students the parlous state of his own heavily assaulted kidneys.

2. The Emergence of Bangladesh

If Phillips had not voluntarily left Dacca by the end of 1970 he would have been obliged by other circumstances to leave a few months later. By the beginning of the seventies East Pakistan had been troubled for many years with political unrest. About 56 percent of the population of Pakistan, mainly Bengalis, lived in the East Wing of Pakistan under the conviction that they were being imposed upon by the 1,000-mile distant West Wing. For years the Awami League in the East Wing had demanded greater economic benefits from the West Wing. There had been numerous riots in Dacca in 1968 and 1969 (and members of the Directing and Technical Committees and their consultants have memories of travelling to Dacca airport in the PSCRL ambulances, this being the only safe method of transport when public transport was on strike and private cars and taxis were being stoned).

In the second week of November 1970 a hurricane accompanied by a tidal wave devastated a number of offshore islands and part of the mainland of East Pakistan. The magnitude of the damage and the problems of saving the survivors were not recognized for several days, and consequently the response to the disaster was delayed. When it did come, several members of the PSCRL staff, along with other volunteers from the expatriate community, went to the devastated area to help provide food and shelter for the survivors. They also organized efforts to get clothing, food and medicine sent by voluntary relief agencies. The slowness of response by the government contributed to the large swing in the elections in December 1970, when the Awami League won the majority of seats in the Pakistan National Assembly, which was committed to draft a new Pakistani Constitution. But Pakistan President Yahya Kahn postponed the assembly sessions, and this led to further general strikes and riots in East Pakistan. On 25 March 1971 West Pakistani troops attacked the rebellious Bengalis. The next day the leaders of the Awami League declared independence and set up a government-in-exile in Calcutta. Months of fighting followed, in which it is estimated that at least a million people died. India joined in the struggle against the West Wing, and in a war lasting from 3 to 16 December 1971 inflicted a crushing defeat. Thus on that latter date East Pakistan became the People's Republic of Bangladesh. Thus also the PSCRL lost its first two initials, for Pakistan and SEATO, and became the CRL.

3. The CRL

Phillips was replaced as Director of the PSCRL by Dr. W. Kendrick Hare, who had been head of the physiology division since 1966. A few months previously, with the biennial rotation of U.S. Public Health Service fellows, Nalin and Cash had been replaced by Richard Guerrant and Lincoln Chen, and Geoffrey Sharp had come on a visit from Harvard University. The newcomers were not able to achieve much, because by February 1971 effective research at the PSCRL was seriously disturbed by the strikes and riots in East Pakistan, and towards the end of March it came to a halt when the country was attacked by West Pakistani troops. There was a huge exodus of people from Dacca to country areas, and early in April the entire American and other non-Pakistani staffs were evacuated from Dacca to Tehran, with the exception of three members who remained in the laboratory as caretakers. These were Mosley, Head of the Epidemiology Division; P. G. Talmon, Executive Officer of the Laboratory; and M. P. Tucker, Maintenance Officer. Hare and his wife, Ruth Hare (a member of his division), went to the United States for consultations and returned to Dacca in early June to relieve Mosley, who had been serving as Acting Director in the interim. Mosley then returned to the United States to take up the post of Chairman and Professor in the Department of Population Dynamics of the Johns Hopkins University School of Hygiene and Public Health. By September two new members who had joined the staff in October 1970, Doyle Evans and his wife, Dolores Evans, had managed to return to the laboratory. In December 1971, when the intensive fighting took place, the remaining Americans, the Hares, the Evanses, Talmon and Tucker, were evacuated from Dacca, but within a few weeks the Hares and Tucker were back again, together with G. Eddy, Special Advisor for Supply Management, and in the late spring of 1972 they were joined by Sister Torrance, the British Nursing Supervisor.

Throughout the war the indigenous staff remained at their posts at the laboratory, inspired by the examples of Mujibur Rahaman, the Deputy Director now in charge of the laboratory in the absence of the Americans, and of Jamiul Alam and K.M.S. Aziz. There were no casualties reported among the staff of the laboratory, but most of the Hindu staff had fled to India. Communication with the field hospital at Matlab Bazaar broke down, and it was closed down on 1 July. The laboratory remained virtually untouched during the war, but with bombing all around it between March and December it was difficult for staff to remain on duty and not flee for their lives. But Rahaman and the other senior officers decided that the staff should try and stay and keep the laboratory going somehow. There was at the time some political antagonism towards the laboratory and they feared that if once it was deserted it would be seized and would then be closed forever. They decided therefore to stay on duty, even if the laboratory were bombed, and even if there was hardly any money, since the financing which had previously come from the West Wing was cut off. They would work without salary and live on a subsidy amounting to $6 to $12 a month, derived from the sum of about 1.5 million rupees in the laboratory's bank account in Bangladesh. This idea was supported by all the employees of the laboratory.

During this difficult period the laboratory provided for the treatment of the greatest number of cholera patients in its history. More than 4,000 patients were treated, nearly 1,500 of them in the month of

November 1971 alone. There were also other diseases to deal with, and a very high mortality among children in the slums around Dacca. There was malnutrition, kwashiorkor and diarrhoea, most of it caused by organisms other than cholera. All this good work earned the approval of Sheikh Mujibur Rahman, and the political antagonism to the laboratory died down.

While the laboratory was able to fulfill its function as a centre for the treatment of cholera patients during the difficult days of the war, it was unable to keep up its function to carry out research. But the function was not forgotten by Rahaman and his colleagues and they did all they could do under the circumstances, which was to keep all the refrigerators and deep-freezers going to protect the frozen biological chemical specimens until they could be used again when better times came.

In the meantime there was concern in the United States about the continuation of the laboratory. A number of those interested, including Benenson, Gordon, Greenough, Hirschhorn, Mosley, Nalin, Cash, Craig, Chen and Carpenter, met within a week of the emergence of Bangladesh, i.e., on 22 December 1971, to discuss the situation and to form a Committee for the Continuation of the Cholera Research Laboratory (CCCRL), with Greenough as chairman. The committee expected American support for the CRL in the near future, and were eager to encourage the early return of American workers to Dacca. In the event the first American to return to the scene was David Nalin, working under the Johns Hopkins ICMR program. He cabled Greenough from the laboratory on 11 January 1972: "Everyone well, hospital functioning normally, money for two months, outlook excellent with proper attention to details—urge Hare return soon." Indeed the Hares did return within a few weeks, and so did Richard Cash.

Lincoln Chen visited Bangladesh from 13 to 16 January 1972 and sent a report to Greenough and others in America. He thought that the Bangladesh authorities viewed the laboratory with favour, but was concerned about funding. The current rate of spending at the laboratory was about 400,000 rupees (U.S. $50,000) per month which meant that the 1.5 million rupees in its account in Bangladesh would be exhausted by the end of March, and unless additional funds were found before April the laboratory would be bankrupt. Mujibur Rahaman and K. A. Monsur (head of the Institute of Public Health) had been making considerable efforts, and believed that the new government would be willing to contribute about the same as the previous provincial government of East Pakistan had contributed, i.e., about 600,000 rupees. The United Kingdom was anxious to continue its support of the laboratory and would contribute its previous share of about 20,000 pounds. In

March and April 1972 Greenough made a tour of Bangladesh as a consultant to the International Rescue Committee (IRC),[1] studying its programs concerned with relief and rehabilitation of the country. Greenough was, and still is, deeply concerned with Bangladesh. He had been the second physician to arrive at PSCRL, and his wife was a citizen of Bangladesh. He had many friends in the country, some of whom now occupied important positions in the government. On 10 May 1972 he reported to the CCCRL that as far as the laboratory was concerned, the most urgent need was to reestablish an effective chain of command with an efficient system of funding. This would require negotiations with the government of Bangladesh. The CRL had been rescued from bankruptcy by interim funding from U.S. Department of State, supplied by AID through the IRC. This arrangement was largely due to the CCCRL and Jean Rogier of the AID Technical Bureau, and Colin MacLeod with the State Department just before he set off for Dacca on a mission to assess the work of the laboratory. On his way he died suddenly in London on 11 February 1972, at the age of 63. The first cheque for $75,000 was passed in April and the next would be given in May. There was to be a total of $500,000 to continue the operation of the laboratory for 6 months. It was now apparent that everyone at NIH and at AID who was connected with the laboratory was working towards its reestablishment and the revitalization of its research activities. Greenough believed—and Seal agreed—that the CCCRL had a right to most of the credit for the momentum that generated this interim funding and for the sense of urgency that pressed for the continuation of the laboratory. Since the committee had achieved its object there was no longer any need for it.

In his annual report on the SEATO Cholera Research Program (dated 19 October 1972) to Sunthorn Hongladarom, Secretary-General of the Southeast Asia Treaty Organization, the Director of NIH, Robert Q. Marston (successor to Shannon), commented on the deletion of the P and S from PSCRL and expressed the hope the CRL could be restaffed by the summer of 1973. This was his last report to SEATO of work done under the auspices of the SEATO Cholera Research Program, and he awaited the SEATO Council of Ministers' decision on the continuation of the program. He believed "that Southeast Asia Treaty Organization

---

1. The IRC was founded in 1933 in New York out of a merger of the International Relief Association and the Emergency Rescue Committee. It is a "nonsectarian, nonpartisan voluntary agency supported by foundations, corporations, unions, community groups and the general public to resettle, rehabilitate and assist refugee victims of totalitarian oppression and war on five continents".

can take pride in having stimulated research in cholera which has developed an inexpensive but highly effective treatment, has clearly defined the abilities and shortcomings of present-day vaccines, has trained physicians and paramedical personnel in the care and treatment of the cholera patient, has contributed much basic knowledge on both cholera and other diarrhoeal diseases, and has created a body of experience which has been influential in the application of improved treatment and control measures in many countries as cholera has continued its spread throughout Asia, the Near East and Africa during the past decade. It has also been influential in removing some of the restrictions on commerce and communication which have attended the spread of cholera in the past". The idea that Phillips had discussed with Conroy in Bangkok in 1958 had borne much fruit.

In the six months' breathing space provided by the grant of $500,000 through the IRC, the NIH was engaged in working out a longer range future for the laboratory. At the meeting of the Cholera Advisory Committee in March 1972 the Director of NIH asked the committee to determine whether there was a sound scientific justification for maintaining access to a population in which cholera was endemic. By the end of the meeting the committee was able to tell the Director that they believed that the NIH did have such a valid stake because although access to a cholera endemic population was not necessary for physiological and pharmacological research, it was necessary to carry out field trials on the protective capacity of cholera toxoid in Bangladesh, or elsewhere. The expected cost of $1,500,000 per year to maintain such a capability "did not bother them" because there were many additional studies that could be made in the field, such as a single method for rehydrating children, or studies on other toxin-induced diarrhoeal diseases, such as that caused by *Escherichia coli*.

This was to be the last meeting of the Cholera Advisory Committee. The committee did not meet again in the second half of 1972 because the CRL in Dacca had not been able to resume research activities since no agreement had yet been made with the new government of Bangladesh, and since the development of the toxoid had not reached a stage that needed a discussion by the committee. Responsibility for the Cholera Research Program, including the laboratory in Dacca, was transferred internally within the NIAID from Seal's office (as scientific director of NIAID) to the Geographic Medicine Branch, which had been supporting cholera research under the U.S.-Japan Cooperative Medical Science Program. Carl Miller was to be cholera program officer of the Geographic Medicine Branch, and the Ad Hoc Cholera Toxoid Committee would continue to advise. Under congressional pressure to reduce the number of advisory committees, the NIH decided formally to abolish the Cholera Advisory Committee, which it did on 21 March 1973.

The short-term support for the CRL from the IRC came to its due end, and new arrangements were necessary for the continuation of the laboratory. The U.S. government had recognized the government of Bangladesh in May 1972, and in August of that year Jean Rogier of AID (who had long been AID representative in Dacca) had gone to Dacca to discuss new arrangements for the CRL. He learned there that the government of Bangladesh had decided that the CRL would hence-forth be a Bengali laboratory, directed and operated by Bengalis and responsive to the Ministry of Health. Rogier succeeded in obtaining a considerable modification of this stand after discussion with represen-tatives of the planning commission and the Ministry of Health, including K. A. Monsur, an old friend of the laboratory, who, as well as being Director of the Institute of Health where the CRL was housed, was also Director of Health Services (Preventive) in the Ministry of Health, and a draft agreement was concluded. This agreement was not acceptable to the NIH because it reduced its role to little more than that of a procurement agency. After an exploratory exchange of cables and correspondence which appeared to indicate that the government of Bangladesh might be more flexible, Seal, Miller and Rogier went to Dacca in February 1973 with the object of reaching agreement on the future operation of the CRL that would be acceptable to the NIH, AID and the government of Bangladesh, and would thus enable AID to negotiate financing of the laboratory. They saw Monsur, who made it clear that the Bengalis wanted a much bigger role both in the management and the scientific affairs of the CRL, in accordance with the general national policy of independence after many years of colonialism. He also stated that the government of Bangladesh was anxious for the CRL to continue, with participation by the NIH as the preeminent medical scientific institution in the world. Seal's party in their turn expressed their desire to see the continuation of a fine institution, but did not see how the Director of the NIH could play an effective part in the scientific leadership of the laboratory unless he played a major part in the selection of the Director of the CRL. Monsur made it clear that the Directing Council of the CRL, of which he was to be chairman, would decide the scientific program of the Laboratory, as well as administrative and financial matters. Seal pointed out that since the new proposals specified that the U.S. members of the Directing Council would have to be resident in Bangladesh, they would either have to be non-medical people outside the laboratory, which would be unacceptable, or members of the laboratory staff, which would also be unacceptable because the U.S. could not nominate subordinates of the Director of the CRL to policymaking positions above him. In other words, negotiations for the perpetuation of the CRL were at an impasse.

In the autumn of 1973, Seal, Miller and Rogier again went to Dacca to try and find a way out of the impasse. With the help of former and present Bangladeshi members of the CRL, and especially with Monsur's help, agreement was reached that was approved by the Ministry of Health before they left. With this assurance that a bilateral agreement would emerge, AID was able to continue funding. On 15 May 1974 a new bilateral agreement between the governments of Bangladesh and the United States was signed to cover the period until the end of the fiscal year 1977. It was agreed that the CRL be established by the government of Bangladesh as an autonomous body which would serve as an institution for the implementation of a co-operative program of cholera research between the governments of both countries through AID and NIH. It would operate under the general direction of a Directing Council which would be provided by the NIH with the services of a Scientific Review and Technical Advisory Committee. In this co-operative program the participation of United Nations organizations (such as WHO), of other nations, and of private and public organizations would be welcomed, provided that any arrangement was agreed upon by the contributing party and the government of Bangladesh, after consultation with the concerned agencies of the U.S. government. The Directing Council would consist of three members from the government of Bangladesh, two from the United States and one member from each other participating nation or organization, with a chairman elected by the members of the Council. The Director of the CRL would be an ex-officio non-voting member and secretary to the Council. Since it was considered desirable that the Council should meet frequently (i.e., not less than once a month) it was necessary that its members should reside in Bangladesh.

The Scientific Review Committee would be organized by the NIH in consultation with the Directing Council. It would consist of three to five distinguished investigators, with the Chairman of the Directing Council and the Director of the CRL as ex-officio members. Other distinguished scientists could be invited to advise on specific problems. The committee would meet at least once a year to review the current and proposed research program prepared by the Director of the CRL and to provide technical guidance to the Directing Countil.

The Director of the CRL would be selected by NIH, subject to the approval of the Bangladesh Ministry of Health, and in all major decisions he would be guided by the Directing Council.

The financing of the CRL would be derived from a number of sources: (a) participating agency service agreements between AID and NIH which would provide salaries of non-Bangladeshi scientists not paid by other agencies, and dollar funds for imported equipment and other commitments of the CRL research program that could not be paid in local currency; (b) the CRL general operating fund, created by pooled Bangladesh currency received from the participating nations, supplemented by local currency funds supplied by international agencies and private foundations; (c) the capital reserve fund, created from unspent or unreserved money remaining to the credit of the general operating fund at the end of each financial year.

The laboratory staff, appointed by the Director, would be international in character. Semi-professional scientific staff would be chosen from scientists of the Bangladesh government, or provided by NIH or recruited from other countries on personal service contracts with the CRL. Visiting scientists from other nations, multilateral and regional organizations and agencies could be invited or accepted by the Director for special studies.

The new agreement for the future of the CRL was to continue until the end of the fiscal year, with the possibility of its being extended beyond that date. This support was in fact extended by the Asia Regional Board of AID to the end of the financial year 1978, by which time new plans for the laboratory were evolved.

4. The ICDDR/B

The PSCRL in theory had involved the participation of all the SEATO nations; in practise, participation had been limited largely to Pakistan and the United States, with limited involvement of the United Kingdom. The post-war agreement between the governments of Bangladesh and the United States for the continuation of the CRL made provision for participation by any nation that wished, as well as the United Nations organizations and private and public agencies, but in practise, participation was again largely limited to Bangladesh and the United States. Towards the end of the first period of the new agreement the move towards internationalization of the Laboratory grew stronger. Between April 1976 and February 1978 five reports were published, recommending the broadening both of international participation in the Laboratory and of the scope of its activities.

The Verwey Proposal

W. F. Verwey, Director of the CRL from 1974 to the end of June 1977, when he was obliged by ill health to resign, produced the lengthy (about 50,000 words) "Proposal for the Program of the Cholera Research Laboratory in Bangladesh for the Period of Fy [financial year] 77-Fy

81, inclusive". This proposal was made in response to a request from AID for "a multidisciplinary five-year plan which would broaden the CRL activities to include not only major continuing research on cholera and other diarrhoeal diseases but also research on other problems of Bangladesh and similar countries focussing on demography [population control] and the medical aspects of nutrition". Proposals in the areas of environmental sanitation and rural development had also been suggested. It had been requested that the proposal should be specific and capable of being accomplished within the funding available at that time.

The proposals made by Verwey fell into four groups: (1) diarrhoeal diseases, including general studies (e.g., diarrhoeas of "unknown" etiology, unsupervised oral rehydration, cholera, shigellosis [bacillary dysentery] and the establishment of a network of information on diarrhoeal diseases); (2) demography, including demographic surveillance of the Matlab field area and studies on population control; (3) nutrition, including studies on the effects of diarrhoeal diseases on the growth and development of children, the effects of malabsorption and diarrhoea on the absorption of orally administered medications, and the relationship between nutritional status, immunity and infectious diseases; (4) separately funded collateral studies on such subjects as contraception, the effect of domestic tubewells on health, and diarrhoeal disease infectivity in man.

Verwey suggested a change in the management of the laboratory. (1) There should be a Board of Directors experienced in science and in the management of research. Each country, agency or organization providing significant and continuing support could appoint a member of the Board from its own people experienced in the policies and procedures of their own organizations (e.g., AID and NIH—regarded as two agencies as far as the United States was concerned). (2) The Board of Directors would meet twice a year, once at the CRL and once in a location to be decided. It would elect its own chairman and call in consultants when necessary. (3) The present Directing Council would continue as at present with the management of local administrative and fiscal matters. (4) The Chairman of the Directing Council and the Director of the Laboratory would be ex-officio members of the Board of Directors.

The total operating expenses of the CRL for the five-year period under consideration were calculated to be somewhat over $12 million.

The Mosley Proposal

In a paper also invited by AID, dated April 1976, W. H. Mosley, at that time Chairman of the Department of Population Dynamics of the Johns Hopkins University School of Hygiene and Public Health, also proposed a five-year plan for the CRL, and the plan also envisaged the inclusion of programs of research in human reproduction and in human nutrition in addition to research on cholera and other enteric diseases. These three fields of activity were considered to be interdependent because diarrhoeal disease, as well as the supply of food, affects the nutritional state of a population, and the health of the population determines both its reproductive and its productive potential. Mosley proposed that such a remodelled institution should operate under a broadly based international health and population research program supported by multiple sources of funding from a variety of international agencies and interested governments. He suggested that a model to consider was the Consultative Group on International Agricultural Research consisting of the International Rice Research Institute and other international agriculture institutes throughout the world. The membership of the Directing Council of the revamped laboratory should consist of representatives of the major donors, such as, possibly, the Ford and Rockefeller Foundations, the International Development Research Corporation of Canada, the World Bank, and governments of the United States, Bangladesh, the United Kingdom, Australia and other countries that might be interested. He proposed that the enlarged scope of, and participation in, the new institution should be indicated by a new name such as the International Health and Population Research Institute or (perhaps because such a name could apply to a national institute interested in international health and population) the International Institute for Health and Population Research.

The AID Proposal

Verwey and Mosley's proposals were incorporated in a proposal next made by AID, and Mosley's suggested alternative name for the laboratory was borrowed. In a paper prepared for AID's Asia Regional Bureau, dated August 1976, two members of the Bureau of Technical Assistance of AID's Office of Health, A. J. Davidson and Jean Rogier, put forward the "Proposal for an International Institute of Health and Population Research (IIHPR) in Bangladesh". In November 1976 a somewhat abbreviated version of the paper was put out anonymously as a "preliminary Prospectus", and the word "Nutrition" was inserted between the words "Health" and "Population Research", with the initials now IIHNPR. The prospectus proposed that the CRL should be replaced by an IIHNPR by 1979. "The IINHPR would serve as (a) a world center for the development of new and improved technologies for the reduction of morbidity and mortality resulting from enteric diseases, for the reduction of malnutrition, and for the purpose of slowing population growth, and (b) a center for the development and demonstration of methods which will optimize the application of the technologies learned". The new institution would be a private, non-profit international organization under a charter to be granted by the government of Bangladesh. It would be governed by a Board of Trustees made up of "distinguished individuals and scientists". This Board would solicit and receive funds for the IIHNPR from "the donor community", and it would select the Director of the Institute. There would be a Technical Advisory Committee to advise the Board and the Director. The prospectus pointed out that the CRL was already engaged in demographic and nutritional studies. Since 1974 the Laboratory had been collaborating with the Ministry of Health of the government of Bangladesh and with the Department of Population Dynamics of the Johns Hopkins University in studies, funded by AID, involving clinical trials in Matlab thana on various systemic and hormonal contraceptives. There had also been a study of the growth and development of children in the village of Meharan. In the field of nutrition the Laboratory had started enquiries into nutritional status in the development of children and in their susceptibility to infectious disease, into the nutritional status of mothers in relation to lactation and infant feeding practices, and into the relationship between nutrition and enteric disease, and vice versa. Further to implement the CRL's unique potential to conduct research in the areas of enteric disease, human reproduction and malnutrition, the Laboratory required a degree of permanence. It also required a truly international character that was not attainable under the current bilateral technical assistance arrangement between AID and the government of Bangladesh. Therefore, to "achieve permanence, to develop the potential of the CRL, to attract high quality scientists from the international community and to obtain broad-based support for operating and capital costs from multiple dangers, it [was] proposed that there should be created by 1979 an International Institute for Health, Nutrition and Population Research in Dacca, Bangladesh".

The prospectus' estimate of budget requirement for the five-year period from 1979 of $14 million was made on the assumption that the United States government and the government of Bangladesh, together with other donor nations, foundations (e.g., Ford, Rockefeller) and international organizations, would provide sufficient long-term support.

The prospectus stated: "Action has already been taken to assure the continuity and strengthening of the research program of the CRL and its assimilation into the IIHNPR. Dr. W. Henry Mosley, Chairman of the Department of Population Dynamics, School of Hygiene and Public Health, The Johns Hopkins University, Baltimore, Maryland, has been nominated to the position of Director beginning in July 1977". Behind this statement lay the sad fact that the Director of the CRL, Willard

Foster Verwey, was seriously ill and due to retire prematurely. He died in Flagstaff, Arizona, on 17 May 1979. It should also be noted that the prospectus stated that another CRL alumnus, William B. Greenough III, Associate Professor of Medicine at the Johns Hopkins University School of Medicine, had been nominated to the position of Director of the Clinical Division.

The ICHR Proposal

The initials continued to proliferate. In October 1977 an apparently hastily prepared, flowery rather than precise, draft prospectus for re-placement of the CRL by an International Center for Health Research (ICHR) was issued from the CRL. With the expiry of the existing charter, and with a concurrent change in AID funding policy, the proposal outlined in this prospectus had been made by the authorities of the Bangladesh government and the CRL, and the creation of the ICHR had been approved in principle by the council of advisers to the President of Bangladesh in April 1977. A report of an international scientific review committee (see below) subsequently recalled that the CRL had "taken the opportunity to invite expert opinion on its re-chartering, and on its research objectives, emphasis and relationships with other institutions in Bangladesh and elsewhere". The laboratory had "expe-rienced conflicts of direction and emphasis among its staff and potential conflicts with the development of other institutes in Bangladesh. There had been some public criticism of the CRL's role in health research and training with accusations that the CRL by its very presence [was] retarding health research and development in Bangladesh. Although matters of opinion, the CRL [had] taken these criticisms seriously enough to invite views on their validity". As with the other proposals, it was proposed that the ICHR should be concerned with enteric diseases, malnutrition and overpopulation (in this case, perhaps to be more tactful, called high fertility). The centre would strive "not to intensify and extend research activities, but to develop a program of cooperation with other authorities and organizations in developing countries for collab-orative projects of research and for the broad dissemination and ap-plication of research results". It would be governed by an international board of trustees which would be self-perpetuating. Three members of the board would be designated by the government of Bangladesh, another member would be nominated by the WHO and the Director of the centre would be a non-voting ex-officio member. There would be a majority of as yet unspecified board members, but "some means presumably should be found to permit participation in the selection process by organizations in areas to be served by ICHR and by funding agencies". There is no specific reference to American participation. The estimate for cost was higher than those previously made, viz., nearly $18 million for a four-year period.

The ICDDR/B

From 6 to 14 February 1978 a review meeting was held at the CRL, attended by 20 international and 6 Bangladeshi scientists and the senior staff of the CRL, to review the current scientific program of the CRL, to examine the rationale for transforming it into an ICHR, and to review the objectives of the ICHR and make recommendations for the fulfillment of those objectives. As to diarrhoeal disease, the meeting, "while acknowledging the strengths of past and proposed diarrhoeal disease studies, wishes to emphasize the need for stronger collegiate cooperation with other institutions in Bangladesh and abroad in all further investigations in the area". As to population studies the meeting "favours biological and demographic population studies at the center provided that they are relevant to diarrheal diseases and related topics". Again it was recommended that collegiate cooperation with other institutions in Bangladesh and abroad was desirable. As to nutrition, it was noted that epidemiological observations in several countries indicated that, even when given adequate food, chronically malnourished, intestinally infected and parasitised children did not grow normally, and that this defective caloric intake could be overcome by partial control of infection; on the other hand, improved nutrition could lead to increased capacity to cope with diarrhoeal disease. It was therefore recommended that the centre should address itself to the study of diarrhoeal diseases as they related to nutrition, and vice versa, and that nutritional studies should focus on maternal and foetal malnutrition, breast feeding and weaning. It was also recommended that research on health services should be carried out with the view to improving child feeding practices, child care, early home rehydration, personal and environmental sanitation, and other relevant factors that would lead to improved resistance to disease and improved nutrition.

It was also recognized that the centre should share its technical activities in relation to diarrhoeal disease and related fields of health with its host country and with the rest of the world. This could be achieved by long-term training of potential research workers in equal numbers from Bangladesh and other developing and developed countries. There should also be national and international short-term training through short courses, seminars and workshops, both on research and on its implementation.

The meeting finally recommended that rather than call the internationalized Laboratory the International Center [sic] for Health Research, it should be called the International Centre [sic] for Diarrheal [sic]

Diseases [sic] Research (ICDDR). This name was later to alter slightly. The word "International" had been included in recognition of the fact that diarrhoeal diseases are a major world health problem. Since WHO had initiated a global diarrhoeal disease control programme, including research, the ICDDR would make significant contributions. The more specific title, referring to diarrhoeal disease only, was preferred because it indicated "the focal concern on the institution". These words were presumably intended to indicate that nutrition and population studies were concerned only in so far as they related to diarrhoeal disease; it was important that the ICDDR should not tread on the toes of those institutions in the Ministry of Health of Bangladesh that were already independently concerned with other nutritional and demographic studies.

A draft ordinance to establish the International Centre for Diarrhoeal [sic] Disease [sic] Research, Bangladesh—note the revisions in the title— was prepared by an interim international committee consisting of representatives of WHO and of governments and organizations providing resources for the CRL at the time, viz., Australia, Bangladesh, the Ford Foundation, the International Development Research Corporation, the United Nations Fund for Population Activities, the United Nations Children's Fund, the United Kingdom and the United States, under the chairmanship of the resident representative of the United Nations Development Program (UNDP). The ordinance was promulgated by the President of the People's Republic of Bangladesh on 6 December 1978 establishing the ICDDR/B. This action was followed by a plenary meeting of the Interim International Committee under the chairmanship of the UNDP convened at WHO headquarters in Geneva on 13–14 February 1979 [75, 161]. At this meeting the ICDDR/B was endorsed and 15 members of the first Board of Trustees were elected, representing Bangladesh (entitled to 3 representatives), WHO, Australia, Canada, Costa Rica, India, Indonesia, Kenya, Kuwait, Poland, Sweden, the United Kingdom and the United States; the 16th member of the Board was the Director of the centre, ex-officio. The Board is required to meet at least twice a year. Its function is rather generally defined, largely to approve and authorize actions rather than initiate them. The more immediate supervision of the Centre would seem rather to be in the hands of the Executive Committee designated by the Board, consisting of the Director, and at least one Bangladeshi trustee and presumably some other members. The Board is aided by an External Scientific Review Committee from developed and under-developed countries meeting at least once in two years, a program coordination committee and an ethical review committee.

The ICDDR/B was formally inaugurated by President Ziaur Rahman of Bangladesh on 26 June 1979. The first Director of the ICDDR/B was W. H. Mosley, the Deputy Director was M. Mujibur Rahaman and the three Scientific Directors were K.M.S. Aziz, Lincoln C. Chen, and W. B. Greenough III. Mosley resigned his appointment and left Dacca three days after the inauguration in order to take up an appointment as visiting professor in the Population Studies and Research Institute of the University of Nairobi in Kenya. W. B. Greenough III was appointed Director from 1 July 1979.

References

1. Al-Awqati, Q., Cameron, J. L., Field, M., and Greenough, W. B., III: Response of human ileal mucosa to choleragen and theophylline. J. clin. Invest. 49, 2a, 1970.

2. Annotation: The cholera germ and its discoverer. Lancet 2, 203, 1884.

3. Annual Register of World Events, 1959. London, Longmans, p. 179, 1960.

4. Anon.: Report of cholera at Warrington. Superiority of the saline treatment. London med. Gaz. 10, 731, 1832.

4a. Anon.: On the changes the animal secretions undergo during cholera morbus. By Mr. R. Itermann, of Moscow. Edinburgh New Philosoph. J. 12, 128, 1831.

5. Arnon, S. S., Midura, T. F., Damus, K., Thompson, B., Wood, R. H., and Chin, J.: Honey and other environmental risk factors for infant botulism. J. Pediatr. 94, 331, 1979.

6. Aziz, K.M.A.: Kinship in Bangladesh, ICDDR/B, Dacca, 1979.

7. Banwell, J. G., Gorbach, S. L., Pierce, N. F., Mitra, R., and Mondal, A.: Acute undifferentiated human diarrhea in the tropics. II. Alterations in intestinal fluid and electrolyte movements. J. clin. Invest. 50, 890, 1971.

8. Banwell, J., Pierce, N. F., Mitra, R., Caranasos, G. J., and Keimowitz, R. I.: A study of small intestinal water and solute movement in acute and convalescent human cholera. Symp. on Cholera, U.S.-Japan CMSP, Palo Alto, June 1967, p. 187.

9. Banwell, J. G., Pierce, N. F., Mitra, R., Caranasos, G. J., Keimowitz, R. I., Mondal, A., and Manji, P. M.: Preliminary results of a study of small intestinal water and solute movement in acute and convalescent human cholera. Ind. J. med. Res. 56, 633, 1968.

10. Banwell, J. G., Pierce, N. F., Mitra, R. C., Caranasos, G. J., Keimowitz, R. I., Fedson, D. S., Thomas, J., Gorbach, S. L., Sack, R. B., and Mondal, A.: Intestinal fluid and electrolyte transport in human cholera. J. clin. Invest. 49, 183, 1970.

11. Barr, M., and Glenny, A. T.: Some practical applications of immunological principles. J. Hyg. 44, 135, 1945.

12. Bart, K. J., Huq, A., Khan, M., and Mosley, W. H.: Seroepidemiologic studies during a simultaneous epidemic of infection with El Tor Ogawa and Classical Inaba *Vibrio cholerae*. J. infect. Dis. 121, S17, 1970.

13. Barua, D., and Mukherjee, A. C.: Observations on the El Tor vibrios isolated from cases of cholera in Calcutta. Bull. Calcutta Sch. trop. Med. 12, 147, 1964.

14. Basu Mallik, K. C., and Ganguli, N. C.: Some observations on the pathogenesis of cholera. Ind. J. med. Res. 52, 894, 1964.

15. Bayless, T. M., Iber, R. L., Hendrix, T. R., McGonagle, T., and Serebro, H. A.: Glucose absorption in the rabbit and dog with cholera toxin-induced diarrhea. Symp. on Cholera, U.S.-Japan CMSP, Palo Alto, June 1967, p. 181.

16. Beckman, B., Flores, J., Witkum, P. A., and Sharp, G.W.G.: Studies on the mode of action of cholera to toxin effects on solubilised adenylate cyclase. J. clin. Invest. 53, 122, 1974.

17. Benenson, A. S.: Review of experience with whole-cell and somatic antigen vaccines. Symp. on Cholera, U.S.-Japan CMSP, Sapporo, 1976, p. 228.

18. Benenson, A. S., Joseph, P. R., and Oseasohn, R. O.: Cholera vaccine field trials in East Pakistan. 1. Reaction of antigenicity studies. Bull. WHO 38, 347, 1968.

19. Benenson, A. S., Mosley, W. H., Fahimuddin, M., and Oseasohn, R. O.: Cholera vaccine field trials in East Pakistan. 2. Effectiveness in the field. Bull. WHO 38, 359, 1968.

20. Benenson, A. S., Saad, A., Mosley, W. H., and Ahmed, A.: Serological studies in cholera. 3. Serum toxin neutralization—Rise in titre in response to infection with *vibrio cholerae*, and the level in the "normal" population of East Pakistan. Bull. WHO 38, 287, 1968.

21. Bennett, V., and Cuatrecasas, P.: Mechanism of action of Vibrio cholerae enterotoxin. Effects on adenylate cyclase of toad and rat erythrocyte plasma membranes. J. Membrane Biol. 22, 1, 1975.

22. Bennett, V., and Cuatrecasas, P.: Mechanism of activation of adenylate cyclase by Vibrio cholerae enterotoxin. J. Membrane Biol. 22, 29, 1975.

23. Bennett, V., O'Keefe, E., and Cuatrecasas, P.: Mechanism of action of cholera toxin and the mobile hormone receptor theory of hormone receptor-adenylate cyclase interactions. Proc. Nat. Acad. Sci. 72, 33, 1975.

24. Benyajati, C.: Experimental cholera in humans. Brit. med. J. 1, 140, 1966.

25. Berczi, I.: Stability of *Escherichia coli* endotoxin in the rat gastrointestinal tract. J. Path. Bact. 96, 487, 1968.

26. Berger, E. Y.: Intestinal absorption and excretion. In: Mineral Metabolism, ed. Courar. London, Academic Press, 1960, p. 249.

27. Bernard, C.: Leçons sur les phénomènes de la vie communs aux animaux et aux végétaux. Paris, J.-B. Baillière et Fils, Vol. 1, 1878, p. 112.

28. Bhide, M. B., and Modak, M. J.: Additional site for the action of cholera toxin. Nature, 223, 842, 1969.

29. Biology Data Book, Fed. Amer. Soc. exp. Biol. 2nd ed., Vol. 1, 1972.

30. Blankenhorn, D. H., Hirsch, J., and Ahrens, E. H., Jr.: Transintestinal intubation: Technic for measurement of gut length and physiologic sampling of known loci. Proc. Soc. exp. Biol. Med. 88, 356, 1955.

31. Blume, A. J., and Foster, C. J.: Neuroblastoma adenylate cyclase. Role of 2-chloro-adenosine, prostaglandin E, and guanine nucleotides in regulation of activity. J. biol. Chem. 251, 3399, 1976.

32. Boivin, A., and Mesrobeanu, L.: Recherches sur les antigènes somatiques et sur les endotoxines des bactéries. 1. Considérations générales et exposé des techniques utilisées. Rev. d'Immunol. 1, 553, 1935.

33. Boivin, A., and Mesrobeanu, L.: Recherches sur les antigènes somatiques et sur les endotoxines des bactéries. 2. L'Antigène somatique complet (antigène 0) de certaines bactéries est le constituant principal de leur endotoxine. Rev. d'Immunol. 2, 113, 1936.

34. Botelho, S. Y.: Tears and the lacrimal gland. Scientific American 211, No. 4, 78, 1964.

35. Braude, A. I.: Absorption, distribution, and elimination of endotoxins and their derivatives. In: Bacterial Endotoxins, ed. Landy, M., and Braun, W. New Brunswick, N.J., Rutgers, The State University, p. 98, 1964.

36. Bretonneau, P.: "Fifth Memoir. On the means of preventing the development and progress of diphtheria. To Drs. Bloche and P. Guersant". Arch. générales de Médecine, Jan. and Sept. 1885; English translation by R. H. Semple, in Memoirs on Diphtheria. London, The New Sydenham Society, 1859.

37. Brieger, L.: Untersuchungen über Ptomaine, dritter Theil. Berlin, 1886.

38. Brieger, L., and Fraenkel, C.: Untersuchungen über Bakteriengifte. Berliner Klin. Wochenschr. 27, 268, 1890.

39. Bryceson, A.D.M.: Cholera, the flickering flame. Proc. Roy. Soc. Med. 70, 363, 1977.

39a. Bull. bacteriol. Nomenclature Taxon. 15, 185, 1965.

40. Bulloch, W.: The History of Bacteriology. London, Oxford University Press, 1938, reprinted 1960, p. 376.

41. Burnet, F. M., and Stone, J. D.: Desquamation of intestinal epithelium by *V. cholerae* filtrates. Characterization of mucinase and tissue disintegrating enzymes. Austral. J. exp. Biol. med. Sci. 25, 219, 1947.

42. Burrows, W.: Endotoxins. Ann. Rev. Microbiol. 5, 181, 1951.

43. Burrows, W.: Cholera toxins. Ann. Rev. Microbiol. 22, 245, 1968.

44. Cantani, A.: Giftigkeit der Cholerabacillen. Deutsch. med. Wochenschr. 12, 789, 1886.

45. Carle and Rattone: Studio sperimentale sull'etiologia del tetano. Giorn. dell. R. acad. di. Med. di Torino 32, 174, 1884.

46. Carpenter, C.C.J.: Pathophysiology of cholera. Ind. J. med. Res. 52, 887, 1964.

47. Carpenter, C.C.J.: Canine gut response to cholera exotoxin. Symp. on Cholera, U.S.-Japan CMSP, Palo Alto, June 1967, p. 179.

48. Carpenter, C.C.J.: Treatment of cholera—Tradition and authority versus science, reason, and humanity. Johns Hopkins med. J. 139, 153, 1976.

49. Carpenter, C.C.J., Barua, D., Sack, R. B., Wallace, C. K., Mitra, P. P., Khanra, S. R., Werner, T. S., Duffy, T. E., and Oleinick, A.: Clinical studies in Asiatic cholera. 5. Shock-producing acute diarrheal disease in Calcutta: a clinical and biochemical comparison of cholera with severe non-cholera diarrhea, 1963–1964. Bull. Johns Hopkins Hosp. 118, 230, 1966.

50. Carpenter, C.C.J., Barua, D., Wallace, C. K., Mitra, P. P., Sack, R. B., Khanra, S. R., Wells, S. A., Dans, P. E., and Chaudhuri, R. N.: Clinical studies in Asiatic cholera. 4. Antibiotic therapy in cholera. Bull. Johns Hopkins Hosp. 118, 216, 1966.

51. Carpenter, C.C.J., Barua, D., Wallace, C. K., Sack, R. B., Mitra, P. P., Werner, A. S., Duffy, T. P., Oleinick, A., Khanra, S. R., and Lewis, G. W.: Clinical and physiological observations during an epidemic outbreak of non-vibrio cholera-like disease in Calcutta. Bull. WHO 33, 665, 1965.

52. Carpenter, C.C.J., Chaudhuri, R. N., and Mondal, A.: A simple effective therapy of cholera. Ind. J. med. Res. 52, 924, 1964.

53. Carpenter, C.C.J., and Greenough, W. B., III: The effect of blood flow and metabolic inhibitors on electrolyte loss induced by cholera exotoxin. J. clin. Invest. 47, 15a, 1968.

54. Carpenter, C.C.J., and Greenough, W. B., III: The response of the canine duodenum to intraluminal challenge with cholera exotoxin. J. clin. Invest. 47, 2600, 1968.

55. Carpenter, C.C.J., Greenough, W. B., III, and Sack, R. B.: The relationship of superior mesenteric artery blood flow to gut electrolyte loss in experimental canine cholera. J. infect. Dis. 119, 182, 1969.

56. Carpenter, C.C.J., Mitra, P. P., and Sack, R. B.: Clinical studies in Asiatic cholera. 1. Preliminary observations, November 1962–March 1963. Bull. Johns Hopkins Hosp. 118, 165, 1966.

57. Carpenter, C.C.J., Mitra, P., Sack, B., Wells, S., Dans, P., Saxena, R. S., and Mondal, A.: Metabolic and therapeutic studies on cholera: Preliminary report. Bull. Calcutta Sch. trop. Med. 11, 87, 1963.

58. Carpenter, C.C.J., Mondal, A., Sack, R. B., Mitra, P. P., Dans, P. E., Wells, S. A., Hinman, E. J., and Chaudhuri, R. N.: Clinical studies in Asiatic cholera. 2. Development of 2:1 saline:lactate regimen. Comparison of the regimen with traditional methods of treatment, April and May, 1963. Bull. Johns Hopkins Hosp. 118, 174, 1966.

59. Carpenter, C.C.J., Sack, R. B., Freeley, J. C., and Steenberg, R. W.: Site and characteristics of electrolyte loss and effect of intraluminal glucose in experimental canine cholera. J. clin. Invest. 47, 1210, 1968.

60. Carpenter, C.C.J., Sack, R. B., Mitra, P. P., and Mondal, A.: Tetracycline therapy in cholera. Bull. Calcutta Sch. trop. Med. 12, 30, 1964.

61. Cash, R. A., Nalin, D. R., Rochat, R., Reller, L. B., Haque, Z. A., and Rahman, A.S.M.M.: A clinical trial of oral therapy in a rural cholera-treatment center. Amer. J. trop. Med. Hyg. 19, 653, 1970.

62. Cassel, D., and Pfeuffer, T.: Mechanism of cholera toxin action: Covalent modification of the guanyl nucleotide-binding protein of the adenylate cyclase system. Proc. Nat. Acad. Sci. 75, 2669, 1978.

63. Cassel, D., and Selinger, Z.: Catecholamine-stimulated GTPase activity in turkey erythrocyte membranes. Biochem. Biophys. Acta 452, 538, 1976.

64. Cassel, D., and Selinger, Z.: Mechanism of adenylate cyclase activation by cholera toxin: Inhibition of GTP hydrolysis at the regulatory site. Proc. Nat. Acad. Sci. 74, 3307, 1977.

65. Chakravarti, H. S., and Chaudhuri, R. N.: Plasma sodium, potassium

and chloride changes in cholera and their significance in prognosis and treatment. J. Ind. med. Assoc. 23, 488, 1954.

66. Chambers, J. S.: The Conquest of Cholera—America's Greatest Scourge. New York, The Macmillan Company, 1938.

67. Chandavimol, P.: Thai Health Organization in 1958 for recognition, emergency treatment and transportation of cholera cases. SEATO Conference on Cholera, Dacca, 1960. Bangkok, The Post Publishing Co. Ltd. 1962, pp. 15–18.

68. Chatterjee, N. H.: Control of vomiting in cholera and oral replacement of fluid. Lancet 2, 1063, 1953.

69. Chatterjee, N. H., and Sarkar, J.: Biochemical study of blood of cholera patients. Trans. Roy. Soc. trop. Med. Hyg. 34, 379, 1941.

70. Chaudhuri, R. N.: Notes on some remedies. 34. Dehydration and its treatment. Part 5. Treatment of cholera. Ind. med. Gaz. 85, 257, 1950.

71. Chaudhuri, R. N., Gosal, S. C., Mondal, A., and Chakravarty, N. K.: The treatment of cholera with oral and intravenous chloromycetin. Ind. med. Gaz. 87, 455, 1952.

72. Chen, L. C., Rohde, J. E., and Sharp, G.W.G.: Intestinal adenyl cyclase activity in human cholera. Lancet 1, 939, 1971.

73. Chen, L. C., Rohde, J. E., and Sharp, G.W.G.: Properties of adenyl cyclase from human jejunal mucosa during virtually acquired cholera and convalescence. J. clin. Invest. 51, 731, 1972.

74. Chisholm, C.: An essay towards an enquiry how far the effluvia from dead animal bodies passing through the natural process of putrefaction are efficient in producing malignant pestilential fever. Edinb. med. and surg. J. 6, 389, 1810.

75. Cholera Research Laboratory Annual Report, Dacca, May 1979.

76. Clements, J. D., and Finkelstein, R. A.: Isolation and characterization of homogeneous heat-labile enterotoxins with high specific activity from *Escherichia coli* cultures. Infect. Immun. 24, 760, 1979.

77. Code, C. F.: Absorption of water and electrolyte in healthy persons: A brief review. Proceedings of the Cholera Research Symposium, Jan. 1965, Honolulu. Washington, D.C., U.S. Government Printing Office, 1965, p. 87.

78. Cohnheim, J. F.: Lectures on General Pathology—a Handbook for Practitioners and Students. Translated from the 2nd German edition by A. B. McKee. London, 1889–90.

79. Collier, R. J. Diphtheria toxin: Mode of action and structure. Bacter. Rev. 39, 54, 1975.

80. Collier, R. J.: Inhibition of protein synthesis by exotoxins from *Corynebacterium diphtheriae* and *Pseudomonas aeruginosa*. In: The Specificity and Action of Animal, Bacterial and Plant Toxins, ed. P. Cuatrecasas. London, Chapman and Hall, 1977.

81. Craig, J. P.: The effect of cholera stool and culture filtrates on the skin of guinea pigs and rabbits. Proceedings of the Cholera Research Symposium, Jan. 1965, Honolulu. Washington, D.C., U.S. Government Printing Office, 1965, p. 153.

82. Craig, J. P.: A permeability factor (toxin) found in cholera stools and

filtrates and its neutralization by convalescent cholera sera. Nature, Lond. 207, 614, 1965.

83. Craig, J. P.: Preparation of the vascular permeability factor of *Vibrio cholerae*. J. Bact. 92, 793, 1966.

84. Craig, S. W., and Cebra, J. J.: Peyer's patches: An enriched source of precursors for IgA-producing immunocytes in the rabbit. J. exp. Med. 134, 18, 1971.

85. Craig, S. W., and Cuatrecasas, P.: Mobility of cholera toxin receptor on rat lymphocyte membranes. Proc. Nat. Acad. Sci. 72, 3844, 1975.

86. Creighton, C.: A History of Epidemics in Britain. Vol. 2. From the Extinction of Plague to the Present Time. Cambridge, University Press, 1894.

87. Critchley, D. R., and Macpherson, I.: Cell density dependent glycolipids in NIL2 Hampster cells, derived malignant and transformed cell lines. Biochem. Biophys. Acta 296, 145, 1973.

88. Crosby, W. H., and Kugler, H. W.: Intraluminal biopsy of the small intestine. Amer. J. Digest. Dis. 2, 236, 1957.

89. Cuatrecasas, P.: Gangliosides and membrane receptors for cholera toxin. Biochem. 12, 3558, 1973.

90. Cuatrecasas, P.: Vibrio cholerae cholergenoid. Mechanism of inhibition of cholera toxin action. Biochem. 12, 3577, 1973.

91. Curlin, G., Levine, R., Aziz, K.M.A., Rahman, A. M., and Verwey, W. F.: Serological aspects of a cholera toxoid field trial in Bangladesh. Proc. 12th Joint Conference U.S.-Japan CMSP, Cholera Panel, Sapporo, 1976, p. 276.

92. Curran, P. F.: Na, Cl, and water transport by rat ileum *in vitro*. J. gen. Physiol. 43, 1137, 1960.

93. Darrow, D. C., Pratt, E. L., Flett, J., Jr., Gamble, A. H., and Wiese, F.: Disturbances of water and electrolytes in infantile diarrhea. Pediatrics 3, 129, 1949.

94. Das, A., Ghosal, S., Gupta, S. K., and Chaudhuri, R. N.: Terramycin in cholera. Ind. med. Gaz. 86, 437, 1951.

95. De, S. N.: Enterotoxicity of bacteria-free culture filtrate of *Vibrio cholerae*. Nature 183, 1533, 1959.

96. De, S. N.: Cholera: Its Pathology and Pathogenesis. Edinburgh and London, Oliver and Boyd, 1961.

97. De, S. N., Bhattacharya, K., and Sarkar, J. K.: A study of the pathogenicity of strains of *Bacterium coli* from acute and chronic enteritis. J. Path. Bact. 71, 201, 1956.

98. De, S. N., and Chatterjee, D. N.: An experimental study of the mechanism of action of *Vibrio cholerae* on the intestinal mucous membrane. J. Path. Bact. 66, 559, 1953.

99. De, S. N., Ghose, M. L., and Chandra, J.: Further observations on cholera enterotoxin. Trans. Roy. Soc. trop. Med. Hyg. 56, 241, 1962.

100. De, S. N., Ghose, M. L., and Sen, A.: Activities of bacteria-free preparations from *Vibrio cholera*. J. Path. Bact. 79, 373, 1960.

101. De, S. N., Sarkar, J. K., and Tribedi, B.: An experimental study of the action of cholera toxin. J. Path. Bact. 63, 707, 1951.

102. Dianin, S.: Borodin. Oxford, University Press, 1963, p. 142.

103. Diarrhoea Dialogue. Published by AHRTAG, Appropriate Health Resources and Technologies Action Group Ltd., 85 Marylebone High Street, London.

104. Dolman, C. E.: Botulism as a world health problem. In Botulism. U.S. Public Health Service Publication No. 999-FP-1, pp. 5–30, 1964.

105. Donta, S. T., King, M., and Sloper, K.: Induction of steroido-genesis in tissue culture by cholera enterotoxin. Nature (New Biol.) 243, 246, 1973.

106. Dutta, N. K.: Investigation on the behaviour of kidney in cholera. Calcutta med. J. 38, 621, 1941.

107. Dutta, N. K., and Habbu, M. K.: Experimental cholera in infant rabbits: A method for chemotherapeutic investigation. Brit. J. Pharmacol. 10, 153, 1955.

108. Dutta, N. K., Panse, M. V., and Kulkarui, D. R.: Role of cholera toxin in experimental cholera. J. Bact. 78, 594, 1959.

108a. Editorial: Edinburgh New philosoph. J. 12, 128, 1831.

109. Editorial: Water with sugar and salt. Lancet 2, 300, 1978.

110. Ehrlich, P.: On immunity with special reference to cell life. Proc. Roy. Soc. London 66, 424, 1900.

111. Elliott, H. L., Carpenter, C.C.J., Sack, R. B., and Yardley, J. H.: Small bowel morphology in experimental canine cholera. A light and electron microscopic study. Lab. Invest. 22, 112, 1970.

112. Engelman, R. C., and Joy, R.J.T.: Two Hundred Years of Military Medicine. Washington, D.C., U.S. Government Printing Office, 1975-672-885.

113. Evans, D. G., Evans, D. J., Jr., and Pierce, N. F.: Differences in the response of rabbit small intestine to heat-labile and heat-stable enterotoxins of *Escherichia coli*. Infect. Immun. 7, 873, 1973.

114. Faber, K.: Die Pathogenese der Tetanus. Berliner Klin. Wochenschr. 27, 717, 1890.

115. Farrel, J. G.: The Siege of Krishnapur. London, Weidenfeld and Nicolson, 1973.

116. Feeley, J. C., and Pittman, M.: Laboratory assays of cholera vaccine used in field trial in East Pakistan, 1963. Lancet 1, 449, 1965.

117. Felsenfeld, O.: Some observations on the cholera (El Tor) epidemic in 1961–62. Bull. WHO 26, 289, 1963.

118. Felsenfeld, O.: The Cholera Problem. St. Louis, Missouri, Warren H. Green Inc., 1967.

119. Férran, J.: Nota sobre la profilaxis del cólera por medio de inyecciones hipodermicas de cultivo puro del bacilo virgula. Siglo méd. 32, 480, 1885.

120. Field, M.: Intestinal secretion: Effect of cyclic AMP and its role in cholera. New Engl. J. Med. 284, 1137, 1971.

121. Field, M.: Model of action of cholera toxin: Stabilization of actecholamine-sensitive adenylate cyclase in turkey erythrocytes. Proc. Nat. Acad. Sci. 71, 3299, 1974.

122. Field, M.: Regulation of active ion transport in the small intestine. In: Acute Diarrhoea in Childhood (Ciba Foundation Symposium, new series; 42), ed. Elliott, K., and Knight, J.; Amsterdam, Oxford, New York, Elsevier–Excerpta Medica–North-Holland, 1975, p. 109.

123. Field, M., Fromm, D., Al-Awqati, Q., and Greenough, W. B., III: Effect

of cholera enterotoxin on ion transport across isolated ileal mucosa. J. clin. Invest. 51, 796, 1972.

124. Field, M., Fromm, D., Wallace, C. K., and Greenough, W. B., III: Stimulation of active chloride secretion in small intestine by cholera toxin. J. clin. Invest. 48, 249, 1969.

125. Field, M., Plotkin, G. R., and Silen, W.: Effects of vasopressin, theophylline and cyclic adenosine monophosphate on short-circuit current across isolated rabbit ileal mucosa. Nature 217, 469, 1968.

126. Fine J.: The Bacterial Factor in Traumatic Shock. Springfield, Illinois, Thomas, 1954.

127. Finkelstein, R. A.: Cholera. CRC Critical Reviews in Microbiology 2, 553, 1973.

128. Finkelstein, R. A., Boesman, M., Neoh, S. H., LaRue, M. K., and Delaney, R.: Dissociation and recombination of the subunits of the cholera enterotoxin (choleragen). J. Immunol. 113, 145, 1974.

129. Finkelstein, R. A., and Lankford, C. E.: Nutrient requirements of Vibrio cholerae. Bact. Proc. 1955, p. 49.

130. Finkelstein, R. A., LaRue, M. K., and LoSpalluto, J. J.: Properties of the cholera exo-enterotoxin: Effects of dispersing agents and reducing agents in gel filtration and electrophoresis. Infect. Immun. 6, 934, 1972.

131. Finkelstein, R. A., and LoSpalluto, J. J.: Pathogenesis of experimental cholera. Preparation and isolation of choleragen and choleragenoid. J. exp. Med. 130, 185, 1969.

132. Finkelstein, R. A., and LoSpalluto, J. J.: Preparation of highly purified choleragen and choleragenoid. J. infect. Dis. 121, Suppl., S63, 1970.

133. Finkelstein, R. A., Norris, H. T., and Dutta, N. K.: Pathogenesis of experimental cholera in infant rabbits. 1. Observations on the intraintestinal infective and experimental cholera produced with cell-free products. J. infect. Dis. 114, 203, 1964.

134. Finkelstein, R. A., Peterson, J. W., and LoSpalluto, J. J.: Conversion of cholera exo-enterotoxin (choleragen) to natural toxoid (choleragenoid). J. Immunol. 106, 868, 1971.

135. Finkelstein, R. A., Vasil, M. L., and Holmes, R. K.: Studies on toxinogenesis in Vibrio cholerae. 2. Isolation of mutants with altered toxigenicity. J. infect. Dis. 129, 117, 1974.

136. Fisher, R. B., and Parsons, D. S.: A preparation of surviving rat small intestine for the study of absorption. J. Physiol. 110, 36, 1949.

137. Fisher, R. B., and Parsons, D. S.: Glucose absorption from the surviving rat small intestine. J. Physiol. 110, 281, 1950.

138. Fisher, R. B., and Parsons, D. S.: Galactose absorption from the surviving small intestine of the rat. J. Physiol. 119, 224, 1953.

139. Fishman, P. H., and Brady, R. O.: Biosynthesis and function of gangliosides. Science 194, 906, 1975.

140. Flores, J., Witkum, P., and Sharp, G.W.G.: Activation of adenylate cyclase by cholera toxin in rat liver homogenates. J. clin. Invest. 57, 450, 1976.

141. Florey, H. W., Wright, R. D., and Jennings, M. A.: The secretions of the intestine. Physiol. Rev. 21, 36, 1941.

142. Formal, S. B., Kundel, D., Schneider, H., Kuner, N., and Sprinz, H.: Studies with Vibrio cholerae in the ligated loop of the intestine. Brit. J. exp. Path. 42, 504, 1961.

143. Fraenkel, E.: Uber Choleraleichenbefunde. Deutsch. med. Wochenschr. 19, 157, 1893.

144. Franceschini, P.: La scoperta del bacillo del cholera: Firenze, 29 Agosto 1954. Physis 18, 349, 1976.

145. Freter, R., and Gangarosa, E. J.: Oral immunization and production of copro antibody in human volunteers. J. Immunol. 91, 724, 1963.

146. Fuhrman, G. J., and Fuhrman, F. A.: Inhibition of active sodium transport by cholera toxin. Nature 188, 71, 1960.

147. Fujita, K., and Finkelstein, R. A.: Antitoxic immunity in experimental cholera: Comparison of immunity induced perorally and parenterally in mice. J. infect. Dis. 125, 647, 1972.

148. Gallut, J.: Contribution à l'étude de la toxine cholérique: variation du pouvoir toxique de *Vibrio cholerae* (*Ogawa*) au cours de la malade. Ann. Inst. Pasteur 86, 561, 1954.

149. Gamaleia, N.: Sur la vaccination preventive du choléra asiatique. C. R. Acad. Sci. (Paris) 107, 432, 1888.

150. Gamaleia, N.: Du choléra chez les chiens. C. R. Soc. Biol. (Paris), 9th ser. 4, 739, 1892.

151. Gangarosa, E. J., Beisel, W. R., Benyayati, C., Sprinz, H., and Piyaratn, P.: The nature of the gastrointestinal lesion in Asiatic cholera and its relation to pathogenesis: A biopsy study. Amer. J. trop. Med. Hyg. 9, 125, 1960.

152. Gangarosa, E. J., and Mosley, W. H.: Epidemiology and Surveillance of Cholera. In: Cholera, ed. Barua, D., and Burrows, W. Philadelphia, W. B. Saunders Co., 1974, p. 381.

153. Gascoyne, N., and van Heyningen, W. E.: Unmasking of actual and potential receptor sites for cholera toxin in intestinal mucosal homogenates. J. infect. Dis. 139, 235, 1979.

154. Gautier, A.: Les Toxines microbiennes et animales. Paris, Société d'Editions Scientifiques 1896, p. 342.

155. Gill, D. M.: The arrangements of subunits in cholera toxin. Biochemistry 15, 1242, 1976.

156. Gill, D. M.: Multiple roles of erythrocyte supernatant in the activation of adenylate cyclase by *Vibrio cholerae* toxin in vitro. J. infect. Dis. 133, S55, 1976.

157. Gill, D. M., and King, C. A.: The mechanism of action of cholera toxin in pigeon erythrocyte lysates. J. biol. Chem. 250, 6424, 1975.

158. Gill, D. M., and Meren, R.: ADP-ribosylation of membrane proteins catalysed by cholera toxin: Basis of the activation of adenylate cyclase. Proc. Nat. Acad. Sci. 75, 3050, 1978.

159. Giono, J.: Le Hussard sur le toit. Paris, Editions Gallimard, 1951.

160. Glimpse (ICDDR/B Newsletter) 1, No. 3, 1979.

161. Glimpse (ICDDR/B Newsletter) 1, No. 4, 1979.

162. Glimpse (ICDDR/B Newsletter) 1, No. 6, 1, 1979.

163. Goodner, K., Stempen, H., Smith, H. L., and Monsur, K. A.: Immu-

nological aspects of cholera. SEATO Conference on Cholera, Dacca, East Pakistan, December 1960. Bangkok, The Post Publishing Co. Ltd., 1962. pp. 104–110.

164. Goodpasture, E. W.: Histopathology of intestine in cholera. Philippine J. Sc. (Sect. B) 22, 413, 1923.

165. Gorbach, S. L., Banwell, J. G., Chatterjee, B. D., Jacobs, B., and Sack, R. B.: Acute undifferentiated human diarrhea in the tropics. 1. Alterations in intestinal microflora. J. clin. Invest. 50, 881, 1971.

166. Gorbach, S. L., Kean, B. H., Evans, D. G., Evans, D. J., Jr., and Bessudo, D.: Travellers' diarrhea and toxigenic *Escherichia coli*. New Engl. J. Med. 292, 933, 1975.

167. Gordon, R. S., Jr.: Advantages and disadvantages of methods to evaluate amino acid requirements. Fed. Proc. 23, 52, 1964.

168. Gordon, R. S., Jr.: The failure of Asiatic cholera to give rise to "exudative enteropathy". SEATO Conference on Cholera, Dacca, East Pakistan, December 1960. Bangkok, The Post Publishing Co., Ltd., 1962, pp. 54–57.

169. Gorman, M.: Sir William O'Shaughnessy, Lord Dalhousie, and the establishment of the telegraph system in India. Technology and Culture 12I, 581, 1971.

170. Gowans, J. L., and Knight, E. J.: The route of recirculation of lymphocytes in the rat. Proc. Roy. Soc. London B. 159, 257, 1964.

171. Gradwohl, R.B.H., Benitez Soto, L., and Felsenfeld, O.: Clinical Tropical Medicine. St. Louis, C. V. Mosby Co., 1951, pp. 477–506.

172. Grady, G. F., and Chang, M. C.: Cholera enterotoxin free from permeability factor? J. infect. Dis. 121, (Suppl.) S92, 1970.

173. Grady, G. F., Madoff, M. A., Duhamel, R. C., Moore, E. W., and Chalmers, T. C.: Sodium transport inhibition by cholera toxin: The role of nonionic diffusion of ammonia. J. infect. Dis. 118, 263, 1968.

174. Graf, L. H., Smith, P. L., and Field, M.: Cholera toxin activation of adenylate cyclase in turkey erythrocyte membranes: Dependence on NAD and cytosol. Fed. Proc. 35, 1356, 1976.

175. Graybill, J. R., Kaplan, M. M., and Pierce, N. F.: Hormone-like effects of cholera exotoxin (CE). Clin. Res. 18, 454, 1970.

176. Greenough, W. B., III: Mortality and fertility: Causal link. Science 167, 237, 1970.

177. Greenough, W. B., III, and Carpenter, C.C.J.: Fluid loss in cholera: A current perspective. Texas Rep. Biol. Med. 27, 302, 1969.

178. Greenough, W. B., III, Gordon, R. S., Rosenberg, I. S., Davies, B. I., and Benenson, A. S.: Tetracycline in the treatment of cholera. Lancet 1, 355, 1964.

179. Greenough, W. B., III, Hirschhorn, N., Gordon, R. S., Jr., Lindenbaum, L., and Ally, K. M.: Pulmonary oedema associated with acidosis in patients with cholera. Trop. geog. Med. 28, 86, 1976.

180. Greenwood, M.: Epidemics and Crowd-Diseases. An Introduction to the Study of Epidemiology. London, Williams and Norgate Ltd. 1935.

181. Greenwood, M., and Yule, G. U.: The statistics of anti-typhoid and anti-cholera inoculations, and the interpretation of such statistics in general. Proc. Roy. Soc. Med. 8, pt. 2, 113, 1915.

182. Greig, E.D.W.: The treatment of cholera by intravenous saline infections; with particular reference to the contribution of Dr. Thomas Aitchinson Latta of Leith (1832). Edinburgh Med. J. 53, 256, 1946.

183. Guerrant, R. L., Moore, R. A., Kirschenfeld, P. M., and Saude, M. S.: Role of toxigenic and invasive bacteria in acute diarrhoea of childhood. New Engl. J. Med. 293, 567, 1975.

184. Haffkine, W. M.: Innoculation de vaccins anticholériques à l'homme. C. R. Soc. Biol. (Paris), 9th ser. 4, 740, 1892.

185. Haffkine, W. M.: Anti-cholera inoculation. Report to the Government of India. Calcutta, Thacker, Spink and Co., 1895.

186. Haffkine, W. M.: Inoculations against cholera in India. Brit. med. J. 2, 735, 1895.

187. Haffkine, W. M.: On preventive inoculation. Proc. Roy. Soc. London 65, 252, 1899.

188. Haffkine, W. M.: Protective Inoculation against Cholera. Calcutta, Thacker, Spink and Co., 1913.

189. Haksar, A., Maudsley, D. V., and Peron, F.: Neuraminidase treatment of adrenal cells increases their response to cholera enterotoxin. Nature 251, 514, 1974.

190. Harvey, R. M., Enson, Y., Lewis, M. L., Greenough, W. B., III, Ally, K. M., and Panno, R. A.: Hemodynamic studies on cholera—Effects of hypovolemia and acidosis. Circulation 37, 709, 1968.

191. Hendrix, T. R.: The pathophysiology of cholera. Bull. N.Y. Acad. Med. 47, 1169, 1971.

192. Hendrix, T. R., and Bayless, T. M.: Digestion: Intestinal secretion. Ann. Rev. Physiol. 32, 139, 1970.

193. Heremans, J. F., and Crabbe, P. A.: Gamma globulin structure and control of biosynthesis. Proc. Nobel Symp. 3, 129, 1967.

194. Hermann, R.: Ueber die Veränderungen die Secretionen des menschlichen Organisms durch Cholera erleiden. Poggendorf's Ann. 22, 161, 1831.

195. Hindustan Times Weekly, 5 Jan. 1964.

196. Hirschhorn, N., Cash, R. A., Woodward, W. E., and Spivey, G. H.: Oral fluid therapy of Apache children with acute infectious diarrhoea. Lancet 2, 15, 1972.

197. Hirschhorn, N., and Denny, K. M.: Oral glucose-electrolyte therapy for diarrhea: A means to maintain or improve nutrition? Amer. J. clin. Nutr. 28, 189, 1975.

198. Hirschhorn, N., Kinzie, J. L., Sachar, D. B., Taylor, J. O., Northrup, R. S., and Phillips, R. A.: Reduction in stool output in cholera by glucose and electrolyte lavage. Symp. on Cholera, U.S.-Japan CMSP, Palo Alto, July 1967, p. 195.

199. Hirschhorn, N., Kinzie, J. L., Sachar, D. B., Northrup, R. S., Taylor, J. O., Ahmad, S. Z., and Phillips, R. A.: Decrease in net stool output in cholera during intestinal perfusion with glucose-containing solution. New Engl. J. Med. 279, 176, 1968.

200. Hirschhorn, N., McCarthy, B. J., Ranney, B., Hirschhorn, M. A., Woodward, S. T., Lacapa, A., Cash, R. A., and Woodward, W. E.: Ad libitum oral

glucose-electrolyte therapy for acute diarrhea in Apache children. J. Pediatr. 83, 562, 1973.

201. Hirschhorn, N., and Westley, T. A.: Oral rehydration of children with acute diarrhoea. Lancet 2, 494, 1972.

202. Hollenberg, M. D., and Cuatrecasas, P.: Epidermal growth factor: Receptors in human fibroblasts and modulation of action by cholera toxin. Proc. Nat. Acad. Sci. 70, 2964, 1973.

203. Hollenberg, M. D., Fishman, P. H., Bennett, V., and Cuatrecasas, P.: Cholera toxin and cell growth: Role of membrane gangliosides. Proc. Nat. Acad. Sci. 71, 4224, 1971.

204. Holmgren, J.: Comparison of the tissue receptors for *Vibrio cholerae* and *Escherichia coli* enterotoxins by means of gangliosides and natural cholera toxoid. Infect. Immun. 8, 851, 1973.

205. Holmgren, J., Lonnroth, I., Mansson, J. E., and Svennerholm, L.: Interaction of cholera toxin and membrane GM1 ganglioside of small intestine. Proc. Nat. Acad. Sci. 72, 2520, 1975.

206. Holmgren, J., Lonnroth, I., and Svennerholm, L.: Fixation and inactivation of cholera toxin by GM1 gangliosides. Scand. J. infect. Dis. 5, 77, 1973.

207. Honda, T., and Finkelstein, R. A.: Selection and characteristics of a *Vibrio cholerae* mutant lacking the A (ADP-ribosylating) portion of the cholera enterotoxin. Proc. Nat. Acad. Sci. 76, 2052, 1979.

208. Howard-Jones, N.: Cholera therapy in the nineteenth century. J. Hist. Med. 27, 373, 1972.

209. Howard-Jones, N.: Cholera nomenclature and nosology: A historical note. Bull. WHO 51, 317, 1974.

210. Howard-Jones, N.: The scientific background of the International Sanitary Conferences 1851–1938. Geneva, World Health Organization, 1975.

211. Huber, G. S., and Phillips, R. A.: Cholera and the sodium pump. Proceedings of SEATO Conference on Cholera, Dacca, 1960. Bangkok, The Post Publishing Co., 1962.

212. Iber, F. L., McGonagle, T. J., Serebro, H. A., Luebbers, E. H., Bayless, T. M., and Hendrix, T. R.: Unidirectional sodium flux in small intestine in experimental canine cholera. Amer. J. Med. Sci. 258, 340, 1969.

212a. Jaehnichen: Animadversiones anatomico-pathologicae de cholera-morbo mosquae grassante . . . Moscow 1830 (reprinted in Mittheilungen ub. d. morgenländ. Brechruhr 1832).

213. Jaehnichen: Memoire sur le cholera-morbus qui regne en Russie. Gazette méd. Paris 2, 85, 1831.

214. Jameson, J.: Report on the epidemic cholera morbus as it visited the territories subject to the Presidency of Bengal in the years 1817, 1818 and 1819. Calcutta, Printed at the Government Gazette Press, 1820.

215. Jenkin, C. R., and Rowley, D.: Possible factors in the pathogenesis of cholera. Brit. J. exp. Path. 40, 474, 1959.

216. Jensen, K. E.: Immunologic characterization of a mucinolytic enzyme of *Vibrio cholerae*. J. infect. Dis. 93, 107, 1953.

217. Johnson, G. L., and Bourne, H. R.: Influence of cholera toxin on the

regulation of adenylate cyclase by GTP. Biochem. Biophys. Res. Com. 78, 792, 1977.

218. Johnson, M. K., Weaver, R. H., and Phillips, R. A.: The treatment of cholera. J. Egypt. Public Health Assoc. 23, 15, 1948.

219. Judicial Commission of the International Commission on Bacteriological Nomenclature. Bull. Bacteriol. Nomenclature Taxon. 15, 185, 1965.

220. Kamal, A. M.: Cholera. In: Epidemiology of Communicable Diseases, by A. M. Kamal. Cairo, Anglo-Egyptian Bookshop, Publisher, 1958, p. 138.

221. Karnow, S.: "These Americans must be gods". Saturday Evening Post, 25 April 1964, p. 72.

222. Keenan, T. W., Schmid, E., Franke, W. W., and Wiegandt, H.: Exogenous glycosphingolipids suppress growth rate of transformed and untransformed 3T3 mouse cells. Exp. Cell. Res. 92, 259, 1975.

223. Kimberg, D. V., Field, M., Johnson, J., Henderson, A., and Gershorn, E.: Stimulation of intestinal mucosal adenylate cyclase by cholera enterotoxin and prostaglandin. J. clin. Invest. 50, 1218, 1971.

224. King, C. A., and van Heyningen, W. E.: Deactivation of cholera toxin by a sialidase resistant monosialosyl ganglioside. J. infect. Dis. 127, 639, 1973.

225. King, C. A., and van Heyningen, W. E.: Evidence for the complex nature of the ganglioside receptor for cholera toxin. J. infect. Dis. 131, 643, 1975.

226. King, C. A., van Heyningen, W. E., and Gascoyne, N.: Aspects of the interaction of cholera toxin with the pigeon red cell membrane. J. infect. Dis. 133, S75, 1976.

227. Kitasato, S.: Ueber den Tetanusbacillus. Zeitschr. für Hygiene 7, 225, 1889.

228. Kitasato, S., and Weyl, Th.: Zur Kenntnis der Anaëroben, zweite Abhandlung. Der Bacillus Tetani. Zeitschr. für Hygiene 8, 404, 1890.

229. Klebs, E.: Über Diphtheria, ihre parasitäre Natur, Verhaltniss des localen Prozesses zur algemeinen Infektion, Contagiosität, Therapie (Chirurgie), und Prophylaxie. Verhandl. Congress. Inn. Med., Wiesbaden, 2 Abt. 1883, p. 143.

230. Klenk, E.: On the discovery and chemistry of neuraminic acid and gangliosides. Chem. Phys. Lipids 5, 193, 1970.

231. Koch, R.: Untersuchungen über der Aetiologie der Wundinfectionskrankheiten. Leipzig, Vogel, 1878, p. 27.

232. Koch, R.: Der zweiter Bericht der deutschen Cholera-Commission. Deutsch. med. Wochenschr. 9, 615, 1883.

233. Koch, R.: Sechster Bericht der deutschen wissenschaftligen Commission zur Erforschung der Cholera. Deutsch. med. Wochenschr. 10, 191, 1884.

234. Koch, R.: Die Conferenz zur Erörterung der Cholerfrage. Deutsch. med. Wochenschr. 10, 499, 519, 1884.

235. Koch, R.: Zweite Serie der Conferenzen zur Erörterung der Cholerafrage. Deutsch. med. Wochenschr. 11, 329, 1885.

236. Kohn, L. D.: Relationships in the structure and function of receptors for glycoprotein hormones, bacterial toxins and interferon. In: Receptors and Recognition, ed. Cuatrecasas and Greaves. London, Chapman and Hall, 1978.

237. Kolle, W.: Die aktive Immunisierung der Menschen gegen Cholera, nach Haffkine's Verfahren in Indien ausgefuhrt. Zbl. Bakt. i. Abt. Orig. 19, 217, 1896.

238. Kuhn, R., Wiegandt, H., and Egge, H.: Zum Bauplan der Ganglioside. Angew. Chem. 73, 580, 1961.

239. Kuno, Y.: Human Perspiration. Springfield, Illinois, C. C. Thomas, 1956.

240. Kurosky, A., Markel, D. E., Peterson, J. W., and Fitch, W. M.: Primary structure of cholera toxin B-chain: a glycoprotein analog? Science 195, 299 1977.

241. Lai, C., Mendez, E., Chang, D., and Wang, M.: Primary structure of cholera toxin B-subunit. Biochem. Biophys. Res. Com. 74, 215, 1977.

242. Landsteiner, K., and Botteri, A.: Über Verbindungen von Tetanustoxin mit Lipoiden. IV. Zbl. Bakt. (Orig.) 42, 562, 1906.

243. Latta, T.: Letter from Dr. Latta to the Secretary of the Central Board of Health, London, affording a view of the rationale and results of his practice in the treatment of cholera by aqueous and saline injections. Lancet 2, 274, 1831–32.

244. Leading Article: Polyamines as markers of response to chemotherapy of cancer. Brit. med. J. 1, 1619, 1977.

245. Ledley, F. D., Lee, G., Kohn, L. D., Habiq, W. H., and Hardegree, M. C.: Tetanus toxin interactions with thyroid plasma membranes. J. biol. Chem. 252, 4049, 1977.

246. Ledley, F. D., Mullin, B. R., Lee, G., Aloj, S. M., Fishman, R. H., Hunt, L. T., Dayhoff, M. O., and Kohn, L. D.: Sequence similarity between cholera toxin and glycoprotein hormones: Implications for structure activity relationships and mechanism of action. Biochem. Biophys. Res. Com. 69, 852, 1976.

247. Leighton, G.: Botulism and Food Preservation (The Loch Maree Tragedy). London, Collins, 1923.

248. Levey, G. S.: Solubilisation of myocardial adenylcyclase. Biochem. Biophys. Res. Com. 38, 86, 1970.

249. Levine, M. M., Nalin, D. R., Craig, J. P., Hoover, D., Bergquist, E. J., Waterman, D., Holley, H. P., Hornick, R. B., Pierce, N. F., and Libonati, J. P.: Immunity to cholera in man: Relative role of antibacterial versus antitoxic immunity. Trans. Roy. Soc. trop. Med. Hyg. 73, 3, 1979.

250. Levine, M. M., Nalin, D. R., Bergquist, E. J., Waterman, D. H., Young, C. R., Scotman, S., and Rowe, B.: Escherichia coli strains that cause diarrhoea but do not produce heat-labile or heat-stable enterotoxins and are non-invasive. Lancet 1, 1119, 1978.

251. Levinson, S. L., and Blume, A. J.: Altered guanine nucleotide hydrolysis as basis for increased adenylate cyclase activity after cholera toxin treatment. J. biol. Chem. 252, 3766, 1977.

252. Lindenbaum, J.: Small intestine dysfunction in Pakistanis and Americans resident in Pakistan. Amer. J. clin. Nutr. 21, 1023, 1968.

253. Loeffler, F.: Untersuchungen über die Bedeutung der Mikroorganismen für die Entstehung der Diphtherie beim Menschen, bei der Taube und beim Kalbe. Mitth. Kaiserl. Gesundheitsamte 2, 421, 1884.

254. Loeffler, F.: The history of diphtheria. In: The Bacteriology of Diphtheria,

ed. Nuttall, G.H.F., and Grahame-Smith, G. S., Cambridge, University Press, 1908, p. 1.

255. Londos, C., Salomon, Y., Lin, M. C., Harwood, J. P., Schramm, M., Wolff, J., and Rodbell, M.: 5'-Guanylylimidodiphosphate a potent activator of adenylate cyclase systems in eukaryotic cells. Proc. Nat. Acad. Sci. 71, 3087, 1974.

256. Longmate, N.: King Cholera. The Biography of a Disease. London, Hamish Hamilton, 1966.

257. Lonnroth, I., and Holmgren, J.: Subunit structure of cholera toxin. J. gen. Microbiol. 76, 417, 1973.

258. LoSpalluto, J. J., and Finkelstein, R. A.: Chemical and physical properties of cholera exo-enterotoxin (choleragen) and its spontaneously formed toxoid (choleragenoid). Biochem. Biophys. Acta 257, 158, 1972.

259. Love, A.H.G.: The effect of glucose on cation transport. Proceedings of the Cholera Research Symposium, Honolulu, Jan. 1965. Washington, D.C., U.S. Government Printing Office, 1965, p. 144.

260. Love, A.H.G.: Water and sodium absorption by the intestine in cholera. Gut, 10, 63, 1969.

261. Lowenthal, J. P.: Stability of a fluid cholera mucinase preparation when combined with a commercially prepared cholera vaccine. Proc. Soc. exp. Biol. Med. 93, 103, 1956.

262. Lutzker, E.: Waldemar Mordecai Haffkine, C.I.E. Bull. Haffkine Inst. 1, 11, 1974.

263. Macallum, A. B.: The paleochemistry of the body fluid and tissues. Physiol. Rev. 6, 316, 1926.

264. McCluer, R. H.: Chemistry of gangliosides. Chem. Phys. Lipids 5, 220, 1970.

265. McIntyre, O. R., Feeley, J. C., Greenough, W. B., III, Benenson, A. S., Hassan, S. I., and Saad, A.: Diarrhoea caused by non-cholera vibrios. Amer. J. trop. Med. Hyg. 14, 412, 1965.

266. MacLeod, C. M.: Relation of the incubation period and the secondary immune response to lasting immunity to infectious diseases. J. Immunol. 70, 421, 1953.

267. MacLeod, C. M.: Some requirements for a field trial of cholera vaccines. SEATO Conference on Cholera, Dacca, Dec. 1960. Bangkok, Post Publishing Co., 1962, pp. 111–113.

268. Mahalanabis, D., Chaudhuri, A. B., Bagchi, N. G., Bhattacharya, A. K., and Simpson, T. W.: Oral fluid therapy of cholera among Bangladesh refugees. Johns Hopkins med. J. 132, 197, 1973.

269. Mahalanabis, D., Sack, R. B., Jacobs, B., Mondal, A., and Thomas, J.: Use of an oral glucose-electrolyte solution in the treatment of pediatric cholera— A controlled study. J. trop. Pediat. envir. Child. Health 20, 82, 1974.

270. Manson, P.: Tropical Diseases, 4th ed. London, Cassell and Co. Ltd., 1907.

271. Marcuk, L. M., Nikiforv, V. N., Scerbak, Ja. F., Levitor, T. A., Kotljarova, R. I., Naumsina, M. S., Davydov, S. U., Monsur, K. A., Rahman, M. A., Latif, M. A., Northrup, R. S., Cash, R. A., Huq, I., Dey, C. R., and Phillips, R. A.:

Clinical studies of the use of bacteriophage in the treatment of cholera. Bull. WHO 45, 77, 1971.

272. Markus, F.C.M.: Rapport sur le cholera-Morbus de Moscou. Moscow, Semen, 1832.

273. Martin, B. R., Honslay, M. D., and Kennedy, E. L.: Cholera toxin requires oxidised nicotinamide–adenine dinucleotide to activate adenylate cyclase in purified rat liver plasma membranes. Biochem. J. 161, 639, 1977.

274. Martin, S.: The proteids of the seeds of *Abrus precatorius* (Jecquirity). Proc. Roy. Soc. Lond. 42, 331, 1897.

275. Mata, L. J., Kronmal, R. A., Garcia, B., Butler, W., Urrutia, J. J., and Murillo, S.: Breast-feeding, weaning and the diarrhoeal syndrome in a Guatemalan Indian village. In: Acute Diarrhoea in Childhood, ed. Elliott, A., and Knight, I. Amsterdam, Oxford, New York, Elsevier–Excerpta Medica–North Holland, 1975, p. 311.

276. Matsuda, M., and Yoneda, M.: Antigenic substructure of tetanus neurotoxin. Biochem. Biophys. Res. Comm. 77, 268, 1977.

277. Matuo, Y., Wheeler, M. A., and Bitensky, M. W.: Small fragments from the A subunit of cholera toxin capable of activating adenylate cyclase. Proc. Nat. Acad. Sci. 73, 2654, 1976.

278. Memoirs on Diphtheria (ed. R. H. Semple). London, New Syndenham Soc., 1859.

279. Metchnikoff, E.: Recherches sur le choléra et les vibrions. Sur l'immunité et la receptivite vis-à-vis du choléra intestinal. Ann. Inst. Pasteur 8, 529, 1894.

280. Milner, K. C., Rudbach, J. A., and Ribi, E.: General characteristics. In: Microbial Toxins. Vol. 4. Bacterial Endotoxins, ed. Ajil, S. J., Ciegler, A., Montie, T. C., Wainbaum, G. New York and London, Academic Press, 1961, p. 1.

281. Minneman, K. P., and Iverson, L. L.: Cholera toxin induces pineal enzymes in culture. Science 192, 803, 1976.

282. Mosley, W. H., Aziz, K.M.S., and Ahmed, A.: Serological evidence for the identity of the vascular permeability factor and ileal loop toxin of *Vibrio cholerae*. J. infect. Dis. 121, 243, 1970.

283. Mosley, W. H., Aziz, K.M.A., Rahman, A.S.M.M., Choudhuri, A.K.M.A., Ahmed, A., and Fahimuddin, M.: Report on the 1966–67 cholera vaccine trial in rural East Pakistan. 4. Five years observation with a practical assessment of the role of a cholera vaccine in cholera control programmes. Bull. WHO 47, 229, 1972.

284. Mosley, W. H., Aziz, A.K.M., Rahman, A.S.M.M., Chowdhury, A.K.M.A., and Ahmed, A.: Field trials of monovalent Ogawa and Inaba cholera vaccines in rural Bangladesh—Three years of observation. Bull. WHO 49, 381, 1973.

285. Mosley, W. H., Benenson, A. S., and Barui, R.: A serological survey for cholera antibodies in rural East Pakistan. 1. The distribution of antibody in the control population of a cholera-vaccine field-trial area and the relation of antibody titre to the pattern of endemic cholera. Bull. WHO 38, 327, 1968.

286. Mosley, W. H., Benenson, A. S., and Barui, R.: A serological survey for cholera antibodies in rural East Pakistan. 2. A comparison of antibody titres in the immunized and control population of a cholera-vaccine field area and the relation of antibody titre to cholera case rate. Bull. WHO 38, 335, 1968.

287. Mosley, W. H., McCormack, W. H., Fahimuddin, M., Aziz, K.M.A., Rahman, A.S.M.M., Chowdhury, A.K.M.A., Marlin, A. R., Feeley, J. C., and Phillips, R. A.: Report of the 1966–67 cholera vaccine field trial in rural East Pakistan. 1. Study and results of the first year of observation. Bull. WHO 40, 177, 1969.

288. Mosley, W. H., Woodward, W. E., Aziz, K.M.A., Rahman, A.S.M.M., Chowdhury, A.K.M.A., Ahmed, A., and Feeley, J.C.: The 1968–69 cholera vaccine field trial in rural East Pakistan. Effectiveness of monovalent and Inaba vaccines and purified Inaba antigen, with comparative serological and animal protective tests. J. infect. Dis. 121, S1, 1970.

289. Moss, J., Manganiello, V. C., and Vaughan, M.: Hydrolysis of nicotin-amide adenine dinucleotide by choleragen and its A protomer. Possible role in the activation of adenylate cyclase. Proc. Nat. Acad. Sci. 73, 4424, 1976.

290. Moss, J., and Vaughan, M.: Mechanism of action of choleragen. Evidence for ADP-ribosyltransferase activity with arginine as an acceptor. J. biol. Chem. 252, 2455, 1977.

291. Nakashima, Y., Napiorkowski, P., Schafer, D. E., and Konigsberg, W. H.: Primary structure of B subunit of cholera enterotoxin. FEBS Letters 68, 275, 1976.

292. Nalin, D. R.: Sucrose in oral therapy for cholera and related diarrhoeas. Lancet 1, 1400, 1975.

293. Nalin, D. R.: A spoonful of sugar. Lancet 2, 264, 1978.

294. Nalin, D. R. and Cash, R. A.: Studies in experimental cholera in animals. Report to the Technical Committee, Pakistan-SEATO Cholera Research Labo-ratory, 27–29 November 1967.

295. Nalin, D. R., and Cash, R. A.: Oral or nasogastric maintenance therapy for diarrhoea of unknown aetiology resembling cholera. Trans. Roy. Soc. trop. Med. Hyg. 64, 769, 1970.

296. Nalin, D. R., and Cash, R.: Oral or nasogastric maintenance therapy in pediatric cholera patients. J. Pediat. 78, 355, 1971.

297. Nalin, D. R., Cash, R. A., Islam, R., Motta, M., and Phillips, R. A.: Oral maintenance therapy for cholera in adults. Lancet 2, 370, 1968.

298. Nalin, D. R., Cash, R. A., and Rahman, M.: Oral (or nasogastric) maintenance therapy for cholera patients in all age-groups. Bull. WHO 43, 361, 1970.

299. Nalin, D. R., Cash, R. A., Rahman, M., and Ynus, M.: Effect of glycine and glucose on sodium and water absorption in patients with cholera. Gut, 11, 768, 1970.

300. Nalin, D. R., Levine, M. M., Hornick, R. B., Bergquist, E. J., Hoover, D., Holley, H. P., Waterman, D., VanBlerk, J., Matheny, S., Sotman, S., and Rennals, M.: The problem of emesis during oral glucose-electrolyte therapy given from the onset of severe cholera. Trans. Roy. Soc. trop. Med. Hyg. 13, 10, 1978.

301. Nalin, D. R., Levine, M. M., Mata, L., de Cespader, C., Vargas, W., Lixano, C., Loria, A. R., Simhorn, A., Mohs, E.: Comparison of sucrose with glucose in oral therapy of infant diarrhoea. Lancet 2, 277, 1978.

302. Nalin, D. R., and Russel, R.: Vitamin A, xerophthalmia and diarrhoea. Lancet 1, 1411, 1980.

303. Nellans, H. N., Frizzel, R. A., and Schultz, S. G.: Coupled sodium-chloride influx across the brush border of rabbit ileum. Amer. J. Physiol. 225, 467, 1973.

304. Neptune, E. M., and Mitchell, T. G.: Ammonium toxicity, a potential artifact in the preparation of toxins. Proceedings of the Cholera Research Symposium, Honolulu, Jan. 1965. Washington, D.C., U.S. Government Printing Office, p. 299.

305. Nicati, W., and Rietsch, M.: Odeur et effets toxiques des produits de la fermentation produite par les bacilles en virgule. C. R. Acad. Sci. (Paris) 99, 928, 1884.

306. Nicati, W., and Rietsch, M.: Sur l'inoculation du bacille virgule du choléra. Sem. méd. (Paris), 2nd ser. 4, 370, 1884.

307. Nicolaier, A.: Ueber infectiosen Tetanus. Deutsche med. Wochenschr. 10, 842, 1884.

308. NIH Record 17, 17 Aug. 1959.

309. Niles Weekly Register, 28 July, 27 October, 24 November, 1832.

310. Norris, H. T., Dutta, N. K., Finkelstein, R. A., Formal, S. B., and Spring, H.: Morphological alterations of the intestine of ten day old rabbits given intact and ultrasonically disrupted cholera vibrios or cholera endotoxin. Fed. Proc. 22, 512, 1963.

311. Ohtomo, N., Muraoka, T., Tashiro, A., Zinnaka, Y., and Amako, K.: Size and structure of the cholera toxin molecule and its subunits. J. infect. Dis. 133, S31, 1976.

312. Ohtomo, N., Muraoka, T., Tashiro, A., Zinnaka, Y., and Amako, K.: Size and structure of the cholera toxin molecule and its subunits. J. infect. Dis. 133, S31, 1976.

313. Olmsted, J.M.D.: Francois Magendie. New York, Schumans', 1944.

314. Olsnes, S., and Pihl, A.: Abrin, ricin, and their associated agglutinins. In: The Specificity and Action of Animal, Bacterial and Plant Toxins, ed. Cuatrecasas, P. London, Chapman and Hall, 1977, p. 129.

315. Orth, G. L.: Notes on the occurrence of Vibrio cholerae in Thailand in 1959. SEATO Conference on Cholera, Dacca, 1960. Bangkok, The Post Publishing Company, 1962, p. 124.

316. Oseasohn, R. O., Benenson, A. S., and Fahimuddin, M.: Field trial of cholera vaccine in rural East Pakistan. Lancet 1, 450, 1965.

317. O'Shaughnessy, W. B.: Proposal of a new method of treating the blue epidemic cholera by the injection of highly-oxygenised salts into the venous sytem. Lancet 1, 366, 1831–32.

318. O'Shaughnessy, W. B.: Letter to the Editor of The Lancet. Lancet 1, 401, 1831–32.

319. O'Shaughnessy, W. B.: Experiments on the blood in cholera. Lancet 1, 490, 1831–32.

320. O'Shaughnessy, W. B.: Chemical pathology of cholera. Lancet 2, 225, 1831–32.

321. O'Shaughnessy, W. B.: Report of the chemical pathology of the malignant

cholera; containing analyses of the blood, dejecta, etc. of patients labouring under the disease in Newcastle and London, London, S. Highley, 1832.

322. Osler, W.: The Principles and Practice of Medicine. New York, D. Appleton Company, 1892, p. 121.

323. Oza, N. B., and Dutta, N. K.: Experimental cholera produced by toxin prepared by ultrasonic disintegration of *Vibrio* comma. J. Bact. 85, 497, 1963.

324. Pacini, F.: Osservazioni microscopiche e deduzioni patologiche sul colera asiatico. Gazz. med. italiana 6, 405, 1854.

325. Pappenheimer, A. M., Jr., and Gill, D. M.: Diphtheria. Science 182, 353, 1973.

326. Parkinson, D. K., Ebel, H., DiBona, D. R., and Sharp, G.W.G.: Localisation of the action of cholera toxin on adenyl cyclase in mucosal epithelial cells of rabbit intestine. J. clin. Invest. 51, 2292, 1972.

327. Pecker, P., and Hanoune, J.: Activation of epinephrine sensitive adenylate cyclase in rat liver by cytosolic protein–nucleotide complex. J. biol. Chem. 252, 2784, 1977.

328. Pelling, M.: Cholera, Fever and English Medicine 1825–1865. Oxford, The University Press, 1978.

329. Peterson, J. W., LoSpalluto, J. J., and Finkelstein, R. A.: Localization of cholera toxin in vivo. J. infect. Dis. 126, 617, 1972.

330. Pfeiffer, R.: Untersuchungen über das Choleragift. Zeitschr. Hyg. Infect. Kr. 11, 393, 1892.

331. Pfeiffer, R.: Ein neues Grundgesetz der Immunität. Deutsche. med. Wochenschr. 22, 97, 119, 1896.

332. Pfeiffer, R., and Wassermann, A.: Untersuchungen über die Wesen der Cholera Immunität. Zeitschr. Hyg. Infect. Kr. 14, 46, 1893.

333. Pfeuffer, T.: GTP binding proteins in membranes and the control of adenylate cyclase activity. J. biol. Chem. 252, 7224, 1977.

334. Philippines Cholera Commission: A controlled field trial of the effectiveness of cholera and cholera El Tor vaccines in the Philippines. Preliminary report. Bull. WHO 32, 603, 1965.

335. Philippines Cholera Commission: A controlled field trial of the effectiveness of various doses of cholera El Tor vaccine in the Philippines. Bull. WHO 38, 917, 1968.

336. Philippines Cholera Commission: A controlled field trial of the effectiveness of monovalent classical and El Tor cholera vaccines in the Philippines. Bull. WHO 49, 13, 1973.

337. Phillips, R. A.: The dehydration of cholera—Therapeutic implications. In: SEATO Conference on Cholera, Dacca, East Pakistan, December 5–8, 1960. Bangkok, The Post Publishing Co. Ltd., 1962. p. 49.

338. Phillips, R. A.: The patho-physiology of cholera. Bull. WHO 28, 297, 1963.

339. Phillips, R. A.: Water and electrolyte losses in cholera. Fed. Proc. 23, 705, 1964.

340. Phillips, R. A.: Cholera in the perspective of 1966. Ann. intern. Med. 65, 922, 1966.

341. Phillips, R. A.: Twenty years of cholera research. J. Amer. med. Assoc. 202, 610, 1967.

342. Phillips, R. A., Van Slyke, D. D., Hamilton, P. B., Dole, V. P., Emerson, K., Jr., and Archibald, R. M.: Measurement of specific gravities of whole blood and plasma by standard copper sulphate solutions. Bur. Med. News Letter U.S. Navy 1, 1, 1943.

343. Phillips, R. A., Van Slyke, D. D., Hamilton, P. B., Dole, V. P., Emerson, K., Jr., and Archibald, R. M.: Measurement of specific gravities of whole blood and plasma by standard copper sulphate solutions. Bull. U.S. Army Med. Dept. 71, 66, 1943.

344. Phillips, R. A., Van Slyke, D. D., Hamilton, P. B., Dole, V. P., Emerson, K., Jr., and Archibald, R. M.: Measurement of specific gravities of whole blood and plasma by standard copper sulphate solutions. J. biol. Chem. 183, 305, 1949.

345. Phillips, R. A., Wallace, C. K., and Blackwell, R. Q.: Water and electrolyte absorption by the intestine in cholera. Proceedings of the Cholera Research Symposium, Honolulu, Jan. 1965. Washington, D.C., U.S. Government Printing Office, p. 299.

346. Pierce, N. F.: Differential inhibitory effects of cholera toxoids and ganglioside on the enterotoxins of Vibrio cholerae and Escherichia coli. J. exp. Med. 137, 1009, 1973.

347. Pierce, N. F., Banwell, J. G., Mitra, R. C., Caranosos, G. J., Keimowitz, R. I., Mondal, A., and Manji, P. M.: Oral maintenance of water electrolyte and acid-base balance in cholera; a preliminary report. Ind. J. med. Res. 56, 640, 1968.

348. Pierce, N. F., Banwell, J. G., Mitra, R., Keimowitz, R. I., and Caranosos, G. J.: Studies on oral maintenance of water electrolyte and acid-base balance in cholera. Symp. on Cholera, U.S.-Japan CMSP, Palo Alto, July 1967, p. 197.

349. Pierce, N. F., Banwell, J. G., Mitra, R. C., Caranosos, G. J., Keimowitz, R. I., Mondal, A., and Manji, P. M.: Effect of intragastric glucose-electrolyte infusion upon water and electrolyte balance in Asiatic cholera. Gastroenterology 55, 333, 1968.

350. Pierce, N. F., Banwell, J. G., Mitra, R. C., Sack, R. B., Brigham, K. L., Fedson, D. S., Mondal, A., and Manji, P. M.: Oral replacement of water and electrolyte losses in cholera. Ind. J. med. Res. 57, 848, 1969.

351. Pierce, N. F., Cray, W. C., Jr., and Engel, P. F.: Antitoxic immunity to cholera in dogs immunized orally with cholera toxin. Infect. Immun. 27, 632, 1980.

352. Pierce, N. F., Cray, W. C., Jr., and Sircar, B. M.: Induction of mucosal antitoxin response and its role in immunity to experimental canine cholera. Infect. Immun. 121, 185, 1978.

353. Pierce, N. F., and Gowans, J. L.: Cellular kinetics of the intestinal immune response to cholera toxoid in rats. J. exp. Med. 142, 1550, 1975.

354. Pierce, N. F., Graybill, J. R., Kaplan, M. M., and Bouwman, D. L.: Systemic effects of parenteral cholera enterotoxin in dogs. J. Lab. clin. Med. 79, 145, 1972.

355. Pierce, N. F., Greenough, W. B., III, and Carpenter, C.C.J.: Vibrio cholerae enterotoxin and its mode of action. Bact. Rev. 35, 1, 1971.

356. Pierce, N. F., Kaniecki, E. A., and Northrup, R. S.: Protection against experimental cholera by antitoxin. J. infect. Dis. 126, 606, 1972.

357. Pierce, N. F., and Reynolds, H. Y.: Immunity to experimental cholera. 2. Secretory and humoral antitoxin response to local and systemic toxoid administration. J. infect. Dis. 131, 383, 1975.

358. Pierce, N. F., Sack, R. B., and Mahalanabis, D.: Management of cholera in adults and children. In: Principles and Practice of Cholera Control. Geneva, World Health Organization, 1970, p. 61.

359. Pierce, N. F., Sack, R. B., Mitra, R. C., Banwell, J. G., Brigham, K. L., Fedson, D. S., and Mondal, A.: Replacement of water and electrolyte losses in cholera by an oral glucose-electrolyte solution. Ann. intern. Med. 70, 1173, 1969.

360. Pollitzer, R.: Cholera. Geneva, World Health Organization, 1959.

361. Rappaport, R. S.: Observations on the mechanism of release of heat-labile *E. coli* enterotoxin. Proceedings of the U.S.-Japan CMSP Conference on Cholera, Atlanta, 1977, 1978.

362. Rappaport, R. S., Bonde, G., McCann, T., Rubin, B. A., and Tint, H.: Development of a purified cholera toxoid. 2. Preparation of a stable antigenic toxoid by reaction of purified toxin with glutaraldehyde. Infect. Immun. 9, 304, 1974.

363. Rappaport, R. S., Pierzchala, W. A., Bonde, G., McCann, T., and Rubin, B. A.: Development of a purified cholera toxoid. 3. Refinements in purification of toxin and methods for the determination of residual somatic antigen. Infect. Immun. 14, 687, 1976.

364. Rappaport, R. S., Rubin, B. A., Tint, H.: Development of a purified cholera toxoid. 1. Purification of toxin. Infect. Immun. 9, 294, 1974.

365. Rappaport, R. S., Sagin, J. F., Pierzchala, W. A., Bonde, G., Rubin, B. A., and Tint, H.: Activation of heat-labile *Escherichia coli* enterotoxin by trypsin. J. infect. Dis. 133, S41, 1976.

366. Revesz, T., and Greaves, M.: Ligand induced redistribution of lymphocyte membrane ganglioside GM1. Nature 257, 103, 1975.

367. Rodbell, M., Birnbaumer, L., Pohl, S. L., and Krans, H.M.J.: The glucagon-sensitive adenyl cyclase system in plasma membranes of rat liver. An obligatory role of guanyl nucleotides in glucagon action. J. biol. Chem. 246, 1877, 1971.

368. Rodbell, M., Krans, H.M.J., Pohl, S. L., and Birnbaumer, L.: The glucagon-sensitive adenyl cyclase system in plasma membranes of rat liver. J. biol. Chem. 246, 1872, 1971.

369. Rogers, L.: The variations in the pressure and composition of blood in cholera. Proc. Roy. Soc. B. 81, 291, 1909.

370. Rogers, L.: The further reduction of the mortality of cholera to 11 percent by the addition of atropine hypodermically to the hypertonic and permanganate treatment, with an addendum summarising the system of treatment. Ind. med. Gaz. 51, 7, 1916.

371. Rogers, L.: Further work on the reduction of the alkalinity of the blood

in cholera; and sodium bicarbonate injections in the prevention of uraemia. Ann. trop. Med. Parasitol. 10, 139, 1916–17.

372. Rogers, L.: Bowel Diseases in the Tropics—Cholera, Dysenteries, Liver Abscess and Sprue. London, Henry Frowde and Hodder and Stoughton, 1921.

373. Rogers, L., Cholera. In: Tropical Medicine, 6th ed, ed. Rogers, L., and Megaw, J.W.D. London, J. and A. Churchill Ltd., 1952.

374. Roggin, G. M., Banwell, J. G., Yardley, J. H., and Hendrix, T. R.: Unimpaired response of rabbit jejunum to cholera toxin after selective damage to villus epithelium. Gastroenterology 63, 981, 1972.

375. Rohde, J.: Child health and family planning. Lancet 2, 705, 1972.

376. Rohde, J. E., and Northrup, R. S.: Taking science where the diarrhoea is. In: Acute Diarrhoea in Childhood, ed. Elliott and Knight. Amsterdam, Oxford, New York, Elsevier–Excerpta Medica–North-Holland, 1975, p. 339.

377. Rosenberg, C. E.: The Cholera Years. The United States in 1832, 1849, and 1966. Chicago, University of Chicago Press, 1962.

378. Rosenberg, I. H., Greenough, W. B., III, Lindenbaum, J., and Gordon, R. G.: Nutritional studies in cholera. Influence of nutritional status on susceptibility to infection. Amer. J. clin. Nutr. 19, 384, 1966.

379. Roux, E., and Yersin, A.: Contribution à l'étude de la diphthérie. Ann. Inst. Pasteur 2, 629, 1888.

380. Sachar, D. B., Taylor, J. O., Kinzie, J. L., and Saha, J. R.: Transmural electric potentiates and their response to sugars in the intestine of acute cholera patients and normal subjects. Symp. on Cholera, U.S.-Japan CMSP, Palo Alto, July 1967, p. 183.

381. Sack, R. B., and Carpenter, C.C.J.: Experimental canine cholera. 1. Development of the model. J. infect. Dis. 119, 138, 1969.

382. Sack, R. B., Carpenter, C.C.J., Steinberg, R. W., and Pierce, N. F.: Experimental cholera: A canine model. Lancet 2, 206, 1966.

383. Sack, D. A., Chowdhury, A.K.M.A., Eusof, A., Ali, M. A., Merson, M. H., Islam, S., Black, R. E., and Brown, K. H.: Oral hydration in rotavirus diarrhoea: A double blind comparison of sucrose with glucose electrolyte solution. Lancet 2, 280, 1978.

384. Sack, R. B., Gorbach, S. L., Banwell, J. G., Jacobs, B., Chatterjee, B. D., and Mitra, R. C.: Enterotoxinogenic Escherichia coli isolated from patients with severe cholera-like disease. J. infect. Dis. 123, 378, 1971.

385. Sayhoum, N., and Cuatrecasas, P.: Mechanism of activation of adenylate cyclase by cholera toxin. Proc. Nat. Acad. Sci. 72, 3438, 1975.

386. Schafer, D. E., Lust, W. D., Sircar, B., and Goldberg, N. D.: Elevated concentrations of adenosine-3'5'-cyclic monophosphate in intestinal mucosa after treatment with cholera toxin. Proc. Nat. Acad. Sci. 67, 851, 1970.

387. Schramm, M., and Rodbell, M.: Persistent active state of the adenylate cyclase system produced by the combined actions of isoproterenol and guanylyl imidodiphosphate in frog erythrocyte membranes. J. biol. Chem. 250, 2232, 1975.

388. Schrank, G. D., and Verwey, W. F.: Distribution of cholera organisms in experimental Vibrio cholerae infections: Proposed mechanisms of pathogenesis and antibacterial immunity. Infect. Immun. 13, 195, 1976.

389. Schultz, S. G., and Zalusky, R.: Ion transport in isolated rabbit ileum. 2. The interaction between active sodium and active sugar transport. J. gen. Physiol. 47, 1043, 1964.

390. Scot, W.: Report on the Epidemic Cholera as it appeared in the Territories subject to the Presidency of Fort St. George. Madras, Printed at the Asylum Press, 1824.

391. SEATO Proceedings of the Conference on Cholera, Dec. 1960, Dacca, East Pakistan. Bangkok, The Post Publishing Co., Ltd., 1962.

392. SEATO Proceedings of the Cholera Research Symposium, Jan. 24–29, 1965, Honolulu, Hawaii. Washington, D.C., U.S. Government Printing Office: 1965 0-775-163.

393. Sellards, A. W.: Tolerance for alkalis in Asiatic cholera. Philippine J. Sci. (Sect. B) 5, 363, 1910.

394. Selmi, F.: Sulla esistenza di principii alcalodi naturali nei visceri freschi e putrefatti onde il perito chimico puo essere condotto a conclusioni eronee nella ricerca degli alcaloidi venefici. Mem. Accad. d. Sc. d. Ist. di. Bologna, 3^e ser. ii, 81, 1872.

395. Selwyn, S.: Cholera old and new. Proc. Roy. Soc. Med. 70, 301, 1977.

396. Sharp, G.W.G., and Hynie, S.: Stimulation of intestinal adenyl cyclase by cholera toxin. Nature 229, 266, 1971.

397. Shattuck, G. C.: Diseases of the Tropics. New York, Appleton-Century-Crofts Inc., 1951, p. 327.

398. Sheerin, H. E., and Field, M.: Ileal HCO_3 secretion: Relationship to Na and Cl fluxes and effect of theophylline. Amer. J. Physiol. 228, 1065, 1975.

399. Siddhichai, P.: The epidemiology of the outbreak of cholera in Thailand, 1958–1959. SEATO Conference on Cholera. Bangkok, The Post Publishing Co. Ltd., 1962, p. 116.

400. Smith, H. W., and Gyles, G. L.: The relationship between two apparently different enterotoxins produced by enteropathogenic strains of *Escherichia coli* of porcine origin. J. med. Microbiol. 3, 387, 1970.

401. Smith, H. W., and Jones, J.E.T.: Observations on the alimentary tract and its bacterial flora in healthy and diseased pigs. J. Path. Bact. 86, 387, 1963.

402. Smyth, C. J.: The identification and purification of multiple forms of theta-haemolysins (theta-toxin) of Clostridium perfringens type A. J. gen. Microbiol. 87, 219, 1975.

403. Snow, J.: On the Mode of Communication of Cholera; 2nd edition, much enlarged. London, John Churchill, 1855; reprinted 1965, New York and London, Hafner Publishing Co., 1965.

404. Soergel, K. H., Whalen, G. E., and Harris, J. A.: Passive movement of water and sodium across the human small intestinal mucosa. J. appl. Physiol. 24, 40, 1968.

405. Sommer, A., Khan, M., and Mosley, W. H.: Efficacy of vaccination of family contacts of cholera cases. Lancet 1, 1230, 1973.

406. Sommer, A., and Mosley, W. H.: Ineffectiveness of cholera vaccination as an epidemic control measure. Lancet 1, 1232, 1973.

407. Staerk, J., Ronneberger, H. J., and Wiegandt, H.: Neuraminidase, a

virulence factor in *Vibrio cholerae* infection? Behring Institute Research Commun. 55, 145, 1974.

408. Steel, T.: The Life and Death of St. Kilda. London, Collins, 1975.

409. Stommel, H., and Stommel, E.: The year without a summer. Scientific American 240, 176, 1979.

410. Straus, I., and Roux, E.: Exposé des recherches sur le choléra à Toulon. Bull. Acad. Med., 2e serie, 8, 1047, 1884.

411. Sulzer, B. M., and Craig, J. P.: Cholera toxin inhibits macro-molecular synthesis in mouse spleen cells. Nature (New Biol). 244, 178, 1973.

412. Sutherland, W. E.: On the biological role of cyclic AMP. J. Amer. med. Assoc. 214, 1281, 1970.

413. Tabor, C. W., and Tabor, H.: 1,4-Diaminobutane (putrescine), spermidine, and spermine. Ann. Rev. Biochem. 45, 285, 1976.

414. Tait, R. M., and van Heyningen, S.: The adenylate cyclase-activating activity of cholera toxin is not associated with a nicotinamide-adenine dinucleotide glycohydrolase. Biochem. J. 174, 1059, 1978.

415. Takaki, K.: Über Tetanusgift bindende Bestandteile des Gehirns. Beitr. z. chem. Physiol. 11, 288, 1909.

416. Taylor, J. O., Sachar, D. B., Kinzie, J. L., and Phillips, R. A.: Enhancement of net sodium and water absorption in acute human cholera by intestinal glucose lavage. Symp. on Cholera, U.S.-Japan CMSP, Palo Alto, July 1967, p. 191.

417. Tizzoni, G., and Catani, G.: Über das Tetanusgift. Centralbl. Bakt. Parasiten. 8, 69, 1890.

418. Tizzoni, G., and Catani, G.: Untersuchungen über das Tetanusgift. Arch. exp. Pathol. Pharmakol. 27, 432, 1890.

419. Tomasi, T. B.: Structure and function of mucosal antibodies. Ann. Rev. Med. 21, 281, 1970.

420. Topley, W.W.C., and Wilson, G. S.: The Principles of Bacteriology and Immunity; 1st ed., 1929; 2nd ed., 1936. London, Edward Arnold and Co.

420a. Trans med phys. Soc. Calcutta 8, 1836.

421. van Ermengem, E.: Recherches sur des cas d'accidents alimentaires. Rev. Hyg. Police sanit. 18, 761, 1896.

422. van Ermengem, E.: Über einen neuer anaeroben Bacillus und seine Beziehungen zum Botulismus. Zeitschr. für Hygiene 26, 1, 1897.

423. van Heyningen. S.: Cholera toxin: interaction of subunits with ganglioside GM1. Science 183, 656, 1974.

424. van Heyningen, S.: Activation by cholera toxin of adenylate cyclase solubilized from rat liver. Biochem. J. 157, 785, 1976.

425. van Heyningen, S.: Binding of ganglioside by the chains of tetanus toxin. FEBS Letters 68, 5, 1976.

426. van Heyningen, S.: Activity of covalently cross-linked cholera toxin with the adenylate cyclase of intact and lysed pigeon erythrocytes. Biochem. J. 168, 457, 1977.

427. van Heyningen, S.: Cholera toxin. Biol. Rev. 52, 509, 1977.

428. van Heyningen, S., and King, C. A.: Subunit A from cholera toxin is an activator of adenylate cyclase in pigeon erythrocytes. Biochem. J. 146, 269, 1975.

429. van Heyningen, W. E.: Tentative identification of the tetanus toxin receptor in nervous tissue. J. gen. Microbiol. 20, 310, 1959.

430. van Heyningen, W. E.: The assay of bacterial toxins. Hoppe-Seyler Thierfelder's Handbuch der physiologisch- und pathologisch-chemischen Analyse. 10. Aufl. Bd. IV, 785, 1960.

431. van Heyningen, W. E.: The fixation of tetanus toxin, strychnine, serotonin and other substances by ganglioside. J. gen. Microbiol. 31, 375, 1964.

432. van Heyningen, W. E.: Bacterial Exotoxins. In: International Textbook of Medicine, Vol. 2. Medical Microbiology, ed. Braude. Philadelphia, W. B. Saunders and Co., 1981.

433. van Heyningen, W. E., Carpenter, C.C.J., Pierce, N. F., and Greenough, W. B., III: Deactivation of cholera toxin by ganglioside. J. infect. Dis. 124, 415, 1971.

434. van Heyningen, W. E., and Mellanby: Eliminate tetanus in India. Bull. Haffkine Inst. 1, 7, 1974.

435. van Heyningen, W. E., and Miller, P. A.: The fixation of tetanus toxin by ganglioside. J. gen. Microbiol. 24, 107, 1961.

436. Vaughan, M., Pierce, N. F., Greenough, W. B., III: Stimulation of glycerol production in fat cells by cholera toxin. Nature 226, 658, 1970.

437. Verwey, W. F.: An hypothesis of antibacterial immunity in cholera. Proc. of the U.S.-Japan CMSP Conference on Cholera, Tokyo, 1972, p. 186.

438. Verwey, W. F.: Current concepts of the pathogenesis of cholera infection. Proceedings of the U.S.-Japan CMSP Conference on Cholera, Sapporo, 1976, p. 311.

439. Violle, H.: Sur la pathogenie du choléra. C. R. Acad. Sci. (Paris) 158, 1710, 1914.

440. Violle, H.: Essais sur la pathogenie du choléra. Ann. Inst. Pasteur 28, 759, 1914.

441. Violle, H., and Crendiropoulo: Note sur le choléra experimental. Comptes rendus Soc. Biologie (Paris) 78, 331, 1915.

442. Virchow, R.: Gesammelte Abhandlungen auf dem Gebiete der offentlichen Medizin. 1, 151, 1879.

443. von Behring, E., and Kitasato, S.: Ueber das Zustandekommen der Diphtherie-Immunität und der Tetanus-Immunität bei Thieren. Deutsch. med. Wochschr. 16, 1113, 1890.

444. Wahed, A.K.M. Abdul: Classical features of cholera and its management. SEATO Conference on Cholera, Dacca, Dec. 1960. Bangkok, Post Publishing Co., 1962, pp. 11–14.

445. Wallace, C. K.: Cholera: A continuing threat and challenge. Int. Rev. trop. Med. 3, 159, 1969.

446. Wallace, C. K., Carpenter, C.C.J., Mitra, P. P., Sack, R. B., Khanra, S. R., Werner, A. S., Duffy, T. P., Oleinick, A., and Lewis, G. W.: Classical and El Tor Cholera: A clinical comparison. Brit. med. J. 2, 447, 1966.

447. Wallace, C. K., Cox, J. W., Fabie, A., Primicias, P., Uylangco, C. V., and Phillips, R. A.: The treatment of cholera. Chinese med. J. R.O.C. 9, 15–23 March 1962.

448. Wallace, C. K., Cox, J. W., Fabie, A., Primicias, P., Uylangco, C. V.,

and Phillips, R. A.: The Treatment of Cholera. NAMRU-2 Report 62-2, 1 March 1962.

449. Wallace, C. K., Cox, J. W., Fabie, A., Primicias, P., Uylangco, C. V., and Phillips, R. A.: The Treatment of Cholera. J. Philippine med. Assoc. 38, 297, May 1962.

450. Wallace, C. K., Fabie, A. E., Mangubat, O., Velasco, E., Juinio, C., and Phillips, R. A.: The 1961 cholera epidemic in Manila, Republic of the Philippines. Bull. WHO 30, 795, 1964.

451. Wassermann, A.: Ueber eine neue Art von kunstlicher Immunität. Berliner Klin. Wochenschr. 35, 4, 1898.

452. Wassermann, A., and Takaki, T.: Uber tetanusantitoxische Eigenschaften des normalen Centralnervensystems. Berliner Klin. Wochschr. 35, 5, 1898.

453. Watanabe, Y., and Verwey, W. F.: The preparation and properties of a purified mouse-protective lipopolysaccharide from the Ogawa subtype of the El Tor variety of *Vibrio cholerae*. Proceedings of the Cholera Research Symposium, Honolulu, Jan. 1965. Washington, D.C., U.S. Government Printing Office, 1965, p. 253.

454. Watson Cheyne, W.: Introduction. In: Bacteria in Relation to Diseases, ed. Watson Cheyne, W. London, New Sydenham Society, 1886.

455. Watten, R. H., Blackwell, R. Q., and Phillips, R. A.: The relation of electrolyte concentrations in plasma and excreta of cholera patients. SEATO Conference on Cholera, Dacca, Dec. 5–8, 1960. Bangkok, The Post Publishing Co. Ltd., 1962, p. 41.

456. Watten, R. H., Morgan, F. M., Songkhla, Y. na, Vanikiati, B., and Phillips, R. A.: Water and electrolyte studies in cholera. J. clin. Invest. 38, 1879, 1959.

457. Watten, R. H., and Phillips, R. A.: Potassium in the treatment of cholera. Lancet 2, 999, 1960.

458. Weaver, R. H., Johnson, M. K., and Phillips, R. A.: Biochemical studies of cholera. J. Egypt. Public Health Assoc. 23, 5, 1948.

459. Wheeler, M. A., Solomon, R. A., Cooper, C., Hertzberg, L., Mehta, H., Miki, N., and Bitensky, M. W.: Interaction of *Vibrio cholerae* toxin with sarcoma 180 cell membranes. J. infect. Dis. 133, S89, 1976.

460. WHO Scientific Working Group: *Escherichia coli* diarrhoea. Bull. WHO 58, 23, 1980.

461. Williams, H. R., Verwey, W. F., Schrank, G. D., and Hurry, E. K.: An in vitro antigen-antibody reaction in relation to an hypothesis of intestinal immunity to cholera. Proceedings of the U.S.-Japan CMSP Conference on Cholera, Grand Canyon, Arizona, 1973, p. 161.

462. Wilson, G. S., and Miles, A. A.: Topley and Wilson's Principles of Bacteriology, Immunology and Virology. London, Edward Arnold and Co., editions of 1946, 1955, 1964, 1975.

463. Wilson, T. H.: Intestinal Absorption. Philadelphia, London, W. B. Saunders Company, 1962.

464. Wolff, A.: Ueber Grundgesetze der Immunität. (1. Ueber antitoxische und antiendotoxishe Immunität und über die Eigenschaften der Endotoxine.) Centralbl. Bakt. Parasitenk. Infektionskr. Erste Abt. 37, Orig. 390, 1904.

465. Woodward, T. E.: No substitute for excellence. J. infect. Dis. 137, 498, 1978.

466. Woodward, W. E.: Cholera reinfection in man. J. infect. Dis. 123, 61, 1971.

467. Yu, H., and Chen, K. F.: A suggestive skin test for susceptibility to cholera. Chinese med. J. 46, 799, 1932.

468. Zieve, P. D., Pierce, N. F., and Greenough, W. B., III: Stimulation of glycogenolysis by purified cholera exotoxin in disrupted cells. Clin. Res. 18, 690, 1970.

Index